...ing

THE COMPLETE GUIDE TO

Writing, Producing, and Directing a Low-Budget Short Film

GINI GRAHAM SCOTT

AN IMPRINT OF
HAL•LEONARD®

Published in 2011 by Limelight Editions
An Imprint of Hal Leonard Corporation
7777 West Bluemound Road
Milwaukee, WI 53213

Trade Book Division Editorial Offices
33 Plymouth St., Montclair, NJ 07042

Printed in the United States of America

Book design by Mark Lerner

Library of Congress Cataloging-in-Publication Data

Scott, Gini Graham.
  The complete guide to writing, producing, and directing a low-budget short film / Gini Graham Scott.
     p. cm.
  Includes bibliographical references.
  ISBN 978-0-87910-392-7
  1. Motion picture authorship. 2. Short films--Production and direction. 3. Low budget films--Production direction. I. Title.
  PN1996.S3557 2011
  808.2'3--dc23
                    2011043119

www.limelighteditions.com

Contents

PART II: PRODUCTION

PART III: POST-PRODUCTION

PART IV: PROMOTING YOUR FILM

Introduction

The Complete Guide to Writing, Producing, and Directing a Low-Budget Short Film is based on my experience in writing, producing, and sometimes directing about four dozen short videos for TV pilots, sizzle reels, trailers for books, scripts, and films, five- to nine-minute dramatic shorts, and music videos. Initially I hired producers and directors to make a half dozen music videos for me. Then I wrote the script for *The New Child* and brought in producers and directors to shoot and edit a script trailer for it and wrote and produced a dramatic short, *Cougar and Cub.*

Most recently I have written, produced, and sometimes directed some TV pilots (*Meet and Compete, Behind the Scenes with Debbi and Frankie,* and *The Very Next New Thing*) and some shorts (*I'll Make Some Bread, My Four Presidents, Massage Wash, Heads Up, Zoo Do, Zoo Don't, The Engagement,* and many others). I have also participated as a writer in a several one-day shoots to complete a film in a day or forty-eight hours (*Cats, Zapped, Cracked,* and *The Rat*). Another half dozen projects will be completed in the next few months (*Ironworkers* and the *New Identity Trailer*). I completed filming for several pilots for documentaries—*Hide and Seek* on the sport of geocaching and *Pet Mania* on how much people love their pets.

I am also a founding member of a collaborative film and media group that not only joined together to film the *Do You Look Like Your Dog? Fashion Show*, *The Deal*, *The Consultation*, and *Peace Out*, but is offering services to community groups, corporations, and professionals to produce short films and train others on how to do their videos. I have also organized a half dozen film groups with over 3,000 members through Meetup.com, including The Film and TV Connection, Bay Area Film and TV Connection, The Hollywood Film Industry, and the Bay Area Film Fans, and I have put on feedback forums and promotional events for short films through these groups. A complete bio is in the "About the Author" section at the end of the book.

This book is designed to show you how to write, produce, shoot, and edit your film, at a time when it is easier than ever to get the equipment you need to do it, though I will leave the choice of the equipment and how to operate it up to you. Often the director of photography (also called a DP) or the camera, lighting, or sound people you bring in to shoot the video will have their own equipment or can recommend what to get and where to buy it very cheaply. So the focus here will be on the five key steps to completing and promoting a low- or no-budget project:

Write it—come up with a script or guidelines to help the host or actors improvise, and in some cases, assist the director in doing scene and shot breakdowns.

Produce it—organize and guide the project, including getting the cast and crew together, setting the budget of the project, deciding on the locations for filming, and arranging for editing and post-production.

Direct it—work with the actors so they know what to do—and then work with the editor to edit the completed film—or invite a director to join your team and take on this role under your direction.

Edit it—work with an editor to edit your film, unless you want to do this yourself.

Promote it—get your film shown to individuals or groups.

If you have done a good job in putting the crew together, they will take care of the actual filming and editing, while you supervise or provide some occasional input to make sure they are doing what you want.

Then once the film is created, it's normally up to you to promote it, such as by setting up screening events, entering it in short film competitions or in the short film divisions of larger events, and inviting others to view your video online—usually on YouTube—by using e-mails and social media like Facebook, LinkedIn, and Twitter.

I have focused on these five key non-technical aspects of creating and coordinating the project, though I have touched briefly on some of the technical aspects of filming, such as choosing a camera, operating it, handling lighting and sound, and editing the video yourself. You can find excellent books, courses, and articles on all of these topics, and I have included a selected listing of these in the "Resources and References" chapter.

While I have geared the discussion to the novice filmmaker, others will find many sections of the book helpful in organizing and implementing their own projects. Feel free to skip ahead to those sections that are relevant for you.

Generally don't expect to make any money from these short films, though they are great for promoting what you do, pitching projects like books, scripts, and films, and just having fun.

Normally these short films take one day to shoot, sometimes two, and then a day or two to edit.

Certainly you can take a video camera or SLR with a video function and shoot with little or no planning, and you can edit something in an hour or two, or even post your video online without any editing. But this book is designed to help you create a well-organized, well-shot,

professional-looking film with one or a few cameras and a small supporting cast or crew.

I've divided this discussion into the three stages of production—
pre-production, production, post-production—and promoting your
film. I have also included examples of forms you can use, such as to
list equipment, get cast releases, and log scenes, as well as check-off
lists to help you prepare. The first chapters deal with doing a dramatic
short feature. Additional chapters deal with doing a documentary,
music video, and book and film trailers.

So good luck and have fun.

PART I

Pre-production

Chapter 1

Writing Your Script

Writing your script may seem like the easiest part. You have an idea for a short script that's under ten pages—write it out and it's ready to go. Well, yes and no, because you need to keep in mind a number of considerations in writing a short low- or no-budget script: to make it filmable for low or no cost in one or two days, preferably one.

Also, your script needs to be formatted both as a reading script and as a production or shooting script. The reading script is generally the one you have already written, and this is the one to show to prospective actors and crew members to get them excited about volunteering their time or working for very low pay.

The shooting or production script builds on the reading script you have already written. It also includes scene and shot breakdowns and the order in which these will be shot. Sometimes the director, assistant director (also called the AD), or director of photography (also called a DP) will do these breakdowns. Or as the writer, you may do it. Sometimes two or three team members may work together to decide how to break down the script for shooting different scenes and shots.

There are special programs to create this shooting script, as well as software for creating a storyboard. It's ideal if you can use one of these software programs for the breakdown, but you can create it in any word-processing program, with or without columns. The director, AD, or DP doing the final breakdown may also want to use your script as a guide.

Turning Your Ideas into a Completed Script

When you turn your ideas into a completed script, there are certain guidelines to keep in mind. I'll leave the creative content up to you, though it is helpful to get feedback from people other than close family and friends to see what they think of the idea and help you polish it up. Even though the script itself will often change during filming, as the actors improvise and you get ideas from the DP or others on the set, you generally need a script in advance to start with. The following are some guidelines to keep in mind.

Keep Your Script Under Ten Pages

The usual guideline for turning a script into a film is one page equals one minute of film. So guide your writing accordingly and cut your script to fit the expected length of your film. A good target to aim for with a short is three to seven minutes, unless you need more time to tell your story. People today have short attention spans, and you will be more likely to get viewers to watch a short under five minutes on sites like YouTube or in festivals or short-film programs, where programmers like to include a large number of short films.

Limit the Number of Characters

For ease of filming and to keep costs down, keep the number of characters low. Generally, have one, two, or at most three main characters, and limit the number of supporting characters to two or three so you have at most four or five characters in the film.

As you add more characters, it becomes harder to cast the film, and you'll need more time for rehearsals and blocking the characters' actions when you film. While some directors adjust their camera as the actors go through their lines or improvise, you'll get a more professional-looking film if you do this initial preparation with the actors, so you know what they are doing and can set up the lighting in advance accordingly. That's another reason why it's best to keep down the number of characters, so you can better prepare them and the crew for filming on the set.

Limit the Number of Locations

Since the number of scenes and shots affects the time needed to shoot the film, limit the number of locations. Ideally don't have more than four locations, and keep down the costs by having these locations close together or even in the same house or on the same property. Each location requires another setup of the cameras and lighting, unless you are shooting outdoors without any reflectors. So when you can, write the scenes to take place in the same or nearby locations.

Think About the Different Shots That May Occur in a Scene

Take into account that each scene may have a number of shots, since you are not just shooting a stage play. Rather, there is commonly a wide establishing shot, then medium shots and close-ups on the main characters as they are speaking or to show their reactions. Conversely, you might start with a close-up to pull the viewer immediately into the scene and then pull back to show a medium or wide shot. There also may be over-the-shoulder shots to show the scene from a different character's point of view.

So depending on the number of cameras you use, different cameras might capture different views during a take, or multiple takes might be used to capture different angles. (And, of course, there may be additional takes to get a better performance from the actors).

Thus, to ease the transition from the written to filmed story, take into account how the scene might be filmed cinematically. You might even imagine different shots in your mind as you write. This pre-visualization can also help you see different turning points in the action, such as when one character stands up angrily to yell at another, and the second character responds angrily in return.

Keep the Action and Setting Descriptions Short and to the Point

Remember that writing a script is different from writing a novel, so keep the descriptions of the action and setting short and spare. The director will use the narrative as a guide for shooting the scene, but will decide on the action and what's in the scene based on where the film is actually shot—and that can differ from your imagined location in writing the script (unless you are directing the scene at the exact location described in the script).

So generally include a minimum of detail—only enough to move the story along and suggest the setting. This also makes for a faster, easier read for the actors and others considering participating in the film.

For example, in introducing characters, only give each character's name, approximate age, and a word or two to indicate who they are. And the first time you introduce a character, capitalize their name. For instance, you might write: TONY, 30s, a tough-talking gangster. Unless it's important, leave out the person's height, weight, hair, or dress, since that will depend on who is cast and their wardrobe.

Likewise, describe the setting very briefly, such as saying the location is a "seedy-looking diner by a gas station," rather than going into detail about what the diner looks like inside.

Keep the Dialogue Short

In normal speech, people may go on and on. But in a script, you want to highlight the main points. You can include some of the back-and-forth to suggest a disagreement or escalating confrontation, but avoid repeating some of the same points, even in different words, although this is common in normal discussion.

Also, avoid long monologues or speeches by a single character. Even if the character is giving a speech, you can use "cut ahead" to show that this is a long speech, without having the character say it all.

Generally keep the dialogue to four or five lines or shorter. And as appropriate, let one character jump in and interrupt, so the character who is talking can't finish his or her line.

Use Character Names That Are Different, or Feature a Character's Attribute or Role

Generally use names that are very different for the characters, unless there is a good reason for similar names, such as having twins named Dan and Dave. The reason for using distinctive names is so that it is easier for viewers to keep track of who's who.

If appropriate, have the character say his or her name or the name of another character, though in many shorts, the characters don't have names. If this is the case, you might call them by their attribute or role, such as the Professor, Young Man, Husband, or Wife, since it will be confusing in the credits to list the name of a character that's not stated in the story.

Formatting Your Script

Ideally, use one of the popular screenwriting programs to format your script following the standard conventions for a reading script. The two major programs are Final Draft, now up to Final Draft 8, and Movie Magic Screenwriter, each used by about half of the screenwriters. The software costs about $250 for Final Draft and $170 to $200 for Movie Magic Screenwriter, depending on where you get it. Do a search to get it online. Another recent program is called Celtx, which is available at no charge online, with a few low-cost add-ons, though it lacks some of the formatting features of the professional software.

If you aren't able to get this software, follow this standard script formatting in a word-processing program:

- Set the margins for the dialogue in about one inch on either side, and place the character's name in caps above the dialogue.
- Set your margins at one and a quarter inch and use single spacing.
- Add a line between each section of the script (i.e., after a scene description, after narrative describing the action or setting, and after a character's dialogue).
- Add two lines between the end of one scene and the next.
- Begin each new scene with a brief line in caps about the setting, which includes whether it's an interior (INT.) or exterior (EXT.) shot, followed by the location (DAN'S BEDROOM), which should be identified by the same designation each time, and then the time of day (i.e., DAY, NIGHT, A LITTLE LATER, LATER). I also find it helpful to include time designations for the passage of time, such as: MOMENTS LATER, THE NEXT DAY, or SEVERAL DAYS LATER, to provide a sense of context for the story. Many screenwriters prefer to leave out such designations, since they won't appear in the film, though sometimes they do, such as when a title indicates: "THREE DAYS LATER . . ." or "NEXT WEEK . . ." Use the approach that works best for you.
- Describe the action in a few lines.
- Use the tighter margins to indicate the character speaking and the dialogue. Add (CONT'D) if the same character is speaking the next line of dialogue.
- In the event you add in the name of a character but the dialogue begins on the next page, space-down until the name of the character is on top of the first block of dialogue. It is okay to split up the dialogue in the middle, though split it at the end of a complete sentence, not between lines. The scriptwriting software will automatically do this.
- Add in the next action description using your original margins.
- If the scene changes, indicate it as described previously.
- To cue the actor on how to express a line of dialogue, include a short description in parentheses under the characters name, such

as (annoyed), (angry), (bewildered). But if it's clear from the action or dialogue how the character is feeling, avoid such descriptions, since they slow down the story.

- If something is a flashback or fantasy sequence, indicate this at the beginning and end, such as: FLASHBACK BEGINS . . . and later: FLASHBACK ENDS.
- If you image a series of short shorts, indicate this as a MONTAGE, describe the shots or type of shots to include, and end the series with MONTAGE ENDS.

And that's it. The advantage of script software is that it automatically does all this formatting and spacing for you.

In case you aren't using script software, here are a few pages from a script I wrote to illustrate what this formatting looks like.

```
FADE IN:

EXT. FREEWAY OAKLAND LEADING TO BAY BRIDGE—DAY

A pan shows cars driving toward the toll booth.

EXT. CITY STREET NEAR FREEWAY RAMP IN EAST
BAY—DAY

SAM, 30s, is driving with MARY BETH, 30s,
toward San Francisco. They both dressed
casually, as business professionals might on a
day off.

Sam stops at a light.

EXT. INTERIOR OF CAR—DAY
```

Mary Beth holds up her hand to admire her ring.

> MARY BETH
> It's so nice. I can't wait to show
> it off at the party.

Mary Beth leans over and plants a kiss on Sam's cheek.

> MARY BETH (CONT'D)
> And finally after two years.

Sam looks up at the light, trying to concentrate on the road and listen to Mary Beth.

> SAM
> Yeah, it'll be nice to finally
> announce our own engagement.

The light changes and Sam heads onto the freeway ramp.

EXT. FREEWAY IN OAKLAND HEADING TO THE BAY BRIDGE—DAY

A long shot shows cars on the freeway.

> MARY BETH (V.O.)
> (A little shrewish)
> Yes. Mom and Daddy will be so
> pleased. And I'm sure you'll enjoy
> working for Daddy. So much better

than the crappy jobs you've had for
the past year.

                    SAM (V.O.)
I know. But it's been so hard being
a writer.

EXT. INTERIOR OF CAR—DAY

Mary Beth waves her hand around, looking at her
ring, as Sam drives.

                    MARY BETH
    But Daddy to the rescue.

                    SAM
    Yeah, I guess.

EXT. TOLL BOOTH ENTRY TO THE BAY BRIDGE—DAY

A shot shows the toll booth ahead.

EXT. INTERIOR OF CAR—DAY

Sam looks up and sees the toll booth ahead.

                    SAM
                (Half aloud)
    Oh, shit.

Mary Beth looks up.

>   MARY BETH
>   What's wrong?

>   SAM
> Ummm . . . I'm on the wrong road. I don't want
> to go to San Francisco. Damn. And I can't back
> up.

Sam, grudging, grabs his wallet to pay.

Chapter 2

Getting Feedback, Rewriting, and Finalizing Your Script

Once you complete your script, get feedback from others to see what they think of it, and be open to making changes if you get similar suggestions from different people. Often scripts are rewritten and rewritten again, and they are often revised during rehearsals or shooting, when the actors, director, DP, or others make suggestions. And sometimes actors improvise, using the written script as a basis for coming up with ideas. Later the editor, along with the director, writer, or others viewing the footage that has been shot can decide which works best—the original script or the improvised scenes—and use the preferred takes in the final film.

So be ready to leave your ego at the door and be willing to rewrite or incorporate improvs by the actors. At the same time, seek to get the script in as finished a form as possible before shooting the film, since you will want to send the script out to prospective cast and crew members so they can decide if they want to work on the film.

Sources of Getting Feedback

Ideally get suggestions from screenwriters, directors, producers, or others in the film industry. You may find screenwriter or film industry critique meetings through local filmmaker groups. You might find some through Meetup groups or groups like the United Filmmakers Association in your area. Check in Google or Facebook for such groups.

In these critique groups, people typically bring up to ten pages of what they are working on, with sufficient copies so people in the group can read aloud for different characters or follow along as they read to themselves or listen to others read.

Or possibly some of your business associates might be interested in reading your script and giving you feedback. As a last resort, get comments from family and friends, since they are likely to be biased and tell you great things to make you feel good. To counteract that, emphasize that you are looking for critical feedback and would very much like to hear if anything isn't working for them in your script.

Seeking Comments and Having a Script Reading

You can either seek out comments from people individually or in a group.

Getting Individual Comments

Giving your script to some people and asking for feedback is one approach. To help people think about what you want to know, you might include a short checklist or guidelines for comments.

When you ask people to give you comments, emphasize that it's a very short script—only about five to seven pages, which will take only a few minutes to read, and afterward you would like to talk to them briefly on the phone about their reactions—or if people prefer, they can send you an e-mail with their feedback.

When you approach people about reading your script, make sure that they really want to read it and can do so within your time frame for getting comments to edit the script. Otherwise, you may find that people don't get around to reading your script or only do so grudgingly, so they won't give you meaningful comments.

If you find some willing people, follow up after a few days to see if they have read your script or have any comments. If they haven't read it, remind them of your deadline for doing a rewrite and see if they are still able to comment.

Having a Script Reading

Rather than getting individual comments, it's better if you can get feedback from a group in which some participants read the parts of the script aloud. That's an ideal scenario, because then you will hear how the script sounds when read or even acted with feeling, so you can better see how your script will work when turned into a film. It will particularly help you see if the dialogue sounds natural, and if not, you can always make edits as the readers read the various parts.

In some cases, you can find a screenwriters group in your area, in which you each get to bring pages and comment on each other's work. Typically screenwriters bring up to ten pages of a work in progress, so you can bring your complete short script. As previously noted, you can find such groups through Meetup, or try Googling: "screenwriters group [and your city]."

If you can't find such a group, possibly some of your friends and business associates might want to get together on a particular date to read and comment on your script. In this case, you might include your reading as part of a networking or social event, so people have even more of an incentive to attend and give you feedback.

Seeking Suggestions for Rewriting

Whether you ask for individual comments or work in a group, emphasize that you want honest criticisms, along with suggestions for improving the script. If people really like it, you want to hear that too, especially if they can articulate what exactly they most like. But even if people generally like your script, you want to hear their ideas about making it even better.

In a group, you might start with an open-ended question like "What do you think of this?" to see others' initial reactions to the script, note the first comments, and then ask specific questions. Or give them a little guidance about what you are especially interested in hearing about.

In the case of asking for individual comments, you might include your questions in a letter or e-mail that accompanies a copy of the script.

Some of the suggestions to ask for are:

Is any of the action or motivation of the characters unclear? If so, do you have any suggestions on what to change?

Does anything seem repetitious or unnecessary? If so, do you have any suggestions about what to cut?

Do you have any suggestions on things to add to the story, such as more information about a character to explain why he or she is acting in this way?

What do others think about the theme or message of the story? Is it clear what it is? If not, do you have any suggestions on how to better get this across?

If you can give the audience a little guidance, this will help them know what to look for, as well as show that you are serious in getting critical, but helpful, input about your script to improve it—not just hearing praise for it.

However people are responding to your script, individually or in a group, invite them to write their comments directly on your script. Then you can later look at any comments made by each person on each page when you make any revisions.

Preparing for a Script Reading

If you bring your script to a script reading, prepare for the reading in the following ways:

Determine the number of parts in the script and make at least as many copies as there are parts, or readers for the different parts if you are combining some of the parts for a single reader. Include an additional script for the narrator to read the setting and action and one for yourself to follow along. Preferably, you should only listen and not read anything so you can better listen and observe as a member of the audience, as well as jot down notes on the comments and your observations as the reading goes along. If there aren't enough readers for you to just listen and observe, you might read the narration and/or one or more of the very small parts.

As best you can, assign parts to the people who are most like the characters in the script. Take into consideration who are the best, most articulate readers, if you hear them read previous scripts or listen to them talk in the group. Choose the most suitable and best speakers for the lead characters and give other group members the supporting parts.

Using Feedback to Improve Your Script

When you get feedback, take notes on the script. Note general comments in front and specific comments next to the scene to which those comments apply. You can later combine your comments with those that anyone else has written on the script to guide your rewrite.

If you get similar comments from more than one person, consider incorporating these suggestions in making your revisions. However, if the comment comes from only one person or you get varying comments about what people like or suggest for a rewrite, takes these suggestions less seriously, since they are more idiosyncratic comments, which may or may not be good ideas.

Sometimes you will get one-of-a-kind comments, particularly in screenwriter groups, because each person has a different idea about the story and characters. So they may be re-imagining or revising your script to reflect their point of view and turning it into another story. In such a case, unless you really like their idea and want to write something else, it might be best to not include such ideas in your rewrite.

When you get comments, don't be defensive and try to defend yourself. And don't be insulted if someone doesn't like your script and is harshly critical. Just quietly listen, acknowledge people's comments, and absorb what they say. Afterward you can politely thank anyone for their comments.

If people don't understand something or find something confusing or unclear, don't try to explain what the viewer should get out of the script. If people miss a point you are trying to make, this suggests you need to make it clearer in the script so they get it. The script needs to speak for itself.

You may also get some common types of feedback for common scriptwriting mistakes. If so, correct those mistakes in your rewrite. These common mistakes are:

Too much detail in the description of the setting or the action. Cut out the extra detail.

Too much repetition in the action or dialogue. Cut down the repetition.

Too long passages of dialogue so it's more like a speech. Cut down the dialogue to highlight the main points. You can use "cut ahead" to indicate what a person might have said without saying it to avoid a long speech.

The speech pattern for different characters sounds very similar. Revise the dialogue for some of the characters, so they each have a different voice.

The script should start closer to the main turning point or action; there is too much action or dialogue that doesn't go anywhere or doesn't contribute to the main story. Start the script at a later point in time and put the earlier action into a flashback if it's important, or if not, cut it out.

There are too many characters, so it's hard to follow the story or tell who is the main character or characters. Reduce the number of characters by eliminating characters or combining smaller roles together. Decide who is the main protagonist—or the two or three main characters—and focus the story on that character or the two or three main characters.

In some cases, a single rewrite after a cycle of comments may be all you need to feel your script is ready. However, it's a good idea to get some additional feedback to make sure, whether it's from a few other people or from another group reading. Then if no one suggests any further changes or everyone says they like the script as is, that's a good sign that your script really is ready—though as with any script, you may still want to make more changes when you do the scene breakdowns or get feedback from the actors or others on the set.

Chapter 3

Doing Scene Breakdowns

Once you have finalized, or almost finalized, your script to prepare for filming, do a scene and shot breakdown. If you are only writing the script, the director, assistant director, or director of photography will do this. Or you might do it to help them translate your vision into the film.

There are a few different formats you might use, and I'll provide some examples.

Two columns—one for the video (which includes the action, setting, props, and any special effects), the other for the audio (which includes the dialogue and any sound effects).

Three columns—one for the video, a second for audio, and a third for any props or special effects in the scene).

A linear presentation—in which you list by scene the scene line, action, actors, and any props needed, followed by the dialogue.

A producer's checklist.

If you use columns, you can set this up in a word-processing program, such as Word, in Excel, or get a special software that sets up the columns for you, such as Final Draft AV—a companion to the Final Draft scriptwriting software.

Creating Your Shooting Script

A shooting script differs from a reading script, in that it has scene and shot breakdowns and may include information about camera angles. It may also be accompanied by a story board that illustrates the proposed action for each shot. If you want a storyboard and aren't an artist, you can work with an illustrator who is familiar with doing storyboards, or you can obtain some software to create storyboards, such as Storyboard Quick 6, which costs about $200 to $250; Toon Boom, which costs about $200; or even get free software from Celtx. Doing a storyboard is discussed in more detail in chapter 4, "Creating a Storyboard."

Generally a shooting script is used by the director and DP in determining how to shoot the scene and the amount of time it is likely to take. It might also be useful for creating a budget for the shoot, since you can use the shooting script to figure out how long the shoot will take, any props you need to buy, the cost of providing food to the cast and crew, and the like. In some cases, actors might find it helpful to know how the film will be shot, though generally they will only get the reading script.

Numbering Scenes

A good way to start creating a shooting script is to number the scenes (which some script software, such as in Final Draft, will do). For example, when you number the scenes, they will be indicated like in the following. I have used an example from one of my scripts, *The Consultation.* I have indicated the setting and action, but eliminated the dialogue.

1. INT. ANDREA'S OFFICE—DAY

ANDREA, 30s, a marketing consultant, meets with BURT, 40s, an insurance broker. Andrea flips through a printout.

2. INT. ANDREA'S OFFICE—LATER THAT NIGHT
Andrea picks up the paper with Burt's credit card information and clicks some buttons on her credit card machine. A close-up shows $175.00. She clicks some more buttons and a tape prints out the sale.

3. INT. ANDREA'S BEDROOM—THE NEXT MORNING
Andrea wakes up to a ringing phone by her bed. She picks it up groggily.

4. INT. ANDREA'S HALL/LIVING ROOM—THE NEXT MORNING
BARBARA, 30s, and TIM, 30s, are seated the couch or chairs. Cut ahead for snippets of their comments.

5. INT. ANDREA'S OFFICE—A FEW MINUTES LATER
Andrea turns to the computer and writes, reading aloud.

Ordering Scenes and Shots
Unless it makes sense to shoot in sequence, such as when all the scenes are outside or inside in the same place, decide on the order of shooting, which can differ from the original sequence of shots. One common approach is to shoot all of the easiest shots first, though some filmmakers prefer to get the most challenging shots with the most set up out of the way first. It is also a good idea to shoot the scenes with supporting characters who are only in one or two scenes first so they can finish shooting their scenes early and they don't have to stay for the whole shoot.

A good approach is to group together all the shots to be shot outside or inside together, since you can use natural lighting if you are outside, though some filmmakers still use some supplemental lighting or reflectors, whereas you normally have to set up lighting indoors, if not enough light comes in through the windows. (You can't mix the two kinds of light.) Also, group together any scenes that will be shot under different lighting conditions at different times of the day. Finally, group together any scenes in the same location. If there are multiple rooms, each one is a separate location. Group together the rooms that are next to each other or on the same floor.

For example, in the previous example, three scenes in Andrea's office might be combined together, since these are all indoor shots. Also, since the office, hall, and living room are on the same floor, they might be grouped together, while the bedroom, which is on another floor, might be shot at a later time. So the scenes might be rearranged thus:

1. INT. ANDREA'S OFFICE—DAY
ANDREA, 30s, a marketing consultant, meets with BURT, 40s, an insurance broker. Andrea flips through a printout.

5. INT. ANDREA'S OFFICE—MORNING—A FEW MINUTES LATER.
Andrea turns to the computer and writes, reading aloud.

2. INT. ANDREA'S OFFICE—LATER THAT NIGHT
Andrea picks up the paper with Burt's credit card information and clicks some buttons on her credit card machine. A close in shows $175.00. She clicks some more buttons and a tape prints out the sale.

4. INT. ANDREA'S HALL/LIVING ROOM—THE NEXT MORNING
BARBARA, 30s, and TIM, 30s, are seated the couch or chairs. Cut ahead for snippets of their comments.

3. INT. ANDREA'S BEDROOM—THE NEXT MORNING

Andrea wakes up to a ringing phone by her bed. She picks it up groggily.

Breaking Your Scenes into Shots

To make your video more cinematic, figure on using multiple shots for each scene, unless it is a very short scene that doesn't need such shots. Generally a wide or long shot can be used to establish the scene, though sometimes for dramatic effect a scene may begin with a close-up or extreme close-up. Then there will usually be medium shots, such as waist-up shots of two people talking and close-ups from the shoulders up—or even extreme close-ups of the face only, along with close-in shots of things in the area. Another type of shot is an over-the-shoulder shot, taken from the perspective of one person and featuring the back of that person's head or shoulder.

This variety of shots helps to open up the action, so even a scene with a few people talking can become very dramatized by the camera work.

Indicate each shot in the scene with a letter following the scene number. For example, the first shot in the first scene will be 1a, the next shot 1b, the third shot 1c, and so on. The first shot in the second scene will be 2a, the next one 2b, and so on. Another approach is to use 1, 2, and so on for the first master shot, and then 1a, 1b, and so on for the medium and close-up shots or for shots taken from different angles.

If your primary role is as a writer and/or producer, you might consider the scene breakdowns as your suggestions to the director or DP, who will determine the actual scenes, shots, and order for the shoot. Another reason for considering these as only preliminary suggestions is that during the actual shoot the shots may often change, particularly when the actors rehearse and block out their scenes, since the director or DP may see other possibilities or recognize that some shots don't work given the location, lighting, and other shooting conditions.

Estimating the Time for Each Scene

After doing the scene and shot breakdowns, estimate how long each scene or shot might take. This can be especially helpful if you are planning a shoot with a time limit—such as four to six hours or one day. If it looks like the video will run over, the producer, director, or DP can reduce the number of shots or plan for an additional time period for the shoot.

Using Screen Breakdown Software

The advantage of screen breakdown software, such as Final Draft AV, is you can keep the audio and video columns aligned when you add, edit, or delete text.

You begin with a header indicating what this project is and who's involved in creating it. Then you import a script from any word-processing program or from Final Draft. You can now drag and drop text from one place to another, and when you add text to one column, the matching paragraph in the opposite column will automatically stay with it.

While you can match up video and audio in the correct columns in a word-processing program, it is difficult to keep the corresponding text lined up, because when you type in one column, the text in the next column will go down the same number of lines and you have to close up the spacing.

Thus, if you expect to do a number of scene breakdowns and your budget allows it, it's well worth it to get the software to do the breakdown. And if you are already using Final Draft for your script, you can go back and forth between these two programs. The cost is about $150 to download the software or get a boxed copy.

Here's an example of how the columns are set up in this software program.

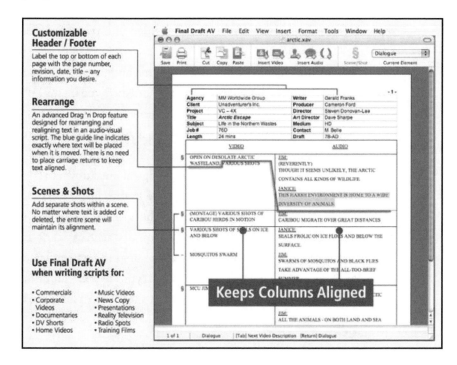

Using Two or Three Columns in a Word-Processing Program or Excel

If you are using Word, another word-processing program, or Excel, first set up the columns with headers. If you are using two columns, use one for video and the other for audio in the usual profile layout. If you use three columns, besides the video and audio columns, set up a third column to list the actors, props, or special effects in a scene, and use a landscape layout to provide extra space for the third column.

On pages 29 and 30 are two examples of how I set this up—the first for a series of videos featuring chapters from a book I wrote, *Want It, See It, Get It!* (see p. 29), the second for a music video for

I'm a Nighttime Man in a Daytime Job (see p. 30). In both cases, I used these two-column set-ups to provide guidelines for a director I hired for each project. The first example shows a table divided into two columns; the second shows a page divided into two columns. You can use either format.

Commonly the video goes in the first column and the audio in the second column, although I put the narration and dialogue on the left and the visual on the right, since I tend to think of the narration or dialogue first and then the video to illustrate it. Set up the columns however you or the people you are working with prefer.

Note that these scripts provide a chronological breakdown of the sequence of action and narrative or dialogue in the shot. To create an actual shooting script, add in scene numbers for each scene in a particular location and break that down into shots, such as Scene 1, Shot 1a; Scene 1, Shot 1b; and so on. Then rearrange them to indicate the order of the scenes that will be shot, since typically films are shot out of order. The video and audio in each of these examples would be rearranged accordingly.

Using a Linear Approach

If you don't have software for formatting the columns, it might be easier to use the linear approach in Word or another word-processing program, because the columns are so difficult to work with and the text shifts in the second column as you type in the first, so it is hard to match up the text in both columns.

When you use a linear approach, first number the scenes and shots in a chronological order, matching the order of scenes in the reading script. Besides listing the location, include the actors and special props for that scene. Next, include the action for that scene and the dialogue, just as laid out in the reading script.

You can suggest different types of shots using these standard symbols on the following page:

WANT IT, SEE IT SCRIPT IDEAS – INTRODUCTION

AUDIO	VIDEO
NARRATOR: The WANT IT, SEE, GET IT approach is a powerful method for determining what you want and getting it. We call it the WSG approach for short.	Narrator is in a comfortable easy chair or couch. Might be me in my living room. Flashing WSG letters
NARRATOR: (V.O) In this first section you'll learn the three basic steps. In subsequent sections, you'll learn how to apply these techniques in different areas of your life to get what you want – from work success to personal relationships.	Image of steps. Images of success, loving relationship
First, determine what you really **want** – and can realistically obtain.	Man or woman getting relaxed in comfortable environment.
Second, **see it** clearly and visualize yourself achieving it.	Images of seeing clearly – ie: microscope, telescope, binoculars; then see more images of success, good relationships.
Third, take the steps to **get it**.	Images of people moving forward – racing horses, boats, planes, on escalator, racing up steps to soaring building.
The key to using this approach effectively is tapping into your powers of visualization or mental imagery. This way you clearly imagine what you want and then go get it.	Image of person relaxing again.
Use whatever images, symbols, or concepts in your visualization that are powerful for you. Even call on your spiritual guides or a favorite teacher.	Collage of symbols
OFF CAMERA INTERVIEWS ON WHAT IMAGES, SYMBOLS DO PEOPLE USE	Clips of people talking about the different images or symbols they use that are powerful to them – such as cross if person is a Christian, good luck charms, etc. Let information come from subject and highlight best clips.
The underlying force for using these WSG techniques is your intuitive creative force and your power of visualization or mental imagery.	Image showing release of energy, mental power (ie: kaleidoscope, shower of sparks, flame.

Wide Shot—WS

Long Shot—LS

Medium Shot—MS

Close-Up—CU

Extreme Close-Up—XCU

Over-the-Shoulder Shot (OSS)

I'M A NIGHTTIME MAN IN A DAYTIME JOB

VERSE
I gotta start the pump at work each day,
Though my own pump's running low.
Then at night when the whole town's asleep,
I'm pumped up and ready to go.

Man who looks like factory worker, redneck
type filling up a car at a gas station.
Guy excitedly walking by bar lights on street
with small town feeling.

CHORUS
'Cause I'm a nighttime man in a daytime job,
So it's sure hard to get ahead.
I get to work and it feels like night,
'Cause I'd sure like to go to bed.
Yeah, I'm a nighttime man in a daytime job,
And I'd rather work nights instead.

Guy looking very bored, tired in an office.
Get arrives in office looking out of it.
Guy puts his head down on desk, or lies down
on desk or couch like a sleep.
Guy working at a nighttime job, such as at a
late night gas station, bar, etc.

VERSE
I like to go to clubs at midnight,
Dancing to the bands till close.
At the diner I like to talk till dawn.
And only then do I want to go home.

Guy going into a nightclub.
Guy dancing in club or on the street in front
of bar. Shot of guy through window of dinner
talking with someone.
Guy walking to or into house late at night.

VERSE
Too bad my wife's asleep when I come alive,
And I'm ready to jump and rock.
I'm just living life in a diff'rent time zone.
My life's set to a different clock.

Guy tries to shake wife awake while she is
sleeping, pulling her up while he's dancing.
Shot of guy throwing clock away, smashing
it.

REPEAT CHORUS

Could repeat imagery from chorus, or a
variation on previous chorus – ie doing same
actions but in another type of work setting.

BRIDGE
So it's time to change.
Turn my nights into days.
Find a way to shift my gears.
And play when other folks play.

See him dancing on a very sunny day in a
park, on a beach – doing kind of dance did at
night.
See lots of people around him. Maybe he
throws a ball or catches a Frisbee from a kid.

REPEAT CHORUS TWICE

TAG
Yeah, I'm a nighttime man in a
daytime job,
And I'd rather work nights instead.

Again, could repeat chorus imagery or a
variation on the theme.

See man very happily doing work at night –
ie: if started with him working at a gas station
during the day, now he's there at night.

Copyright Gini Graham Scott and
Dicky Minor

After you indicate the scenes chronologically, you can rearrange them to reflect the order of scenes you are shooting. Possibly the shots may be further reordered by the director or DP during the actual shooting, but it is easier and less confusing if you order the scenes using the original numbers from the chronological listing. You can do so to make your own suggestions to the director or DP or after talking to them for their input on the order of the scenes.

To illustrate, I've included a scene and shot breakdown from *The Consultation*. I have included a few pages of each scene and shot breakdown sequentially, before they were reordered to suggest the sequence for the actual shoot. The complete scene breakdown is in Appendix A.

Example of Doing a Sequential Scene Breakdown

THE CONSULTATION

by Gini Graham Scott

SCENE BREAKDOWN—SEQUENTIALLY

FADE IN:

1. LOCATION: INT. ANDREA'S OFFICE—DAY (WS)

ACTORS: Andrea, Burt

SPECIAL PROPS: Printout, Paper, Notebook, Chairs

ANDREA, 30s, a marketing consultant, meets with BURT, 40s, an insurance broker.

1a. CLOSE-IN SHOT OF ANDREA (MS)

Andrea flips through a printout.

> ANDREA
> I do have some suggestions after looking through the material about your project.

1b. CLOSE-IN SHOT OF BURT (MS)

> BURT
> Good. And I want to assure you, we'll be paying you.

1c. MEDIUM SHOT OF ANDREA AND BURT (2S)
Andrea whips out a blank sheet of paper.

ANDREA
Thanks. So now if I can get your credit card number.
Burt hesitates, then reluctantly gives it to her.

BURT
Okay. Here it is,

1d. CLOSE-IN SHOT OF ANDREA AND WHAT SHE'S WRIT-
ING (CU)
Andrea begins to write.
Minutes later, Andrea finishes writing and looks at Burt.

ANDREA
Now let me give you my suggestions.

1e. CLOSE-IN SHOT OF BURT (CU)

BURT
Good. I want you to give me the good, the bad, and the
ugly. We have a lot riding on this—millions.

1f: MEDIUM SHOT OF ANDREA AND BURT (MS)
Andrea flips through the book as she talks.

ANDREA
Okay. First, I want to understand what you want me to
do, since you already have a proposal and writer for this.

BURT
Yeah. Now what we need is a publishing consultant to
discuss our strategy.

2. LOCATION: ANDREA'S OFFICE—LATER THAT NIGHT
ACTORS: Andrea, Burt
SPECIAL PROPS: Credit Card Machine, Paper or Bill with Order
Information

2a. LONG SHOT OF ANDREA (WS)
Andrea picks up the paper with Burt's credit card information and
clicks some buttons on her credit card machine.

2b. A CLOSE-UP OF CREDIT CARD MACHINE (CU)
A close in shows $175.00.

2c. A MEDIUM SHOT OF ANDREA (MS)
She clicks some more buttons.

2d. A CLOSE-UP OF THE CREDIT CARD MACHINE (CU)
A tape prints out the sale.

3: LOCATION: INT. ANDREA'S BEDROOM—THE NEXT MORNING (LS)
ACTORS: Andrea, Burt
SPECIAL PROPS: Phone, Bed or Couch

A ringing phone wakes Andrea. She picks it up groggily.

As you'll notice, there are only a few scenes, but multiple shots from
different angles and distances to keep the viewer engaged visually. At
one time, scenes were more likely to feature only one or a very few
shots from one or two camera positions. But today there is much more

quick editing and intercutting between different shots, which mix in wide, medium, close-up, and extreme close-up shots taken from different angles. While the close-up shots draw the viewer in closer to the action and to feel more emotionally involved with the character, the wider and medium shots create a sense of remove, distance, and detachment from what the character or characters are feeling.

Example of Turning a Sequential Scene Breakdown into an Ordered Scene Breakdown

After you have the scenes numbered in sequence, you can move them around based on how you want to shoot the scenes. Later the editor can reassemble them by following the scene numbers.

In this case, instead of doing shot breakdowns for each scene, I designated each shot as a another scene, since much of the video was being shot with a green screen, suggesting a car moving from one place to another. Thus, while the actors might be stationary in the car, they were in a series of different scenes, which changed outside their window, using the green screen to project the changing backgrounds.

I have included an example from *The Engagement*, a film I produced and wrote. The first half provides a scene breakdown sequentially; the second half provides a breakdown based on the order of shooting, which I discussed with the director/DP. I did not further break down the scenes into shots, since I left it up to the director/DP to decide on the order in which he wanted to shoot the scenes. Again, I have included only a few pages, the full breakdown for the script is in Appendix B.

THE ENGAGEMENT
by Gini Graham Scott
SCENE BREAKDOWN—SEQUENTIALLY

1. LOCATION: EXT. FREEWAY OAKLAND LEADING TO BAY BRIDGE—DAY

ACTORS: None
SPECIAL PROPS: None
A pan shows cars driving toward the toll booth.

2. LOCATION: EXT. CITY STREET NEAR FREEWAY RAMP IN
EAST BAY—DAY
GREEN SCREEN—SHOOT ON AMY DRIVE
ACTORS: Sam and Mary Beth
SPECIAL PROPS: Ordinary Sedan
DRESS: Casual Weekend Wear for Professionals
ACTION: SAM, 30s, is driving with MARY BETH, 30s, toward San
Francisco. They are both dressed casually, as business professionals
might on a day off.
Sam stops at a light.

3. LOCATION: EXT. INTERIOR OF CAR—DAY
GREEN SCREEN—SHOOT ON AMY DRIVE
ACTORS: Mary Beth
SPECIAL PROPS: Engagement Ring
Mary Beth holds up her hand to admire her ring.

> MARY BETH
> It's so nice. I can't wait to show it off at the party.

4. LOCATION: EXT. INTERIOR OF CAR—DAY
GREEN SCREEN—SHOOT ON AMY DRIVE
ACTORS: Mary Beth and Sam
Mary Beth leans over and plants a kiss on Sam's cheek.

> MARY BETH
> And finally after two years.

Sam looks up at the light, trying to concentrate on the road and listen
to Mary Beth.

SAM
Yeah, it'll be nice to finally announce it.

5. LOCATION: ENTRANCE TO FREEWAY RAMP—DAY
The light changes and Sam heads onto the freeway ramp.

6. LOCATION: EXT. FREEWAY IN OAKLAND HEADING TO
THE BAY BRIDGE—DAY
ACTORS: Mary Beth and Sam—Doing Voice-Overs
A long shot shows cars on the freeway.

MARY BETH (V.O.)
(A little shrewish)
Yes. Mom and Daddy will be so pleased. And I'm sure
you'll enjoy working for Dad. So much better than the
crappy jobs you've had for the past year.

SAM (V.O.)
I know. But it's been so hard being a writer.

7. LOCATION: EXT: INTERIOR OF CAR—DAY
GREEN SCREEN—SHOOT ON AMY DRIVE
ACTORS: Mary Beth and Sam
SPECIAL PROPS: Engagement Ring
Mary Beth waves her hand around, looking at her ring, as Sam drives.

MARY BETH
But Daddy to the rescue.

SAM
Yeah, I guess.

SCENE BREAKDOWN—SHOOTING SCHEDULE

CITY STREETS, GAS STATION, CONVENIENCE STORE—10:30 A.M.–12:30 P.M.

15. LOCATION: EXT. CITY STREET—DAY
ACTORS: Mary Beth and Sam—Doing Voice-Overs
Sam is driving on a city street.

> MARY BETH (V.O.)
> Now we'll be late. If only you hadn't missed the turnoff.

> SAM (V.O.)
> Well, I was talking to you. I got distracted.

> MARY BETH (V.O.)
> Oh, so it's my fault! Anyway, you know how I hate being late.

20. LOCATION: EXT. GAS STATION—A FEW MINUTES LATER
Passing traffic suggests this is a busy downtown gas station.

21. LOCATION: EXT. GAS STATION—A FEW MINUTES LATER
ACTORS: Sam, Station Attendant, Mary Beth
SPECIAL PROPS: Air Gauge, Low Tire
Sam is next to a pump, starting to pump gas, when the STATION ATTENDANT comes over to him.

> STATION ATTENDANT
> Hey, did you know your tire looks really low?

Close in shows a low tire.
Mary Beth peeks her head out of the car.

> MARY BETH
> Oh no. We're in a rush.

> STATION ATTENDANT
> Oh, it'll just take a minute. Good thing you stopped, or
> you could have had a blowout.

As the station attendant pumps air into the tire, Mary Beth glares at
Sam.

> SAM
> Hey, what can I do? I gotta put air in it.

33. LOCATION: EXT. CONVENIENCE STORE—MINUTES
LATER
ACTORS: Sam and Mary Beth
SPECIAL PROPS: "Closed" Sign
Sam pulls into the store lot, but a sign says "Closed."

35. LOCATION: EXT. CONVENIENCE STORE—MOMENTS
LATER
ACTORS: Mary Beth and Sam
SPECIAL PROPS: Cell Phone, Engagement Ring
Mary Beth gets out, leaving the door open, and pulls out her cell
phone. Sam looks stunned.

> SAM
> Yeah, okay.

Sam looks at the ring, dazed, as Mary Beth walks around the corner
with her phone.

36. LOCATION: EXT. CONVENIENCE STORE—MOMENTS
LATER

ACTORS: Sam, Young Woman
SPECIAL PROPS: Wild Flowers, Cell Phone
Suddenly, a knock on the car door. Sam looks up to see an attractive
YOUNG WOMAN, late 20s, with long, flowing hair, in a loose-fitting
dress. She holds some flowers.

> YOUNG WOMAN
> Hi! I'm sorry to bother you. But I took the wrong turn
> and my car ran out of gas. And this store is closed and
> my cell phone died.

Sam looks at her, obviously attracted and intrigued.

> YOUNG WOMAN
> So can you give me a lift?

Sam perks up and smiles broadly.

> SAM
> Sure. Anywhere you want.

The young woman gets in.

LUNCH AT AMY DRIVE—12:30 P.M.–1 P.M.

SHOOTING VOICE-OVER AND GREEN SCREEN SHOTS IN
CAR—AMY DRIVE—1:00 P.M.–4:30 P.M.

6. LOCATION: EXT. FREEWAY IN OAKLAND HEADING
TO THE BAY BRIDGE—DAY (VOICE-OVER WITH GREEN
SCREEN SHOTS)
A long shot shows cars on the freeway.
ACTORS: Mary Beth and Sam—Doing Voice-Overs

> MARY BETH (V.O.)
> (A little shrewish)
> Yes. Mom and Daddy will be so pleased. And I'm sure
> you'll enjoy working for Dad. So much better than the
> crappy jobs you've had for the past year.

> SAM (V.O.)
> I know. But it's been so hard being a writer.

13. LOCATION: EXT. TOLL BOOTH ENTRY TO THE BAY
BRIDGE—DAY (VOICE OVER WITH GREEN SCREEN SHOTS)
A close-in of the car shot suggests Sam is at the toll booth.
ACTORS: Mary Beth and Sam—Doing Voice-Overs

> MARY BETH (V.O.)
> (Annoyed)
> Geez. How could you end up here?

> SAM (V.O.)
> Don't worry. I'll just turn around.

Using a Producer's Checklist

This is another approach suggested to me by a director/producer I
worked with on one of my films, *Heads Up*. It's a simple one-sheet approach in which you list the number of scenes, the characters in each
scene, and the location. Should you have several scenes with the same
characters in the same location, you would combine them. In addition, you briefly note the props and costumes you need for the shoot,
and any special wardrobe you want for the characters for the shoot.

Following are two examples from two of her shoots. In one, the
characters are indicated by their initials.

Producer's Checklist for *Box of Truth*

Scene	Character	Location
1	Henry, Theodore, Robber	Metro/Lafayette or Pleasant Hill BART
2	Henry & Robber	Outside metro
3	Theodore & Courier	Theodore's house
4	Grandmother & Theodore	Grandmother's house

PROPS AND COSTUME

Box with Theodore's name on it

Small box for dog tag

World War II attire

Clipboard

Letter to Theodore

Pen

Books on Fiji—got it

Artifacts from Fiji

Blood

Pictures of younger Theodore

Picture of Henry

Theodore—student look; preppy attire

Henri—scruffy/grunge look

Courier—polo shirt and khaki shorts

Grandmother—duster

Tiffany—professional work attire

Michelle—professional work attire

Robber—black hooded sweatshirt

"SHORT FILM"

Scene	Character	Location
1	GFX	
2	R & V	Lobby
3, 4, 5, 6	A & V	Kitchen
7, 8, 9	W & V	Living Room
10, 11	D & V	Bedroom
12, 13, 14, 15	M1, 2 & V	Car
16, 17, 18	P & V	Street
19	R & V	Lobby
20, 21, 22	A & V	Porch
23, 24	W & V	Sidewalk
25	M2 & V	Sidewalk
26	P & V	Street Corner
27, 28	M1 & V	Street Corner
29	ALL	Street
30	M1 & V	Street
31	V	Street
32, 33, 34	ALL	Street

PROPS AND COSTUME

Blue outfit	Alcohol bottle
House clothes	Picture of family
Prostitute outfit	Make-up for bruise
Black suit for angels	Clipboard
Blue chalk	Flowers
Gun	Candles
Car	

Chapter 4

Creating a Storyboard

In some cases, a director or DP will want a storyboard, in addition to a scene breakdown, to help visualize the scene. Commonly the director or DP will be responsible for doing the storyboard or having it done, and on feature films, a professional storyboard artist normally does a very detailed illustration for each scene—much like a comic book.

There is storyboard software in which you can adapt graphic images of characters and other objects to various settings. Some of the popular programs include StoryBoard Quick 6, which retails for around $250–$300 (http://www.powerproduction.com or http://www.storyboardquick.com), Toon Boom, which retails for about $200 (http://www.toonboom.com/products/storyboard), and Celtx, which is free, though you can purchase sketch images, such as characters, animals, and vehicles for about $10. (http://www.celtx.com). Basically what all these storyboard programs do is give you storyboard templates, along with images you can manipulate, to create scenes with those characters and objects.

If you are not an artist yourself, consider looking for an artist who might volunteer or do a storyboard for a low cost—say $50 to $100. A good source for such artists might be local art schools or art departments. Or ask friends, neighbors, and business associates, or put an ad on Craigslist under gigs or jobs.

You can also quickly do a simple storyboard, even if you are not an artist. Even stick figures might be enough to give the director or DP an idea of how to compose a shot.

To create a storyboard, turn each shot in the scene breakdown into a visual, and you can even use simple stick figures to do so. Begin by creating a template with small squares—about 2" to 3" square—in which to draw your storyboard, using a portrait or landscape layout. A 4 x 5 or 3 x 4 table in Word or other word-processing program makes an ideal template, and you can print out multiple copies.

Now you are ready to start drawing. You can either write in all of the shots in sequence and afterward fill in the drawings—or create and label each drawing as you go along. These shots should include master or wide shots, medium shots, close-ups, extreme close-ups, over-the-shoulder shots, cutaways for graphic images—basically anything with a different camera position.

To turn your storyboard into a graphics file to send it to others, scan it and save it in one of the graphics formats, such as a JPEG, GIF, or BMP file. It is better to use a .bmp rather than a .jpg format since you will get sharper lines. Then you can either send each page as a separate image or insert a picture of each page into Word or another word-processing document so the whole storyboard is in a single file.

To illustrate, I've included a sample storyboard for a script for *Heads Up*, which was filmed while I was writing this book. The seven-minute short included nineteen scenes, with about seventy-five shots. Since I only sketched very rough stick-figure drawings, it took only about one and a half hours to create all the images. Though a storyboard artist might spend several days creating much more detailed illustrations, these rough drawings were all the director and DP of the shoot needed. So it can be easy to do such simple storyboards yourself.

As the first of the following storyboards illustrates, the scene and shot number is on the bottom left (i.e., 1a, 1b, 1c). I have indicated the initial for the name of each character, along with the beginning of each line of dialogue, which corresponds to the dialogue for that shot in the scene breakdown.

Additionally, I have included a 3 x 3 storyboard used by my *Heads Up* director/DP, Judy Razon, for another shoot.

3x3 Format

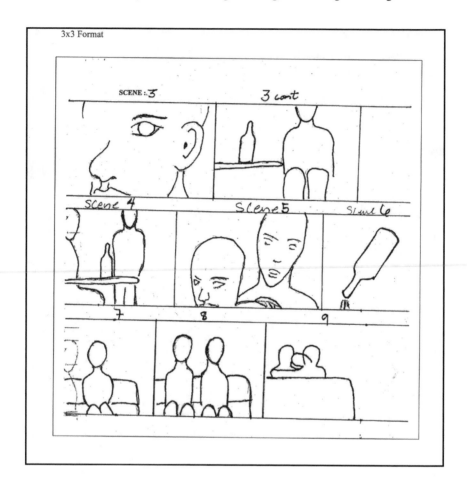

Chapter 5

Finding Locations

When thinking about location, consider each setup for a shot as another location. That's because it takes time to move the cameras, set up lighting and sound, and block the actor's positions again so that everyone is in the shot.

For example, if you plan to shoot at a house, each room is another location. If you shoot two or more scenes in different sections of the room, each one is another location if you have to move the equipment or change the lighting, unless you pan your camera to follow an actor around the room and your lighting and sound is already set up so you can do the pan without stopping to change your setup.

If you are shooting outdoors, you are also dealing with additional locations each time you do another camera setup, unless you are doing a handheld shot where you follow an actor from one place to another.

With outdoor shooting, setups tend to be faster since you normally don't have to worry about setting up and moving lights, although in some cases, you may want to do some fill lighting or have one or more reflectors on a stand or held by one of the PAs.

However, a big concern with shooting outside is controlling the sound. For example, if it's a windy day, you will get sounds from the wind, so unless you want that for ambience, you have to muffle the mikes, so they don't pick that sound—or at least pick up much less of it. Also, if you are near a street, there will be sounds of traffic, which might be fine for ambient sound. But at other times, you may need to stop shooting until a loud sound ends, such as when a large truck or noisy motorcycle roars by.

Determining the Number of Locations for Your Film

Since every location requires another setup, keep that in mind when you write or choose a script for your production. Generally if you plan for a one-day shoot—which is ideal for shorts since it's easiest to get a commitment from a low-pay or no-pay crew and cast for one day—figure on how much time you need for each setup and how many setups you can get in the time planned for the shoot.

For example, say you are planning to shoot from 9 a.m. to 6 p.m., with the crew arriving at 9 a.m. and the actors arriving at 10 a.m. and staying until 5 p.m., with equipment breakdown and cleanup from 5 to 6 p.m.; and an hour for the actor rehearsals while the crew finishes the initial set up. Then if it'll take half an hour to shoot each scene, and one and a half hours for additional setup, plus half an hour for lunch, you can have up to three locations since you are shooting from 11 a.m. to 5 p.m. ($\frac{1}{2} + 1\frac{1}{2} + \frac{1}{2} + \frac{1}{2} + 1\frac{1}{2} = 4\frac{1}{2}$). There's no time for an additional setup, which would take another two hours, unless everyone agrees to stay longer.

If you find that you have too many locations to finish filming in the time allotted, make sure that your actors and crew will agree to a second day of filming, or reduce the number of locations in the script so you can film everything. It's important to time your setups for each location in advance, since otherwise, you are likely to not be able to finish your planned shooting for the day—or you will end up scrambling at the end to complete your short by cutting corners, such as by taking fewer shot angles or takes, to get it done in time.

Deciding What Locations to Use

As you write or choose your script, you may already have certain locations in mind, such as a house, park, street, or shopping center. If so, use them if you can. Otherwise, do some advance scouting so you have your locations set before the day of the shoot.

Permissions and Precautions in Choosing Locations

In deciding on a location, keep in mind the following.

You can't use a private property or shoot from land on a private property unless you have the permission of the owner. Sometimes film groups attempt to film without permission, such as when no one seems around a field or pasture in the countryside, a house seems to be abandoned, an industrial building appears to be closed, or a private beach seems deserted on a cool day. And some groups complete their filming on such private locations without incident. But you are taking a risk of being cited or arrested for trespassing, and you risk the possibility that your film might be destroyed or your equipment confiscated as evidence. So if you decide to shoot anyway, be prepared to run quickly or face any consequences if you are stopped during the shoot.

You are not permitted to use observable trade names, such as a Chevron sign at a gas station or a Safeway sign at a grocery store. The exception is if you are doing a documentary, since there is an exception for news videos. If you use a trade name in other types of shorts, this is trademark infringement, and the owners can ask you not to show the film anymore or seek penalties in a civil action against you. This law may not seem to make sense since many companies with trademarks pay for product placements in films and TV shows as a form of advertising. But they do this in films or programs that will get wide distribution, and they have advance knowledge about the film or show's content and can approve how their product will to be used. But such wide distribution is unlikely for a short, and unless you seek permission, the company will not have seen your script in advance to approve of the use of its name or logo. So there is a risk if the company learns about your film, they can ask you to stop showing it or they might seek monetary penalties. If you expect few people to see your short, such as if it will only be in a portfolio for prospective clients and will not be posted on any place accessible to the public, this may not be a big risk. But given the possible consequences, it is best to use locations where there are no trademarked images or you have an approval to use them.

As long as you are filming on or from public property, you generally don't need permissions, subject to the above exceptions. However, if you are filming on private property or filming what might be a private activity, even if you are on public property, you need permission. An example might be using a zoom lens to film on someone's private backyard where people who can be recognized are having a conversation. This would be considered an invasion of privacy, though some filmmakers take the risk that no one will protest when the film comes out.

As long as you don't interfere with traffic on public streets, you can commonly film there, although some cities require permits, with prices varying per city. For example, in Oakland, I have filmed in the streets in my residential neighborhood. I even had a car painted and outfitted to look like a cop car sitting in front of my house and driving around the neighborhood for two hours without my having to get a permit. I just had to call dispatch and let them know that I would have a cop car on my street for a film project, so if anyone called in about this, the dispatcher could reassure the caller there was no problem in the neighborhood.

By contrast, in LA, such filming not only required a payment to the police but a permit for filming in the city—approximately $1,000. Still, some filmmakers take the risk of being shut down, such as the producers of a short film who filmed on Mulholland Drive for about an hour. While they were shooting a scene, the PA stood in the road and asked the drivers to wait for a few minutes until the director called "Cut." Since few cops patrol Mulholland Drive and the drivers were patient, the filmmakers were able to finish their film without incident. But in another case, as soon as the camera operator started to set up a camera for a scene near the Third Street Promenade in Santa Monica, the local security guards were there within a moment telling the crew to close it down since they had no permit.

Be aware of local permitting requirements for shooting on public property and contact the appropriate agency if you need permission, unless you want to take your chances shooting guerrilla style. For example, in San Francisco, if you film on a city street, you need a permit from the police; if you film in a park under federal jurisdiction, such as the Presidio, you need a permit from the Federal Parks and Recreation Department. If you film in a city park, you need a permit from the San Francisco Parks Department. If it's a quick shot, you may be able to film without a permit, and no one will stop you, such as what occurred when a camera person for the TV pilot of *Behind the Scenes with Debbi and Frankie* went roaming about with her camera to get some B-roll pickup shots to set the scene and no one stopped her from filming. Or if you are stopped, you might try explaining that this is a student film, and commonly you will be told you can't film without a permit, and you just have to end your shoot without a penalty. And by then, you may have already gotten the shot you need. However, if you need to be in a location for any length of time and this is an important shot for your film, it's best to get a permit, and sometimes the cost is fairly low—about $50 for many city permits.

Scouting for Locations

Before you shoot your film, it is best to go to the locations in advance so you know what to expect. Ideally go with whoever will be the director and/or DP, if you aren't going to be the director or DP yourself, so you can all review the location. Alternatively, you can take photos of the suggested locations, and the director or DP can tell you which ones he or she would like to use.

If it's an outdoor location, try to go there around the time of day when you plan to shoot so you can see where the sun is and what the lighting looks like at that time. Then you can determine if this will be a good time to shoot the film, or if not, rearrange the schedule to shoot at a better time.

If it's an indoor location, note what the rooms look like and the amount of space you have for setting up different types of shots. For example, if it's a small space, you may have to use a wide-angle lens to get everything in for a wide shot, or you may have to limit yourself to medium shots and close-ups.

For indoor shots, also note how the furniture is arranged and whether you have to move anything—or if you will be allowed to do this. For example, in shooting *Zoo Do*, we used my living room to create an office environment and did medium shots of a boss by a computer in a corner of the room, so we didn't have to move anything. But for another shoot, *Peace Out*, the DP wanted additional angles of the three actors who were seated in chairs in the middle of the room, so we had to move one of the couches out of the room to have extra space for the lights and cameras on tripods. Some people will be willing to let you use their house but won't let you move anything, so check in advance about what you can and can't do so you can adapt your shoot accordingly or find another location.

Taking Photos of the Proposed Locations

A good way to remember your proposed locations is to take photos of them as you drive or walk around checking them out. You can also use these photos to show others on your team who are deciding where to shoot, such as the director or DP. These photos are especially good in showing off the look of different neighborhoods you are considering for your shoot. These photos can show off important features or places you might want to include in your film, such as a large oak tree or a convenience store hangout. When you take indoor shots, it is helpful to include the dimensions of each room so you will know if a room is large enough for the shoot, and you can better plan how to shoot there.

Photos of my house, which has been used in numerous films, can be found on my website at www.changemakersproductions.com /locations.htm. The exteriors were used in *Cougar and Cub* and *The Engagement*, the side of the house and patio for *The New Child* and *Massage Wash*, the living room for *Ironworkers*, and the living room, den, the downstairs office/den for *Zoo Do, Zoo Don't*, and *My Four Presidents*. My garage was used for the office of a mad scientist in *The New Child*.

Getting Pickup Shots for Your Shoot

Besides taking photos of the proposed locations, your search for locations can be a good time to get B-roll pickup shots, which can be used in your video, so you don't have to take them during or after the shoot. For example, you might take wide or long shots to show what the neighborhood looks like.

One way to easily get these shots is for the person with the video camera to sit in the passenger seat or backseat of a car and shoot out of the window while the other person drives. Or stop briefly to get out of the car to get these shots. Another way to shoot from a car is to use a camera mount, which attaches the camera to the front or side of a car; then the camera rolls as the car drives.

As much as possible, take the pickup shots when you see them, so you don't have to go back and shoot them another time. Or take these pickup shots at about the same time you will be shooting on the set so your lighting in both sets of shots will match.

Considering What You Have to Change in the Shot

In deciding among the various locations, consider what you have to move around to make the shot work and whether you are permitted to make those changes. Also, factor in the time needed to make changes on the set and put everything back as it was after the shoot. If you have to do too much rearranging, you may have to rework the scene so you don't have to make many changes or choose another location.

For example, suppose a friend offers to let you shoot at no charge at his house, but it has all kinds of bric-a-brac on the shelves and Impressionist paintings on the walls. Consider if that décor will work in the scene or not, if you can shoot so you don't show the items, or if your friend can move them for the shoot. If the answer to these questions is no, find another location.

Getting Permissions to Use Special Locations

In some cases, you need special permissions to use certain locations, such as if you want to shoot in an office, store, or bank. Sometimes a friend or business associate may offer you access to their office but may still need the permission of a boss or manager. In that case, be prepared to have a meeting in which you tell the boss or manager what your film is about, how much time you will need for filming, and what you will film there. Sometimes you may get a verbal go-ahead, but other times you will have to sign a written permission form or apply for one, such as if the store manager has to get the approval from a regional or other manager higher up in the organization, which may require a week or two to go through the system. Commonly such written permissions will also include a liability release and agreement to cover any damages, so be prepared to sign—or find another place.

However, even when such written permissions might be required, a friend or associate may give you the permission to film anyway as long as they are present, say because they are in the cast. If so, you might take a chance and hope for the best. For instance, that's what happened in filming *Cracked*, a seven-minute dramatic short. The star of the video was the office manager of a beautiful two-floor office complex, and she permitted us to film in several rooms since we would be filming at night when no one else was there, apart from a few IT techs who were working late. And the filming went off without a hitch.

Considering Liability and Damage Issues

In many cases, you will be asked to sign a release where you assume the responsibility for any damage you cause, although if you are doing a short for a client, ask them to assume the responsibility or have their insurance cover it. But if you are doing your own film, you are responsible. So be willing to sign a form acknowledging your responsibility if asked, and even if not, be willing to assume that responsibility for any damage caused by your cast or crew.

Even if you haven't agreed to be responsible in writing, consider it creating good will or karma to do this. Such a situation occurred when I was on a shoot put on through MMTB (Movie Making Throughout the Bay Area), an organization that brings together writers, directors, actors, and other crew members for one-day shoots. The director didn't have his own camera, so a friend on the crew offered to let him use an extra camera. However, while the director was using the camera for a series of handheld shots, the camera stopped working, though this wasn't apparent during the shoot. Afterward, the crew member who lent his camera discovered this, but when he spoke to the director about the problem, the director claimed the camera wasn't working before the shoot. However, it was a brand-new camera valued at about $1,300, and it had been working when the crew member tested it the day before. To make a long story short, the friend and the director are no longer friends.

I have been on about four dozen shoots, where the issue of liability and damage never came up, because fortunately nothing was damaged. But in case something is, you should have liability insurance to cover this. Check with your insurance company about what they recommend.

Chapter 6

Finding Your Crew

On a low- or no-budget shoot, a crew can range in size from one to nine or ten people, and some people can play multiple roles. But ideally you will have at least three to five people. On a shoe-string shoot, you may not be able to get everyone you want to participate, so be ready to adapt to the people who are available. Also, be ready to adapt, if possible, if someone doesn't show up on the day of a shoot, which sometimes happens because someone has gotten a paying gig or if someone is ill. However, if a key person can't make it or doesn't show up for whatever reason, you will have to cancel or reschedule the shoot, unless you can rework the script to shoot around that person.

The Major Roles in a Film Shoot

These are the main roles in a film shoot, some of which are optional but ideal if you can have someone do it. Besides being the writer and producer, you may sometimes play one or more of the other roles, most notably being the director. But unless you are technically inclined, ideally have other people perform these other roles since this will leave you free to generally oversee the production, which isn't easy if you are tied to other roles, such as running a camera or operating a sound boom.

The Director. The director works with the actors to guide them in their performance and may be involved in rehearsals and blocking out the positions where the actors should be in each scene, such as by telling them where to stand and sometimes using tape on the floor to mark the spot so they always come to their mark in a scene. Also, the director commonly checks the shots in the camera viewer or monitor, although some directors trust the director of photography (DP) and camera people to organize and frame the shot. Once the shot is framed, the director asks if the camera and sound people are ready to shoot, instructs the PA or anyone else who is slating the scene to slate it, and finally calls "Action" once the person slating the scene is out of frame. Lastly, after the action for the scene ends, the director calls "Cut" to end the action for that take, though sometimes the camera and sound will keep rolling so the action can continue without slating another take.

The Director of Photography (or DP). Sometimes called the cinematographer, the DP is responsible for the look of the film. He or she plans out the shots for each scene, and checks the cameras to make sure each camera operator is framing the shots as desired and knows how and when to zoom, pan, or tilt during the shot. Also, the DP may be involved in setting up the scene, including moving around any furniture to clear the way to position the camera or cameras. The DP may additionally be responsible for setting up the lighting and sound or working with whoever is setting this up to make sure the scene is properly lit and the sound equipment is set at the appropriate levels to record the scene. In some cases, the DP will be a camera operator or handle the only camera.

The Camera Operator. Sometimes called the videographer, the camera operator will run one of the cameras and is responsible for framing the shot, and as appropriate, zooming, panning, tilting, or moving the camera (sometimes called "trucking"). Often in low-budget shoots, the sound will be recorded on the camera through a lavalier or shotgun mike, and if so, the camera operator will make sure the sound is recording. Other responsibilities include checking the exposure and focus, and making sure there is a good white balance.

The Lighting Person. Sometimes called a gaffer, the lighting person is responsible for setting up the lighting, although often on a low-budget shoot there won't be a separate person to do this. Instead the DP, director, camera operator, or PAs will all pitch in to help light the set. When you are shooting outdoors, you may not need a lighting person, though sometimes you will want to use reflectors to diffuse or refocus the sun. Then the lighting person will hold a reflector, if there isn't a PA to do this. Generally for an indoor shoot, the lighting person will set up three lights, which include the main or key light, two side lights, and sometimes a fourth backlight, to eliminate shadows behind the actors and create more separation between them and the background. In some cases, a lighting person may use filters and gels on the lights to create special effects, though this is rare on low-budget productions.

The Sound Person. The sound person is responsible for making sure the sound equipment is set to the appropriate level and is recording properly. Ideally you will have a separate sound person to record the sound off of the camera, although commonly on low-budget shoots, you won't record the sound separately but will record directly into the camera using the on-camera mike or an external mike connected to the camera by a cable. In this case, the camera operator or DP is the one who checks the sound, although you might have someone who knows sound well do the checks.

PAs (Production Assistants). The PAs are important for providing various types of support for both the crew and the actors. Generally you should have at least one PA and preferably two or three. Often PAs are new to filmmaking, and this is a good way for them to learn what to do so they can move up to more technical or specialized positions. Some of the things PAs may do include:

- Unpack and log in the equipment and help pack it up.
- Use a clapboard (also called a slate) to slate each take (or use a sheet of paper indicating the take and scene, if you don't have a clapboard).
- Record each take on a scene log form.
- Obtain signed release forms with address and contact information from the actors and crew members.
- Go on errands, as needed, to pick up and drop off actors and crew members arriving by public transportation, or buy needed supplies, such as batteries, water bottles, and lunch.
- Prepare the lunch or dinner for the crew and help with cleanup afterward.
- Hold reflectors or mikes during a shoot.
- Help in moving furniture, pictures, and other things in a room.
- Assist in other ways as needed.

Script Supervisor. The script supervisor does some of the same things as a PA, but is more experienced in already knowing what to do and has additional responsibilities. Among other things, the script supervisor checks for continuity from shot to shot, such as making sure that an object in one scene is in the same place in another or that an actor is wearing the same clothing, which is adjusted in the same way from scene to scene, unless there is a reason to change that. Often the director or DP, or others on the set, will pay attention to continuity too. Additionally the script supervisor may be involved in checking the set design to make sure everything looks good and any props are in place. Often there is no script supervisor on a low-budget film, unless one of the PAs has gained the experience to be given this title.

Assistant Director. The assistant director acts as the right-hand person to the director and DP. Commonly there is no assistant director on a low-budget shoot, unless a PA or script supervisor has become experienced enough to be given this title.

Set or Production Designer. While big-budget films normally have a set or production designer, who contributes to the look of the film by envisioning the visual appearance and style of the set, commonly there is no separate set or production designer on a low-budget shoot. However, any member of the crew who has a good eye for design might help do this.

Makeup Artist. Ideally it would be nice to have someone trained in doing makeup to work with each actor or at least the main characters. But commonly no one does this on a low-budget shoot. Usually makeup artists are paid professionals, and it may be hard to get one to volunteer or work for low pay on a shoot. Still sometimes you may need someone who can do special types of makeup, such as making up someone to look like they have been beaten in a fight or bloodied by a gunshot. Sometimes actors will come with their own makeup kit, and can do the makeup for other actors, too.

Special Effects Artist. Usually there is no special effects artist on a low-budget shoot, since special effects, such as using CGI and green screen technology, become expensive. Thus, most low-budget scripts are written to not require such effects, though if someone is good at certain effects, you might use these on a limited scale.

Determining the Crew You Need

While I have listed numerous possible roles for a film shoot, think about the minimal number of roles you need filled to complete your shoot and the minimal number of people to perform these roles in one, or at most two, days. Focus on what you need to make it happen, tailor your shoot to keep the cost minimal, and if necessary, adapt your script so you can shoot it in fewer locations and with a smaller crew. This may mean you need to forgo the set designer, makeup artist, special effects artist, assistant artistic director, and so on to get your film made.

At a minimum, you need two or three people to handle directing, one camera, sound, and lighting. You can direct if someone else isn't doing this, and the director and camera operator can be one in the same. Whoever's handling the camera might also handle sound if the recording is done from the camera with an on-camera mike, lavalier, or shotgun mike connected directly to the camera, although it is better if you have a separate person to handle sound and lighting. It also helps to have one PA to handle the details of the shoot, though on a very small shoot, you can do this yourself.

Generally it's better to have two cameras—or even three—so one can take the wide and long establishing shots and possibly zoom in to take medium shots too, while a second camera takes the close-in shots and reaction shots from a different angle. In some cases, one camera is set up to take all the establishing shots and the sound, so no one has to operate the camera once it is set up. If there's a third camera, that can be on the other side of the main camera and take still another angle. The extra cameras can also be used to take the pickup or B-roll shots, while the other camera, or cameras, are shooting the main action, thus saving time during a shoot.

An advantage of using two or three cameras is that you don't have to do more takes with one camera to get these additional shots. However, some directors and DPs prefer to use a single camera and do additional takes, and you may not be able to get more than one camera. So when you plan your schedule for the shoot, figure out how long it will take to do the scene based on whether you have one or more cameras.

A good plan is to figure out the minimum crew you need to do the shoot and assign people to additional roles. Once you have your minimum crew or feel confident you will soon have everyone on board, you can find the actors needed for the shoot.

Finding the Crew for Your Shoot

In many low-budget shoots, you will be working with a volunteer crew, although an alternative might be to work with an experienced crew of professionals willing to work for reduced pay, because they like your project or need the work. The options will depend on where you are and your connections in the local film community. As you do more films, it will be easier to find people to work with you—both those who have worked with you before and those who have seen your past productions.

As you put your crew together, it helps to have the locations already in mind, since that will give everyone an idea of what kind of setup and equipment is needed for the shoot so they can let you know if they have this or if you will need to get it. Alternatively you can firm up the exact locations once you have the crew in place while you are recruiting the actors, since you can usually change your locations fairly easily for these small shoots. Getting a committed crew together can be more difficult, so it's usually best to lock in your core crew first.

Finding Volunteers Versus Professionals

In deciding whether to work with volunteers or professionals, a key consideration is cost versus experience, as well as where you are doing the shoot.

For example, when I was in LA it was very difficult to find an all-volunteer crew, because so many film people there are at least part-time working professionals. Thus, when I wrote and co-produced the

TV pilot for *Meet and Compete*, we hired a professional videographer and sound person at the reduced rate of $300 a day each, since they were essential to making a professional quality pilot. But the assistant camera person and PAs were all volunteers.

By contrast, when I returned to Oakland, I found many willing volunteers to be directors, DPs, and sound and lighting people, because many people in this area participate in filmmaking for the love of the art, usually on weekends, since they have regular full-time jobs or because they are putting together portfolios to get paying film industry jobs. So I was able to get much more done in Oakland than in LA because of the large number of willing crew members for volunteer shoots.

Similarly, if you are in a small town or a city outside of LA, you may be better able to find volunteers or individuals willing to work for rock-bottom pay for your crew.

With many volunteers, you can count on their commitment to the shoot because they are doing this to gain the experience and they value being someone others can count on. But with some volunteers, a risk is that they may get a paying job on another project and may cancel shortly before the shoot. So discuss that possibility with any volunteer if they are going to be in a key role, such as being the DP or doing the sound or lighting, because it may not be possible to replace them or their equipment just before a shoot, and you may have to cancel and reschedule the shoot for another time. With PAs and other less essential and more easily replaceable people, this risk is of less concern.

The Cost of Hiring a Professional

If you choose to go with a working professional, figure on about $200–$400 a day for the DP and the sound professional. They may normally make more, but they may be willing to work on your shoot for less when they understand it is for a low-budget short and they can work on an off day on the weekend.

The one crew member I would suggest paying is the editor, since the other crew members can do their work in a one-day shoot of about six to eight hours, or at most two days of six to eight hours each. But the editor is likely to spend ten to twenty hours editing your project with special equipment and software. While you may be able to find editors who will work for free, it will typically take them much longer to edit the project since they will be fitting it in around paid assignments, and they are likely to be less experienced so they can't do as good a job.

To help select an editor, look at examples of their previous work. Typically editors will have examples on their website, YouTube, or Vimeo, which you can look at to determine if you like their style. Then take that past work into consideration in choosing your editor.

Generally editors charge around $35–$50 an hour, though a less experienced editor will work for $10–$25 an hour. Or you may be able to work out a package price for the edit. For example, I have typically paid $100–$300 for editing a five- to seven-minute short and $100–$150 for a one- to two-minute sizzle reel, though in LA I found that the costs tend to be a little higher—about $500 for a short and $250–$300 for the sizzle reel.

Where to Find Crew Members
The various places to find crew members include the following:

- Place an ad on Craigslist under "gigs" in your community.
- Contact a local film school or training center, such as the Berkeley Community Media in Berkeley, California.
- Find a film industry Meetup group in your community through www.meetup.com. After you join the group, you can place an announcement that you are looking for crew members for a project by suggesting an idea or sending a message to other group members, though sometimes you may have to get the approval of the Meetup organizer before your idea is posted or your message is sent.
- Contact film industry groups in your area, which you can find through a Google search or through Facebook or LinkedIn. Put your city or county in the search box and combine it with different

combinations of words, like "film industry" and "filmmakers." Then you can join the film groups that you find.

- Check if there is a chapter for a group, like Making Movies Throughout the Bay Area or the United Filmmakers Association, in your community. Other groups that might have local chapters are Women in Film or Women in Film and Media. If these organizations have a forum, you can generally post your request for help with your film on their Facebook wall or forum on their website. Or you can go to their meetings and network with prospective crew members there.
- Check if there is a directory of filmmakers in your community, such as the Reel Directory for the Bay Area.
- Check if there is a 48-Hour Film Project in your area. If so, you can list your availability to be on a film shoot, go to a recruitment meeting held a week or two before the project begins, or sign up to produce a short film yourself and invite others to join your crew.

Once you find these groups, you may need to join them, and often there is no charge, such as when you join a Meetup, Facebook, or LinkedIn group. Then post your need for crew members or ask the group organizer or coordinator to post your announcement for you. For instance, I have found many crew members through my film industry Meetup groups both in LA (Film and TV Connection and The Hollywood Film Industry) and in the Bay Area (Bay Area Film and TV Connection and the San Francisco Movie Makers).

Still another way to find members is to go to the events put on by these groups, so you can meet and network with prospective crew members. Going to these events is an ideal way to start building relationships so you have a network of potential crew members you can call on for projects again and again. For instance, I have met many prospective crew members through events and mixers put on by Movie Makers Around the Bay Area and the United Filmmakers Association.

As you get more involved with others in the film industry, you may also find opportunities to write, produce, or direct projects that are initiated by others.

Chapter 7

Casting Your Film

The usual approach in casting a short film is to first have the script, then cast the actors based on the different roles. Another approach that some producers and directors use is starting with a team of actors they already know and writing a script for them. Either approach can work well, though the focus here will be on selecting a cast to match your script.

Where to Find Actors

Actors are everywhere, including among family, friends, and business associates. However, unless the people you know have acting talent, it is best to look for actors who can really act—and ask them to audition before you choose them. Actors are used to this selection and frequent rejection process, so don't feel bad about having to turn someone down. Focus on who best fits the film, including fitting in well with other actors you have cast or plan to cast, and is available for the date of the shoot.

Finding Volunteers or Paying Actors

Generally for a short with a one-day—and sometimes two-day—shoot, you can find actors who will volunteer their time. Usually actors are willing to do this to build their portfolios and just have fun, because this is a free-time activity and they have other jobs or are between jobs. Usually the actors willing to volunteer will not be Screen Actors Guild (SAG) members, since SAG has strict requirements for what actors can do. For example, SAG rates for an ultra-low budget film are $100 a day, and you can have SAG and non-SAG actors, as long as the SAG actors get paid for that day or through a deferred pay arrangement (although a short is not likely to make any money, so there is likely to be no deferred pay). Also, when you are working with SAG actors, you are supposed to limit the time on set to eight hours or pay overtime, and you are supposed to fill out certain paperwork agreeing to SAG terms.

However, many SAG actors will work under another name on non-union no-pay projects, and some will simply ignore SAG requirements for a short film. Should a SAG actor want to work under SAG terms, even if they agree to deferred pay, it may be better to simply say, "Thank you, but no thanks," to avoid the hassle.

Just make it very clear when you announce you are seeking actors that this is a no-pay short project scheduled for a short-term shoot (indicate how many days), and generally the actors who apply to be in your film will be willing to volunteer their time, though some may ask if you can make an exception. If an actor does ask, it's generally best to say no. Besides the cost, giving money to one actor can create hard feelings on the set if other actors learn that one actor is getting paid when they aren't. And don't worry; you will usually be able to find many actors.

In some cases, producers do pay actors a small amount, and if so, a common amount is $20 for the main characters and $10 for supporting characters—a budget of about $50–$100 to pay the actors, which is well below the usual SAG rates.

Advertising for Actors

In LA a common expression is "Turn over a rock, and you'll find an actor," because you'll find aspiring actors almost everywhere waiting for that big break. But wherever you are, there are many ways to find actors by advertising or placing announcements in various places. Some of the most common are the following:

- Post an announcement on Craigslist under "gigs" in your community.
- Post an announcement in a film industry group on Facebook, LinkedIn, or Meetup.
- Post an announcement on a community bulletin board in your supermarket.
- Make an announcement in a business networking or referral group.
- Sign up for one of the casting services in your area, such as SF Casting in the Bay Area, and Breakaway Services in LA, and describe what you are looking for.

What to Say in Your Ads for Actors

When you advertise for actors, briefly—in one or two sentences—describe what your script is about and how long it will be (e.g., five- to six-minute short). Indicate that it's a no-pay volunteer project and list the characters or types of characters you are looking for. Explain the perks that come with the no-pay or low-pay project, such as their using the shoot for a promotional reel and your posting the trailer on YouTube and social media sites and entering it in festivals.

If you list the characters by name, indicate the gender if not clear from the name or required by the listing service, the age range, and briefly note any important characteristics, such as occupation or appearance and ethnic group, if relevant. For instance, a description might read:

Harry, 30s, tough Mafia type investment broker
Judy, 30s, mousy secretary

Also indicate when you plan to shoot the film and the dates of the auditions. While you might later reschedule the shoot date or extend the time for auditions, provide prospective actors with your current time frame so they can decide if they can fit the project into their schedule if you cast them. Should your plans change later, you can always let the actors who have already responded know by phone or e-mail to check if they are still available. Likewise, ask them to let you know if their plans change and they are no longer available. While some actors may still audition for a future project, most won't audition if they can't make the shoot.

If you have produced or written scripts for any produced films or shorts before, you can mention these or provide links to where the actors can see your previous work. While this isn't necessary, since I got actors when I first started casting, it contributes to your credibility if you have had any previously produced work, whether as a writer or producer.

If you are placing your own ad or announcement, include an e-mail where actors can write to you and send a head shot and resume (most serious actors will already have these) or send you a link to their portfolio online so you can review these and decide who to contact. It is best not to include a phone number since you don't want a lot of actors calling you for more information about your ad. You want to see information about them first so you can winnow down the number of actors to contact about each role.

Alternatively if you sign up with one of the casting services and place your announcement through it, the interested actors will include their information (usually including a photo and resume and sometimes one or more videos), along with a phone number and sometimes an e-mail, so you can contact them.

Using a Casting Service

Using a casting service to find actors can be very helpful, since you know the actors who respond are serious, and the service streamlines the process so that you don't have to view and download individual headshots and resumes you get by e-mail or regular mail. Instead the photos and background information of the actors interested in each role are shown online so you can review them there and decide on the most promising candidates. Then you can download or print out their information and contact them. I'll use my experience with SF Casting, which I have used to cast over a dozen shorts, to show how the process works. The upcoming shorts I am casting are listed on my Current Projects list, and I have archived those projects that are already completed, such as *Zoo Do, New Identity, Ironworkers,* and *My Four Presidents.*

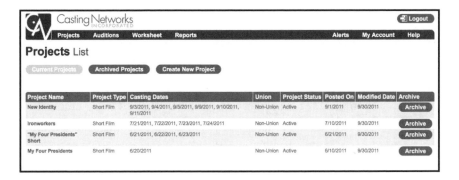

Once archived, the films are indicated like this:

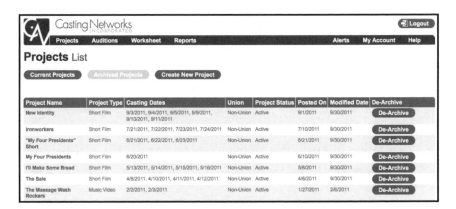

To start the process of looking for an actor through a casting service, enter information about your project, as illustrated below with *Zoo Do*, one of my completed shorts.

First, include a description of the type of film. As a low-budget short, it could be any of the following: a commercial, documentary, industrial, infomercial, Internet, live event, music video, pilot, promo, short film, student film, or student project.

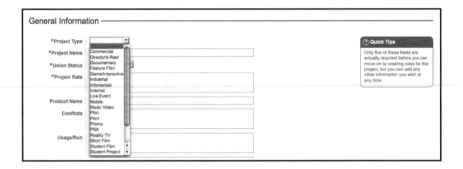

Then include the project name, indicate that it's a non-union project, and explain that there is no pay, though there are other benefits, such as including the clip in one's reel or having fun making this, because of the location, such as at a zoo or on the beach. Also describe how the video will be used, such as on websites and video sharing sites. Include a short synopsis and note the deadline for the actors to submit their material. (See page 73.)

Additionally, include information about when you will hold the auditions and where. If you will hold these at your home or other private location, indicate the general area, and later send the exact address to actors who will be coming to the audition. This way you don't have to reveal a private address publicly.

If you expect to have callbacks, include information about when you plan to do this, though commonly for a one- or two-day shoot, you will decide who to cast after the auditions and won't have callbacks. I have found this process has worked very well in casting actors for my shorts, and I feel it's an imposition to ask actors to return for callbacks for a short, where they are volunteering their time for a one-day shoot.

General Information

*Project Type	Short Film
*Project Name	Zoo Do
*Union Status	Non-Union
*Project Rate	No pay, but can add this to your reel, and there will be a fun day at the zoo for the two leads.
Usage/Run	Plan to enter into film festivals, show on BETV (part of the Berkeley Community Media which is providing some of the equipment for the shoot), post on Websites, make available to anyone involved.
Synopsis	ZOO DO is a 6-7 minute short in which a shy, submissive woman and socially inept guy with tyrant bosses at work separately go to the zoo, and as they see the animals, they gradually open up, become freer, tap into their inner power, are drawn to each other, leave together, and show off their newfound assurance at work.
Project Notes *Please do not include role information here, you will do that on a separate page.*	
Submissions Due By	5/1/2010
Submissions Due By Note	I'm planning to do auditions on 5/2 and 5/3.
*Post On Casting Billboard Through:	5/2/2010

Quick Tips

Only five of these fields are actually required before you can move on to creating roles for this project, but you can add any other information you wish at any time.

Audition Details

Audition Dates	5/2/2010; 5/3/2010;
Audition Note	I'm planning to do auditions on 5/2 and 5/3
Audition Location	Upper Rockridge-Montclair Area of Oakland
Audition Address	Near Proctor and Masonic (private address given to those who audition)
City	Oakland
State	California
Zip	94611
Include Map	Include GoogleMaps Link Preview Map

Quick Tips

Use this section to include any audition information, whether tentative or scheduled.

Callback Details

Callback Dates	
Callback Note	I'll be making a decision after the initial auditions, so no callbacks.
Same As Audition Address	Yes No
Callback Location	
Callback Address	
City	
State	
Zip	
Include Map	Include GoogleMaps Link Preview Map

Quick Tips

Use this section to include any callback information, whether tentative or scheduled.

Additionally, include information about the shoot, such as when it will be and what actors might expect. For instance, for *Zoo Do*, I noted that we would shoot part of the video without sound and would use improv at the zoo, while there would be a few minutes of scripted scenes with dialogue in a home office.

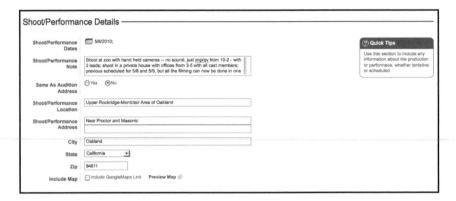

Finally, include information about who you are, including your company name, who to contact there, where you are located, and your e-mail. You don't have to include your phone number if you don't want calls.

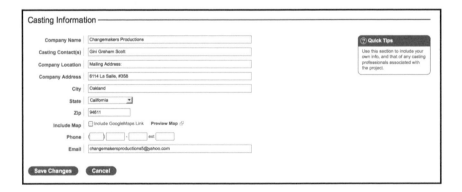

Once you have filled in all of this information, the Project Details (on page 75) will provide an overview of the project.

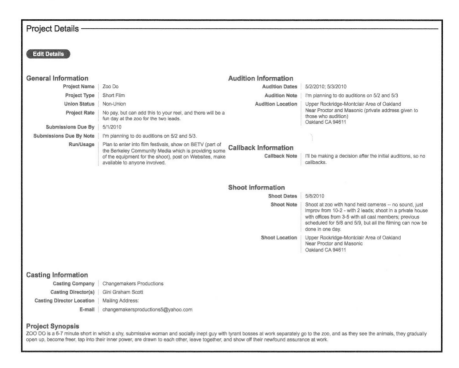

Then describe each role individually by indicating the name of the character, if there's any pay, the age of the character, whether it's a lead, co-star, supporting, or extra role, and any ethnic requirements for the character. You can note any wardrobe requirements or suggestions. (See page 76.)

In describing the character role, there are many possibilities, including being the lead, co-star, supporting, background, or other types of characters. (See page 76.)

After you finish describing the project and the roles of the characters, submit it for approval. Once approved, your information will be listed and actors can decide if they want to audition for it or not should there be a suitable role for them.

Commonly actors check these services for new listings once a day, so you will usually get quick responses if actors are interested in your project. Generally most of the actors who are interested will apply in one

Create Role

*Role Name	
Spot/Episode	
*Pay/Perks	
*Paying Role?	○ Yes ○ No
*Age Range	
*Role Type	▼
*Gender	☐ Female ☐ Male
*Ethnic Appearance	☐ All Ethnicities ☐ African American ☐ Asian ☐ Caucasian ☐ East Indian ☐ Ethnically Ambiguous ☐ Hispanic ☐ Middle Eastern ☐ Native American ☐ Pacific Islander
*Role Description	
*Nudity?	○ Yes ◉ No
*Sexual Situations?	○ Yes ◉ No
Wardrobe	

⑦ Quick Tips

Request Media Submissions: You can view media from talent on the submission page - watch media in one, easy-to-view place!

*Role Type	▼
*Gender	
*Ethnic Appearance	☐ African American ☐ Caucasian ☐ Ethnically Ambiguous ☐ Middle Eastern ☐ Pacific Islander
*Role Description	

Background
Co-Star
Featured
Guest-Star
Lead
Other
Photo Double
Precision Driver
Special
Stand-In
Stunt
Supporting

or two days—some in a matter of hours. Whenever you check your listing, you will see the number of actors who have applied. (See page 77.)

You can see their photos and brief descriptions about all the interested actors, including their names, phone numbers, height, and weight. If you feel an actor seems suitable for the role, you can click on his or her photos, resume, or videos to learn more. As an example, here are some of the submissions I got, though I have cut off their names, phone numbers, and height and weight information for confidentiality. (See page 77.)

You can handle the selection process online by indicating which actors you want to view, select to audition, callback, and finally book. Alternatively I have found it easier to print out the sheets of all the actors interested in a particular role, choose those I'm interested in learning more about based on their photos, view their resumes, and

							Photo View	Worksheet View

Unviewed	Viewed	Selects	Scheduled	Callback Selects	Callbacks	Booked	Role Name/Status	Details
24	0	1	0	0	0	0	Melinda | Edit | Active	Co-Star / Female / Caucasian / 25 - 35 years **Description:** You'll start off being shy and submissive at work, then start expressing yourself through improv as you see the animals at the zoo, and at work again, become newly assertive. **Wardrobe:** Just ordinary clothes for office - look a little mousy for the first scene (about a minute), then wear some layers of clothes so you can take off a jacket, scarf, hat, glasses at the zoo, then look sharply dressed for last scene at the office (about 1 minute). Casting Billboard Role Added 4/26/2010 6:12 PM
5	0	0	0	0	0	0	Jackson | Edit | Active	Co-Star / Male / Caucasian / 25 - 40 years **Description:** You'll start off being shy and socially inept at the office (about 1 minute), then at the zoo, you'll gradually become freer and feel more power as you see different animals; then you'll be more confident in the office the next day and quit for a better job (about 1 minute). **Wardrobe:** Just ordinary clothes for office - look a little mousy for the first scene (about a minute), then wear some layers of clothes so you can take off a jacket, scarf, hat, glasses at the zoo, then look sharply dressed for last scene at the office (about 1 minute). Casting Billboard Role Added 4/26/2010 6:15 PM
40	0	0	0	0	0	0	Melinda's Boss | Edit | Active	Supporting / Male / Female / All Ethnicities / 35 - 50 years **Description:** You'll be a tough, demanding boss in the first scene and the last scene of the film (about 1 minute each). 1 day of shooting. **Wardrobe:** Wear ordinary office clothes. Can be same outfit for both scenes. Casting Billboard Role Added 4/26/2010 6:18 PM
11	0	0	0	0	0	0	Jackson's Boss | Edit | Active	Supporting / Male / Female / All Ethnicities / 35 - 50 years **Description:** You'll be a tough, demanding boss in the first scene and the last scene of the film (about 1 minute each). **Wardrobe:** Ordinary clothes you might wear in an office, can be the same clothes for both scenes. Casting Billboard Role Added 4/26/2010 6:20 PM

decide who to audition based on that information. I keep track of the selection process by making notes when I first contact each actor to indicate if that actor is still interested. Then I ask each actor to bring a resume and picture to the audition when I make the audition arrangements, and I make further notes at the audition to help me select who will be in the cast.

Determining Which Actors to Contact for Each Role

While some producers and directors look carefully at the actor's resume and past experience and focus on that in deciding who to cast, I find it most helpful to first pay the most attention to the actor's photo and imagine how well I can see the actor playing a specific part, assuming the actor performs well in the audition. Then rather than past experience, I focus most on how well the actor plays that character in the here and now. You can combine both approaches to look at the resumes, photos, and any available video clips and decide who to audition. Use whichever approach works best for you.

Another consideration in casting is how many actors to contact for each role. It can sometimes seem overwhelming when you get a large number of submissions for each role. For example, the first time I used a casting service in producing *Cougar and Cub*, I was amazed that I got thirty to forty submissions for the two lead roles since this was a completely volunteer no-pay project. And on other projects, I averaged ten to twenty-five submittals for each part.

To avoid feeling overwhelmed, narrow down your initial selections to up to five or six auditions for each role. Another way to reduce your time in casting is to combine actor auditions when actors submit their information for consideration for two or three roles. You can have each actor read for each role. Or you can audition two or more actors for different parts at the same time. If the actors you initially invite to audition can't make it or later find they can't do the shoot, you can always expand the number of actors you audition.

To help you decide who to audition, you can use a ranking system and extend the invitations to the higher-ranking actors for each role first. To do so, write the number of the ranking on the actor's picture in the display of pictures or on the actor's picture and resume, which you can pick out from the service or request directly from the actor. Use "1" for the actors who initially appear to be the best picks for the role, "2" for the next best picks, "3" for the following best picks, and so on. If an actor is clearly a no, write down a large "O" or "No." If you are wavering between one ranking or another, you can split the difference, such as rating an actor a "1 ½" or "2 ½."

Contacting the Actors and Arranging for Auditions

Once you have found some actors who have expressed an initial interest in being in your short, the next step is to provide the actors you want to contact first (i.e., the 1s and 2s) with more information about your short. If they respond that they are still interested, set up an audition with them.

While some auditions may involve actors coming in one at a time to read for a part, I like to set up auditions with two or three actors reading for different parts, since that gives them a chance to play off each other. This approach can reduce the time you spend on auditions, since rather than taking thirty minutes to separately audition three actors for ten minutes each, you can audition the three actors together in ten to fifteen minutes. Having several actors present also makes it easier to have them improvise together, rather than only doing an improv for you, so you can see how comfortable they are with the other actors.

It's also helpful to create a series of letters to send out with more information about the script or scripts and for follow-up. You can adapt each letter to the particular script and actor you are contacting. While you can send an e-mail to confirm an audition with an actor, I generally use a phone call to the actor to work out the audition arrangements and follow-up with a written confirmation by e-mail.

An Initial Letter Describing the Project and Inviting the Actor to Audition

I generally start with a phone call to determine if the actor is still interested. If necessary, I briefly describe the project to refresh the actor's memory, and, if possible, set up an audition date. Then my initial letter confirms any arrangements, briefly describes the short, and includes a copy of the script to confirm that the actor is still interested. This letter also includes information about where the audition will be, and since I am aiming for two- or three-person auditions, it describes how I hope to arrange for such auditions if the actor's schedule allows for this. Finally, I include both my phone number and e-mail for the actor to contact me, along with my company website for credibility.

Here's an example of the letter I used in setting up auditions for three shorts, where I was hoping to have the same actors take parts in each one. I have blocked out the address and directions for the shoot.

Thanks for your interest in participating in the Peace Out, Deal, and Consultation projects, currently planned for shooting on Saturday, August 28, from 10 to about 5 or 6 p.m. These are three 5–6 minute shorts, which will be shot in one location in one day if possible; if not we will set up a second day for one or two more shorts. We'll be doing Peace Out first, then The Deal, and finally The Consultation. The shorts are designed to be lighthearted with a twist at the end. We'll be shooting in the same location as the auditions in the Upper Rockridge/Montclair area of Oakland.

In *Peace Out*, three community organizers try to organize a peace festival, but have different ideas of what it should be and ultimately end up arguing and fighting.

In *The Deal*, a woman has a phone conversation with a tough-talking investment broker who reneges on a deal, and after she talks to his writer on the project, she and the writer make a deal together.

In *The Consultation*, after a payment dispute, a woman has a phone consultation with an insurance agent, who turns out to be a phony when she investigates who he really is.

We'll be working with the Berkeley Community Media on this project, which will air first on BETV in Berkeley. Then the shorts will be entered in festivals, posted on YouTube and other video sharing sites, and you'll get a copy for your portfolio, which you can post on your own website. It's an all-volunteer shoot.

My address and directions for the auditions (and for the shoot on August 28) is *******. The best way to get here is ********. It is best not to use GPS, MapQuest, or Google Maps, since people tend to get lost.

I'm sending along a copy of the scripts. I would like to arrange group auditions, if possible, so you can act with one or two other people who will be in the scene. I would like to schedule the auditions between 3–7 on Friday, Aug. 20, or 3–6 on Sat., Aug. 21. If necessary, I could schedule other auditions for Sunday morning, the 22nd, from 10 to 12. Can you bring a headshot and resume when you come?

Can you please confirm if still interested, and if so, let me know what times will work for you.

Gini Graham Scott
Changemakers Productions
(510) 339-1625
changemakersproductions@yahoo.com
www.changemakersproductions.com

As another example, here's a letter I used in my initial contact with actors who expressed interest in being in *Zoo Do*.

Thanks for your interest in participating in the *Zoo Do* for Saturday, May 8 and 9. This is a 5–7 minute short about a meek guy who works in IT and an uptight woman with an oppressive boss who separately go to the zoo. There they experience a growing freedom and power as they see the different animals. Then they meet each other and become more powerful at their respective offices. We'll be working with the Berkeley Community Media on this project, which will air first on BETV in Berkeley, then entered in festivals, posted on YouTube and other video sharing sites, and you'll get a copy for your portfolio, which you can post on your own website. It's an all-volunteer shoot, except for a small payment to the editor.

The plan is to shoot at the zoo on May 8 from about 10–2 p.m. with no sound and two to four handheld cameras, with one or two cameras following each actor; and from about 2:30–4:30 p.m. at the offices in my house in Oakland.

My address and directions for the auditions (and the shoot on May 8) is ******. The best way to get here is **********.

I'm sending along a copy of the *Zoo Do* script. I would like to schedule an audition for _____ at ____ or _____. Can you let me know the best time for you and bring a headshot and resume?

Gini Graham Scott
Changemakers Productions
(510) 339-1625
changemakersproductions@yahoo.com
www.changemakersproductions.com

If the actor is still interested after seeing the script, you can work out the details of the audition by e-mail or phone and enter that information on a casting schedule for the time and role, which is what I do. I'd suggest creating your schedule documents in landscape layout so there is more room for each entry (though I have used portrait layout for readability in this book). I list the names of the key characters I am auditioning—usually from two to four characters for the main roles. If there are other roles, I generally cast them from those who auditioned but were not chosen for the main roles.

The casting schedule also includes the time for the audition, and each person's name, phone number, and e-mail. While casting agents with many clients will set up auditions for five to ten minutes, I prefer to set up auditions for fifteen minutes, which allows more time for improvs and to see how actors interact and play off of each other in a group. Setting the audition for fifteen minutes also allows for more flexibility in case actors come late or early due to heavy or light traffic or getting lost along the way.

Besides the person's name, I include their phone number and e-mail on the casting schedule form so I can easily contact them again. I also print out their complete resume and photos for a file with all of the cast members.

Here's an example of the casting schedule form for *Zoo Do*, which I printed out in landscape layout, though it's in profile layout here. I've include a few made-up names as an example.

	CASTING SCHEDULE			
Script(s) Date:		**Reviewers:**		
Time	**Melinda** Name-Phone-E-mail	**Jackson** Name-Phone-E-mail	**Melinda's Boss** Name-Phone-E-mail	**Jackson's Boss** Name-Phone-E-Mail
3:00	Susan Allen (510) 123-4567 susana@yahoo.com	John Jones (510) 456-7891 jjones@gmail.com		
3:15				
3:30			June Williams (925) 321-9876 sweetpea@gmail.com	
3:45				
4:00				
4:15				
4:30				
4:45				
5:00				
5:15				
5:30				
5:45				

It's also important to confirm and reconfirm the arrangement so the actors know they are expected. Then most will take the audition arrangements seriously and show up. Or if they can't, they will usually let you know so that you can make other arrangements or know you have that time free. I only experienced a couple of occasions when actors didn't show up or call to explain—even in LA where people commonly expect only half the actors to show up. Rather those who didn't show up were very apologetic, explaining later that day or the next why they couldn't come, usually because of some unexpected emergency.

In short, if you show you are serious about scheduling auditions, the actors will generally respond in kind and will almost always show up—and in the rare cases when they don't, they will apologize with an explanation and commonly will request to reschedule, if possible.

Here's an example of a reconfirmation letter I sent out, which includes the address and directions for the auditions, just in case.

I just wanted to reconfirm the audition for _____ at _____ and make sure you have the directions.

My address and directions for the auditions (and the shoot on August 28) is *********.

Can you bring a headshot and resume when you come? I'll look forward to seeing you.

Gini Graham Scott
Changemakers Productions
(510) 339-1625
changemakersproductions@yahoo.com
www.changemakersproductions.com

Sending Script Updates

If you get feedback on your script or find other reasons to change anything, you can update your script after you first send it to the actors.

If so, send the actors the latest revised script before their audition so they can read from that, which can contribute to a smoother, more polished performance. However, since not all actors will get the new script or have a chance to review or practice with it, have extra copies at the audition.

Preparing for Auditions

Ideally arrange for two or three actors to audition together so they can play off each other. Otherwise, conduct auditions individually and you read the other parts.

Though you have set a specific time for each actor's audition, often actors may arrive early or late, usually due to unexpectedly light or heavy traffic. So be ready to adjust for early or late arrivals. As possible, audition any actor as soon as he or she arrives, or include the actor by inviting him or her to read for another part while you are auditioning other actors.

Sometimes the actors coming to an audition may know another actor, generally because they have auditioned for or been in other projects together. In some cases, it can be an advantage to cast actors who already know each other to work together, if they fit different roles, since they will have worked together before, and this past performance can add to their on-scene chemistry and off-screen camaraderie. If you have to choose one but not the other, don't worry about this. Choose whoever best fits the part. Actors are used to a rigorous selection process, don't feel they have to be part of a package, and don't feel—or shouldn't feel—any bitterness that an actor they know was selected over them. So if it works for your short, choosing actors that have worked together before can be a big plus; but if not, don't let that affect your choices.

Setting the Time for the Audition

Hold your auditions a week or two before your shoot, and schedule the auditions about a week in advance of when you plan to hold them. This will give the actors time to plan ahead and give you time, if necessary, to change the audition schedules and the actors planned for the shoot. At the same time, you won't set the audition schedule too far ahead of the planned shoot, making it hard for the actors to determine firm plans, since a paying gig, client, or work requirement might come up during this time.

Generally try to set up the auditions to occur over one to, at most, three days, so you can see all the actors at around the same time, which is helpful in thinking about how the different actors will work together, so you can decide soon after the auditions are over.

While auditions for feature films can go all day and into the early evening, since casting involves seeing a large number of actors for many different parts, in a low-budget short you are typically casting only two to four main parts. And often rather than separately casting for the smaller parts, you can invite any actors you don't cast for the main parts to take on any supporting roles. Thus, you can usually conclude casting for a short with just a few hours of seeing up to six actors for each role, or sometimes less.

Since most actors for a volunteer project work at other jobs, scheduling the interviews from 3 p.m. to 7 p.m. on weekdays or during a three- to four-hour block on the weekends works well. Having a limited time block also makes it easier to schedule actors to read together for different parts. It's easier for you too since you will have all the auditions at the same time, not scattered throughout the day.

Once you start scheduling actors, you might be able to further narrow the time frame to conduct all the auditions even more efficiently in a few hours. Even so, be open to accommodating actors who can't come at the planned times by scheduling them for an individual audition at another time.

Telling Actors How to Prepare and What to Bring

While many actors will show up for the audition without any guidance, ready to perform, usually because they have been to many auditions, some will ask what to wear to better fit the part or what to prepare to read in advance.

Generally it's not necessary to have actors wear anything special or engage in any advance preparation, unless they want to do so. Rather actors can wear whatever they are wearing that day, and it is not necessary to rehearse since they can just read from the script.

With feature-length scripts, casting directors and directors frequently give actors a small part of the script, called a "side," in advance or at the audition. But with a short, you normally send them the whole script in advance, and usually they can read their whole part for the audition. If other actors are reading for other parts, they can read with them. If not, plan to read the other parts yourself.

Where to Hold the Audition

A very convenient way to hold auditions for a low-budget short is in your home, if you have a living room or other room that is large enough for two to three people to sit across from you. You can use a hall, dining area, or kitchen for a waiting room. Or if you have a conference room at your office you can use, that's ideal.

Some other low-cost alternatives might be:

- A friend's house
- A room at a community center
- A screening room or community room in your apartment building or friend's apartment building

While there are professional spaces for conducting auditions, such as theaters or audition rooms in centers for filmmaking, and some even have facilities for videotaping auditions, these can be expensive. Rates typically range from $50 to $100 an hour. So generally forget about using such facilities for a low- or no-budget short.

Setting Up for the Audition

If possible, have a hallway or separate room where actors can wait until it is time to audition. Alternatively have a chair or two near the door so the actors can wait there. Then when you are ready, invite them to participate.

Even if you have already sent the actors a script or the latest update, print out several scripts in case the actors don't bring the latest script. If you do provide a script at the audition, ask to get it back if you don't plan to cast a particular actor. But if you think you might cast an actor, let him or her keep the script.

You don't need to provide any refreshments or snacks since the actors are only coming for ten to fifteen minutes. However, have some bottles of water on hand, preferably kept cold in your fridge, in case an actor asks for this.

Also, in advance of the audition, give the actors a phone number to call and have your phone handy so they can call to let you know if they will be late or are lost and need directions. Even if you are in an easy to get to downtown location, give the actors your suggested directions, which are sometimes better than those provided by Google Maps, MapQuest, or a GPS device, which will lead them astray. Be prepared to adjust your audition schedule to accommodate late arrivals and give any directions as needed.

Dealing with Can't-Shows and No-Shows

From time to time, you will get cancellations, usually a day or two before the auditions, but sometimes even the night before or on the day of the audition. Usually a last-minute cancellation is because the actor has found a paying gig for the time of the audition or day of the shoot, though occasionally it is due to illness or problems with traffic.

If an actor can't make the shoot, there's no reason to conduct an audition. Otherwise, if an actor still wants to do the shoot but can't make the audition, you might try to schedule an alternate time, if you haven't yet cast the part. If you can, work the actor into a group interview. If you can't, conduct it as an individual audition.

In some cases, an actor won't be able to make the shoot, but will ask to audition for future projects. In that case, if you have upcoming projects where the actor might be appropriate and can work the actor in, fine; conduct an audition. Then if the actor does a good job, you can keep him or her in mind for the future. And in some cases, an actor's schedule will change, so he or she can now make the shoot if you haven't already cast the part.

Making Arrangements if an Actor's Agent or Manager Calls to Set Up an Audition

Usually in casting volunteer or very low-pay actors, you will deal directly with the actors since they participate in these shoots as a part-time fun activity and don't have agents.

But occasionally an agent or manager will call to make the arrangements. While it can be fine to do so, regard such a call as a possible warning sign that this actor may have an attitude, since he or she is very serious about creating an acting career and may turn out to be a diva at the audition or on the set, if cast. Though the person might be very good, pay attention to any signs of self-importance, which can be a disaster for a low-budget shoot that depends on teamwork. Sometimes the agent or manager will want to accompany the actor to the set, which is another warning sign, since their presence on the set can be disruptive or can undercut the role of the director, if the agent or manager seeks to give input on what the actor should be doing in the film.

For example, at one shoot, although I made it very clear in advance that this was an all-volunteer shoot, an actress arrived at the audition with her manager/agent, who began asking questions as to whether this would be a SAG-approved project or would comply with all the SAG guidelines for ultra-low-budget productions. Though I went ahead with the audition, since the manager/agent stated they had driven for about an hour to get here and I did not want to disappoint them by not conducting the audition, I was relieved when the actress turned out to not be very good so I wouldn't have cast her for that reason. But even if she had been good, I wouldn't have cast her either, since I felt she would have an attitude—or at least her manager/agent might be likely to interfere.

Conducting the Audition

When the actors arrive, take a minute or two to welcome them and make them feel comfortable. You might say things like: "How was your trip here?," "Thanks so much for sending a clip of your video," or "Hi! I'm _____, and I'm so glad to meet you." Some casting directors like to engage in some casual small talk to create more rapport, such as mentioning something about the weather, day, or how they like something the actor is wearing. Do whatever feels comfortable for you.

Then ask if the actor has brought a copy of the script. If not, provide a copy. Also, ask if the actor has brought a headshot and resume. Sometimes the actor may have already sent you a headshot in a JPEG and a resume you can download. But it's better if you can get a printed photo and ideally a resume that is attached on the back. Sometimes directors and casting directors use theses photos and resumes for making notes on the back, or use another sheet for their notes.

Indicate if the actor will just be reading with you or another actor or two. If the other actor or actors are already there, introduce the new actor. Then you can start the reading. Or if the other actor or actors haven't arrived, suggest waiting one or two minutes, then go ahead with an individual audition until the others arrive, if they do. Or start right away and invite the other actors to join you once they arrive.

From Reading to Action to Improv

If an actor asks if you have any suggestions for the reading, you might briefly share your thoughts about the character's major characteristics or motivations for action. Otherwise, it's a good idea to let the actors interpret the part however they want on the first run-through. That way you can see how the actor responds to a role and any other actors without any input from you.

After the first reading, you can make suggestions about how to vary the next reading, such as "Can you do it again with more intensity . . . with more anger . . . with more uncertainty?"

Commonly the actors will start by simply reading the lines. Then some actors will stand up and act out the lines. Usually this stand-up performance is a good sign that the actor is more experienced and feels comfortable with the role. It's ideal when actors get up and act spontaneously, but you can invite them to do so after they do a first reading.

If the part calls for improvisation, you might suggest the scene and ask the actors to do whatever they want for the action, dialogue, or both. For instance, in casting *Zoo Do*, which required the actors to act out dialogue in an office setting and go to the zoo and act like different animals with no dialogue (with the zoo scenes shot first), I asked the actors to imagine they were watching different kind of animals and then act like those animals. The actors had a lot of fun doing this, and I was able to see who was most comfortable with letting themselves go in the scene.

In some cases, you may find that an actor who has applied for one part may be more suitable for another. If so, invite the actor to read for the other part.

In the event that you end up with two actors auditioning for the same part, because one has come early and the other late to the audition, you can have each actor take turns reading for that part while the other reads another part, even if it's not a part they would play. Then they can switch roles. For instance, one time when that happened, instead of my reading a woman's part, I asked each actor in turn to read that while the other read for the part they were each auditioning for. This way, I involved both actors, instead of having one actor wait around while the other reads.

Alternatively if you have a separate waiting area where you can close the door to the audition room, you can have one actor wait outside while the other reads for the part.

Assessing the Actors and Their Fit for the Part at the Audition

As the actors read or act out the part, assess both their fit for the part and their ability to act. Pay attention to how they say their lines and how well they get into a character. You might visualize the character in the actual scene as you listen and observe.

In some cases, actors may change the lines slightly to make them more like something they would say, and that's fine. In fact, you might take notes when the actors do change lines, since this change could suggest a way of further revising and polishing the script so you have more naturalistic dialogue.

There's something of an art to casting since you have to use your intuition to help you decide if someone is right for a part and how the actors will fit together as a team. But as you have more casting sessions, you will feel more comfortable knowing which actors to cast for what roles.

Keep the following considerations in mind as you observe each session:

- Does the actor seem to really slip into character so you can imagine the actor has become this character?
- Or does the actor seem to be *acting* in playing this character so the dialogue sounds flat and hollow or exaggerated, stagey, or forced?

In the event that an actor seems to be acting and not truly inhabiting the character, give some suggestions on how to better get into the role, such as by asking the actor to think about the difficult situation the character is in so he or she feels a sense of anger or danger. Then see if the actor can give a more heartfelt performance. But if the actor still seems flat, stagey, or forced, this actor may not be sufficiently experienced or versatile to truly get into the role. However, if you have a good director who is good at bringing out such qualities in an actor during a rehearsal, it may be worth it to take a chance, particularly if the actor looks ideal for the part and you don't have someone else who is clearly better or any other actor who is available.

As the actor reads or acts at the audition, you can make notes to yourself or rate the performance, say on a scale of 0 (really terrible) to 5 (great). Or make these notes and ratings at the end of the performance. It's best to make this assessment for each actor as you go along, since it can be easy to forget your reactions to individual actors after you have seen a number of performances.

If the actor gives a good performance, let the actor know you appreciate what he or she did. For example, you might say something like "That was a nice job" or "You really showed you understand that character." Even if you later decide not to cast an actor in the role for some reason, actors appreciate this nice feedback since a common experience at auditions is being rejected because there is so much competition for a role—even when it is for a volunteer project.

Concluding the Audition

When the audition ends, you can simply say "Thank you" and "I'll be in touch." You can also let the actor know when you will be making your decision.

If you are sure you want to cast an actor, you can let the actor know on the spot, but this can be awkward if you have auditioned two or more actors at the same time or if you have another actor scheduled to audition that day for the same part. Thus, it's often best to let the actors know that you will call them—either later that day, the next day, or whenever you will make your decision.

If you really do like an actor, but have other actors auditioning for the same part, it might be best to wait until you have concluded the auditions with these other actors before calling this first actor, unless you might have other parts for them in something else. Or if you have them scheduled for the next day, you can let them know you have cast someone so they don't need to come in, unless they want to be considered for something else. Another reason for waiting until you conclude the auditions is that even if you think a particular actor is great, you may find another actor you subsequently audition is even better. Then if the first actor decides not to take the part or is later unable to play it, say due to getting a paying gig or an illness, you have another actor to call on as a last-minute replacement.

Selecting Your Cast

In selecting your cast, think about how the different actors will play against each other. Ask yourself if they will fit together naturally.

This notion of fit is particularly important if they will be playing family members or partners in a relationship or marriage. Even if they may be great actors individually, if they don't look like they belong in the same family or relationship, it is better to cast one of them for one part and choose someone else for the other part.

Once you decide who to cast, it is best to call that person directly rather than sending an e-mail, since the person may not get that right away and you won't know if they have confirmed being in the film or not. If you can reach the person when you call, great. If not, leave a message to call you, since you would like them to play the part, and send an e-mail with the same information to call you. Call back the next day if they haven't returned your call.

Once you reach an actor who confirms he or she will take the part, you can send further details by e-mail—such as when to report for the shoot, what to wear, if there will be a rehearsal before the shoot, such as while the crew is setting up, and so on.

If a selected cast member doesn't get back to you, try contacting them again, and if you still can't get a confirmation, it may be better to select someone else or have someone waiting in the wings to take the role, if you can't reach the selected person in a reasonable length of time.

Saying No to an Actor Who Has Auditioned

If you decide not to cast an actor, it's a nice gesture to thank him or her for coming to the audition, but explain that you have decided to cast someone else, though you would like to keep the actor in mind for future roles. Actors will generally appreciate the gesture and respond back to thank you for the audition and for keeping them in mind for the future.

When you first have to say no, you may find it particularly hard to do so. You may even feel an impetus to write another role for an actor, as I did, when an actor came for a *Zoo Do* audition and I didn't feel he was right for a role as a woman's boss, since I felt a woman who auditioned was a perfect fit. But the actor looked like a great CEO, so I wrote in an extra half-page part for that. However, at the actual shoot, the shot of him talking to an employee was badly framed, and his scene threw off the balance of having two actors interact with a single boss, so his scenes were cut from the film anyway (though they did make a second video called *Zoo Don't,* featuring the bad shots and outtakes from the original footage, showing what not to do in making a film).

So generally if an actor isn't right for the part, don't try to make him or her fit by creating another role. Rather keep that actor in mind for a future project.

When you send these "thanks but no thanks" letters, you can do it efficiently if you have a form letter and adapt it for each actor. This can speed up the process when you have a dozen or more letters to send out. For example, here is a letter I used to say no, and some of the letters I got back from the actors after I did so.

Dear *******

Thank you so much for coming in for an audition for *Zoo Do*. I wanted to let you know that we did cast someone else for the part, but I will be putting together another short film shoot in June or July, and hope to be in touch with you about that then.

Gini Graham Scott

Changemakers Productions

Dear ******

I wanted to thank you so much for coming by for an audition for *Peace Out*, *The Deal*, and *The Consultation*. It was a close decision, but we did decide on another actress (actor) for the part, but I hope to consider you for other projects in the future.

Gini Graham Scott

Changemakers Productions

And some of the responses:

Thanks so much for getting back to me. Please do keep me in mind for future projects.

Thanks again,

BJ

Thank you for your consideration, Gini. Please do keep me in mind for the future.

Sincerely,

AL

Special Situations: Casting Kids or Animals

I've heard many warnings to stay away from casting kids or animals, and they can be more difficult to work with, especially cats. But I have worked with both, and it can be done, though allow some extra time for working with them. Here are some suggestions.

Casting Kids

Many of the kids eager to be in short films are hoping to launch a show business career, so they view shorts as a way to launch their portfolio. Thus, they are quite serious, and so are their parents. Their parents will generally accompany them on the set and watch them perform, so you are also casting their parents—and especially their mothers. Some parents are very easy going and great to work with. But if the parent seems overbearing and domineering, it may be better to cast someone else since that kind of attitude portends possible conflict on the set.

Often kids will be in school and may have homework, so keep the kid roles short, and if possible, film them first, so the kids and their parents aren't waiting for other scenes to be finished. Another reason to film their scenes first is that kids can become especially impatient if they have to wait, especially if they don't have other kids around to talk to while waiting. Then too, since it may be more likely for last-minute problems to come up when you are filming kids—from getting sick to extra homework—it's best to cast an extra kid to be on call or on the set and to do a few extra takes with the extra kid, just in case.

That's what I did in shooting a trailer for *The New Child*, in which there were supposed to be girls of different ages—one seven, one eight, and one fourteen. When the seven-year-old girl canceled the morning of the shoot because her father had a heart attack on their long drive to the set, we changed what the eight-year-old was wearing, and she let her hair down to look younger and played both parts.

Commonly at the casting session, your communication will be with the parent, usually the mother, who has brought the child. So while you may communicate directly with the child when you ask him or her to read or act out a part, you will usually talk to the parent about the shooting schedule and what time the child will be on the set.

As with other actors, at the casting session look for the child to seem natural in the part and not appear like he or she is acting. Also suggest something for the child to improvise to see how comfortable the child is with that. Sometimes a younger child may be especially nervous or inarticulate. In that case, take a little time to talk to the child to help him or her feel more comfortable, but if that isn't working, adapt the scene to what the child can do, or don't cast that child.

In the event you are going to have a number of children in a scene, try to have two or more children come at the same time. That way you can see how comfortable a child is with other children, and often a child will be more relaxed when interacting with other children.

At the end, thank both the child and the parent for coming to the audition, and let the parent know that you will be in touch about your casting decision soon.

Casting Animals

There are a number of sources where you can get animals for your shorts:

- Actors with pets, who you can find through casting services and other channels for finding actors
- Friends, neighbors, or business associates who have pets or know people with pets
- Announcements on Craigslist for your area
- Posting at your local supermarket
- Postings around your neighborhood

Many pet owners like the idea of having their dogs, cats, and other pets in a film, so they can be eager participants. But if the pet plays an important role, it's critical to see how it will respond in a casting session.

For example, it's not necessary to see the pet at an audition if it will be in a walk-on role with the owner, such as in shooting *Cougar and Cub*, when the actress was playing a neighbor walking her dog. Her role was to walk up to a car to see if something was wrong because she heard thumping noises in the trunk. So when we filmed the scene, the dog simply walked along with her, just as if she was walking him on an everyday walk. If the dog had become nervous or skittish on the set, the actress could have easily done the scene without the dog. So there was no need to have her bring the dog to her audition.

But if the animal's role is important, have the owner or whoever will be with the animal on the set come to an audition. Set up the scene as close as possible to the one where you will be filming and see how the animal responds to commands. Or set up a situation where the animal will normally respond with the behavior you want.

Generally it's relatively easy to do a shoot with dogs because they have learned to respond to commands, so they will sit, stay, lie down, run somewhere, walk with someone, jump out of somewhere, and otherwise do what the owner wants them to do. So if the dog does this in an audition, generally the dog will do this when you are filming.

However, it is usually much more difficult to work with cats because you have to set up the situation and entice them to do it. Then if they feel so inclined to cooperate, they will. But when you actually shoot on the set, they may not comply and can be downright ornery. So it can help to have several cats on hand for shooting the scene, in case one doesn't respond, so you can do the scene with another cat.

That's what happened when we were auditioning and later shooting some scenes with cats for the *Cougar and Cub* short. One scene required a cat to jump out of the back of a car trunk to suggest that a woman put into the trunk had turned into a cat and jumped out when the trunk was opened. Two other scenes required two different cats to run across a patio, while the main character massaged two different men, one at a time, in a lounge chair. A different cat was supposed to run across the patio each time.

So for the audition, I got several cat toys to dangle in front of each cat to entice it to run across the patio, though we didn't have the cats jump out of the trunk back, figuring it would be natural for a cat to jump out of the trunk. And during the audition, everything seemed fine. The owners had no problem getting the cats to run across the patio after cat toys or food treats.

However, at the filming, the presence of all the cameras and people changed the dynamic. One cat got very scared and was afraid to do anything, while the other two cats jumped off the patio rather than running across it. So we couldn't use the first cat at all, and we had to adapt the patio scenes to the other. At least one cat jumped out of the trunk just fine, though it scampered under a car rather than running down the street where the owner was waiting with food. Thus, it was good that we chose to have an extra cat after the auditions.

As with kids, it's best to schedule the shots with the animals first so the owners and animals aren't waiting around for other scenes to be shot, which can spook or tire the animals.

Chapter 8

Getting Your Props, Wardrobe, and Costumes

If you need any special props in a scene, get them in advance. This can include anything from vehicles, furniture, and equipment to notebooks, cell phones, paper, and pens. Also, work out arrangements for wardrobe and costumes with the actors, who will usually wear or bring something they already have, but will often want suggestions on what to bring.

Determining the Props You Need

To determine any needed props, go through the script and for each scene list what you already have and what to get. Once you know the location for the shoot, it helps to go there in advance to know what is already there and what you have to bring to the set.

To help you remember what is there, take photos of each setting in a location and include everything that will appear in any shots. If you can't get it all in a single shot, take a series of shots, starting on the left, and make it as much of a panorama as possible. For example, in a room, take a photo of the left wall, then the center wall, and lastly the wall on the right.

Where possible, use what is already at that location. For example, if you are shooting a scene at a desk with a computer, it is likely there are also a notebook, paper, pen, and other objects that normally may be on a desk or in the drawers. Check if these are readily available and where they are, so you can have them easily accessible for a shoot, such as if a character has to pick up a notebook and write something.

Here's an example from one of the scene breakdowns for *The Engagement*, showing how I listed the special props needed and have underlined them where they appear in the action. I haven't included the car as a special prop, since most of the script takes place in a car as the two principal characters drive. But if a car was only used in some of the scenes, it would be listed as a special prop for those scenes.

35. LOCATION: EXT. CONVENIENCE STORE—MOMENTS LATER
ACTORS: Mary Beth and Sam
SPECIAL PROPS: Cell Phone, Engagement Ring
Mary Beth gets out, leaving the car door open, and pulls out her <u>cell phone</u>. Sam looks stunned.

> SAM
> Yeah, okay.

Sam looks at the <u>ring</u>, dazed, as Mary Beth walks around the corner with her phone.

After you make a list of the props for all of the scenes, determine what you have, what you still need, and who will get that prop. If there are more than a few props, create a checklist to indicate what you have, what you need, who will get it, and when obtained, such as in the checklist below. Include a column for any comments about that prop.

PROPS NEEDED FOR ENGAGEMENT				
Prop Needed	Have Now	Need to Get	Who Will Get	Comments
Engagement Ring	X			
Cell Phone	X			
Flowers		X	Alex	Use wildflowers
Map	X			
Notepad	X			
Wrapped Gifts		X	Susan	Should be small, use elegant wrapping
Sunglasses	X			
Scarf	X			
Watch	X			
Hat	X			

Getting the Needed Props

In many cases, you will already have the needed props. Just look around your house and gather them together so they are ready for the shoot. If these are objects you use every day, such as a cell phone, make a note to bring them to the shoot, and once you are there, put them on a table where you have collected the other props.

If you don't have the props yourself, ask others who will be on the shoot if they can bring them. If so, give them a list and send them an e-mail before the shoot to remind them what they are bringing. Often the actors will offer to bring the props they will be using, such as a cell phone, watch, hat, or sunglasses. If so, let them know what they to bring. Give them a list and send an e-mail as a reminder.

If you can't obtain the props yourself or from cast or crew members, plan a shopping trip to pick up what you need. Some good low-cost places for props include the following:

- A thrift store, such as a Goodwill or Salvation Army store. This is especially good for finding clothing, toys, jewelry, kitchen items, and household supplies.
- A CVS pharmacy, Rite Aid, Wal-Mart, K-Mart, or Walgreens
- Local garage sales

If you will be doing a series of shorts, keep the props that you have bought for previous shoots together, since you may be able to use them again. Also, consider making a collection of props, which might inspire future film projects.

Making Wardrobe Arrangements

Generally the actors will bring their own clothing on a low-budget shoot. You just have to give them guidelines on what to wear. In some cases, ask them to bring one or two changes of clothing so you can choose on the day of the shoot. In the event they will do two or more scenes that require a change of clothes, such as when a scene takes place on another day, let the actors know how many changes of clothing they need to bring. Though a change in time or location may be indicated in the script, make sure the actors realize this means a change of clothing too.

A good approach is to give some general style suggestions. Then if the actors want more guidance, suggest particular items of clothing to wear. For example, some general style suggestions might be:

- Casual, sporty
- Office attire
- Professional business attire

Some particular items might include the following.
For women:

- A short cocktail dress

- A pantsuit for the office
- A sweat suit for running

For men:

- A suit and tie
- A jacket, slacks, and turtleneck like an academic might wear
- Khakis and a casual shirt

You might also give some suggestions about color and style, which contributes to better filming, such as:

- Avoid solid blacks and whites, since they are harder to light properly.
- Avoid stripes, since they can vibrate on the screen.
- Wear pastels to suggest a more passive unassertive character.
- Wear strong colors to suggest a more aggressive, assertive character.

Consider any suggestions from the actors too, especially if they have been in other shorts or features before. They will have experience in picking out what to wear for other projects, and they may have a good idea of what would be good for your short.

In the event you need certain items of clothing or accessories for a scene, such as a scarf or tie, ask the actor to wear or bring that item.

Should you need any clothing items or accessories that the actors don't have, a good source is your local thrift store or low-cost stores like Ross or Clothes-4-Less. Keep these items after the shoot, since you may be able to use them for other films.

Getting Costumes

Should you need special costumes, such as masks for a Halloween party, a space suit for an alien, or a gorilla suit, ask if the cast or crew members have something or check with family and friends.

Sometimes you can combine things together to create a costume, such as using a shiny shirt and medallion to suggest a space alien costume.

You might also find costumes in thrift stores, garage sales, and costume shops. In some cases, costume shops will rent costumes, which might be an economical alternative to buying one.

Still another alternative for a hard-to-find costume is revising the script so you don't need that costume.

Chapter 9

Getting Food for the Shoot

A key to having a successful shoot is having food and water on hand for the cast and crew. On the big productions, the food is usually catered buffet style by craft services. Likewise, consider yourself the head of craft services, unless you arrange for a PA, other assistant, or outside food delivery service to handle this.

If you start in the morning, have coffee available to get everyone started, and arrange for lunch between about 11:30 a.m. and 1:30 p.m., whenever you have a good break time. If the shoot goes past 7 or 7:30 p.m., have dinner for everyone too.

If you have access to a kitchen during the shoot, set up the coffee, water, and meals there. Otherwise, arrange for a take-out delivery or pick-up some food and beverages at a nearby fast-food restaurant or convenience store like a Quik Stop or 7-Eleven. It's not necessary to do anything fancy for a low-budget shoot, and a catering service is probably beyond your budget since it averages around $30–$35 a person for three meals for an all-day shoot or about $12–$15 for a single meal.

For water, you can get cases of small water bottles at your local grocery. The standard size is around sixteen ounces, though you can get smaller eight-ounce bottles and even larger thirty-two-ounce and one-gallon sizes. I would recommend getting the standard size, which is most readily available. Don't get the larger sizes, since cast and crew members generally prefer to have their own bottles. You'll find a number of different brands, but I would suggest getting the least expensive one, which may often be the store brand, since, after all, this is just plain water. Buy enough so that you have two or three bottles of water for each person at the shoot.

For coffee, if you have access to a coffeemaker, use ground drip coffee, which is generally preferred because of its fresher taste. If there's no coffeemaker, you can use a microwave or stove and make instant coffee for whoever wants it. If you don't have access to a kitchen, get take-out coffee from a nearby restaurant or convenience store.

For lunch, if you can use a kitchen, shop for the food and beverages a day or two before and put out everything so everyone can help themselves buffet style. PAs can be especially helpful in assisting with setting up the buffet. To keep costs down, buy things from a grocery, put them out on trays or in bowls, and invite everyone to put their sandwiches or salads together themselves. For instance, buy salad fixings and pita bread rather than buying prepared salad platters and sandwiches.

Some examples of good things to serve for lunch include:

- Lettuce or bags of mixed greens
- Cheese slices or cubes, or bags of shredded cheese
- Other salad additions, such as avocados, carrots, mushrooms, croutons, nuts
- Luncheon meats, such as packages of turkey, ham, and chicken
- Pita bread
- Chips and dips
- Cookies
- Apples or bananas
- Pizza

You can use large bowls for salads and large plates or trays for other items.

For beverages, get assorted juices or sodas and avoid anything alcoholic, like wine or beer, since you want everyone to be completely sober until the shoot is over.

To make cleanup easier, get party supplies, such as:

- Paper plates
- Plastic, paper, or Styrofoam cups
- Plastic forks, spoons, and knives
- Paper napkins

Have some serving spoons, knives, and forks available for the salad. If you don't have access to a kitchen, some alternatives are:

- Arrange for a delivery from a local deli.
- Send a PA to pick up some items from a local grocery, deli, or restaurant. Either decide on the menu yourself or invite actors and cast members to list their choices.
- Invite the cast and crew members to go to a local grocery, deli, or restaurant, pick up some items, and bring you the receipts so you can reimburse everyone.

On some low-budget shoots, the producer or director asks the cast and crew members to bring their own lunches, which can work well if you are jointly organizing the shoot. But if you are producing and coordinating the shoot yourself, it's a nice and appropriate gesture to provide the lunch yourself, since everyone is volunteering their time or working for much less than they would normally get paid.

Generally figure on a budget of about $30–$40 for food on a small shoot with about ten actors and cast members, if you buy things at your local grocery, and about $50–$60 if you arrange for a take-out delivery or purchase prepared food at a deli, convenience store, or restaurant.

Chapter 10

Getting Your Equipment and Supplies

This chapter will briefly touch on the equipment you need in only a general way, since many books and courses deal specifically with different types of equipment and how to use it. As a writer, producer, and a director, you don't have be involved with the equipment directly, unless you are also acting as director of photography or camera operator, or helping with sound and lighting.

If you have someone else handling the camera, you might make suggestions on framing the shot and when to zoom in, pan, or tilt, and you might look at the camera viewfinder before everyone prepares to shoot. Otherwise, trust your DP or camera operator to make those choices.

Often you can rely on crew members to bring the necessary equipment so you don't have to supply anything yourself, although you need to determine, commonly with input from the DP, what you need and make sure this is available for the shoot.

In the event you learn just before the shoot that someone can't bring the equipment they planned to bring, try to make other arrangements to get that equipment somewhere else. If that is not possible, try to modify the shooting plans or the script to accommodate that.

Alternatively, reschedule or cancel the shoot if essential equipment is not available.

Sometimes this kind of last-minute cancellation happens in low-budget filmmaking when someone gets ill or lands a last-minute paying job. It's one of the risks of working with volunteers or people who are working for much less than they usually get. But my experience in doing over four dozen shoots for shorts is that this rarely happens when people make a firm commitment to participate in the project. So hope for the best—that you will have all the needed and expected equipment on the day of the shoot.

The main types of equipment you need include:

- Camera equipment, including a tripod and any extra lenses
- Lighting equipment, including reflectors, and sometimes filters and gels
- Sound equipment, including microphones, booms for shotgun mikes, and separate sound equipment (ideal but optional)
- Power strips and extension cables for the cameras, lighting, or sound equipment

The main supplies you will need, which you can provide if others don't plan to bring them, include:

- SD cards or mini-DV tape for video recording, depending on what kind of cameras will be used
- SD cards or CD discs for audio recording, depending on what kind of sound equipment is used
- A slate (also called a clapboard) and chalk, or cards and pens, for recording shots
- A scene log for recording each scene and take
- Masking, electrical, or gaffer tape for positioning lights and making labels

- Pens for marking the SD cards or mini-DV tape to indicate what will be or has been recorded on each card or tape
- An equipment log for noting what equipment has been brought by whom for the shoot
- Release forms for the actors and others to sign, granting permission to use their images—and also ideal for keeping track of the contact information for everyone on the shoot

You can use the forms in this chapter to record what you need and who will be providing what equipment or supplies.

Sources for Equipment

Ideally ask the crew members to bring their own equipment so you don't have to obtain the equipment yourself, especially since the crew member will normally know how to use it. However, crew members will occasionally participate in low-budget shoots to try out new equipment or work with long-unused equipment, so check if the crew member has used that equipment before, and if so, if he or she has done so recently. If not, suggest that the person do some trial runs before coming to the shoot, and possibly help that person to do so, such as driving around with a camera person or DP while he or she takes some shots along the way.

Another possibility is to rent some needed equipment, and usually rental sources have weekend rates or only charge you for one day since they are closed over the weekend—so you get the equipment on Friday and return it on Monday for the one-day price. However, rental costs can add up, as can the costs for extra insurance should the equipment be damaged, so avoid a rental if possible.

Still another option, if you are part of a school or local community media center, is to sign out equipment, if you have the necessary training to qualify to use it. Such equipment is often available at no charge, or at a very low rate, though you have to assume liability if anything happens to it. But if you have a home insurance policy, that may cover any damages after your deductible. Check with your insurance agent if insurance is a consideration.

Finally, if you plan a series of shorts, consider buying some of the equipment, even if you don't use it yourself, so it will be available for other crew members to use when they don't have their own equipment, though they are skilled and interested in doing the shoot.

Getting the Equipment You Need

I'll briefly describe the type of equipment you need. You can discuss this in detail with the crew members bringing their own equipment or with the places providing equipment. You can also find more details at online sites or stores selling this equipment, through classes, or from books, articles, and manuals.

Whoever is bringing any equipment should check it out a few days before the shoot to be sure it works, say, by doing a trial run, since it may not be immediately obvious if something is wrong. For example, on one of my shoots, my associate and I had each picked up a camera, tripod, and other equipment at a local community center, and the access coordinator assured us that everything was fine. However, during the shoot, one of the tripods wouldn't pan or tilt correctly, and we weren't able to fix it. Instead we had to limit the position of the camera once set up so it didn't move.

On other shoots, there have been problems with the sound not recording on one of the cameras. And one time, a DP brought a green screen so that he could later edit in shots that might be seen from a moving car. But he couldn't find the weights that normally hold it upright, so he and a couple of assistants used bricks and even a stone duck ceramic from my front yard to hold it down. However, these ad hoc weights didn't work very well, so they were frequently falling off. Worse, it took five hours of setting up and moving the screen when the sun changed, resulting in the DP only shooting half of the scenes, and later we had to shoot all the shots again without the green screen. That's because it was hard to find a time when all of the actors could come together again for the shoot, and the new director/DP suggested taking the shots with a camera mount on the car rather than using a green screen. He also felt it would be easier to shoot everything again rather than trying to match the shots taken by different cameras on different days.

Thus, it's important for you to not only determine what equipment you need and who will bring it, but ask whoever is bringing that equipment to check that everything works properly at least a day or two before the shoot. Then he or she can make any fixes, if needed, before then, so everything will go smoothly at the shoot.

Camera Equipment, Including a Tripod, and Any Extra Lenses

A key consideration in choosing a camera is whether you are shooting in HD (high definition) or SD (standard definition). Today most of the cameras sold are HD cameras, because they have a higher resolution and now most editing software is made for HD videos. So given the option, shoot in HD.

However, if you can't get an HD camera through your crew or other sources, but have access to SD cameras, say by borrowing a loaner from your local community media center, it may be more economically feasible to use those.

Should you have both HD and SD cameras on the shoot, the HD cameras can be set to shoot standard definition, so you can better match the resolution on both shots, unless you have a reason to have a higher or lower resolution on different shots. For instance, you might use an HD camera to shoot everyday reality shots and the SD camera to shoot grainier fantasy or dream shots.

Another thing to check in using different cameras is that they have or can be set to the same aspect ratio (which refers to the relationship between the horizontal and vertical plane of the picture) so the shots will look the same in editing. Ask the camera people to check this and adjust their cameras accordingly.

As much as possible, the camera people should use a similar exposure and white balance so the color and tone on shots from different cameras look the same. While an editor can make color corrections to match the look of whichever camera is preferred, it is better to have the cameras match during filming since it will take less time to edit.

By the same token, the sound from different cameras should be set as close to the same level as possible so there is a match in editing. Though the editor can adjust sound levels, the editing will take less time if the editor doesn't have to make corrections to the sound level during the edit.

If you are getting cameras from two or more sources, let the DP and camera people know who is bringing what so they can coordinate what will work together and what won't. If necessary, look for additional camera equipment, or alternatively the script might be shot with only one or two cameras, instead of two or three as planned.

Unless you plan to shoot with handheld cameras, use a tripod for each camera, and usually whoever is supplying the camera will have this. If they don't have one, arrange to get one, such as borrowing it from another filmmaker. Generally it is best to take shots on a tripod to eliminate or reduce any camera movement. A tripod is also preferable for breaking up a long scene where the characters move around by moving the camera and tripod to a new position, rather than following the action with a handheld camera and ending up with jerky shots.

Commonly a camera with a zoom lens can be used for everything from wide establishing shots to close-ups. But some DPs and camera operators may want to change lenses during or between shots for some special effects, such as an extreme close-up or a fish-eye view. If so, allow a little extra time in shooting the scene for such a change.

Lighting Equipment, Including Reflectors, Filters, and Gels

If you are shooting outdoors, you may not need extra lighting, though a reflector can diffuse the light or light up an area in the shadows.

Reflectors are typically large white, off-white, or silver circles that range in size from about twelve to twenty-four inches in diameter. However, if you are on a tight budget, you can make your own reflector by putting aluminum foil across a large sheet of cardboard.

For indoor shooting, a typical lighting kit contains three or four lights. You can set up a main, or "key," light to provide the strongest lighting in the area you want to highlight, and two side lights about forty-five degrees on either side of the main light to light up subjects to the right or left of the main subject. Additionally you can add a backlight to provide a fill behind the subjects to eliminate or reduce any shadows on a wall behind them or to help separate them from the background.

You will usually need the much stronger lights made for filming, but if you are doing close-in shooting, a set of photographer's lights for portrait shooting can also work. The lights have to be positioned much closer to the subject—up to about eight feet away, so you have to move your camera close to the subject so you don't get the lights in your shot. The main advantage of using photo lights for shooting film is that they are much less expensive—about $300 for a set plus about $50 for the bulbs, compared to about $1,500 for a set of film lights.

Additionally some lighting people add filters or gels to their lights to create a certain effect, such as using a filter to diffuse the light or a colored red gel to create a reddish cast in the shot.

Check with whoever is doing lighting about what they have and what you may need to get them for the shoot.

Sound Equipment, Including Microphones, Booms for Shotgun Mikes, and Separate Sound Equipment

Although many people focus on getting a good picture, people in the business commonly say that the sound is even more important than the visual and that viewers will be much more forgiving of a bad visual than bad audio. Whether that view is true or not, the sound is critical, so be sure whoever is on the cameras knows how to handle the sound, or arrange for a separate person to record the sound off the camera; later that can be edited in with the video, although it does make it more difficult for the editor to match the sound and video, even when you use a clapper to indicate the beginning of each take. Thus, if you can have a mike on a cable to record sound directly onto the camera, that might be better to keep down time and costs, if the off-camera sound isn't significantly better.

Generally don't rely on the mike on the camera for the best sound. Such a mike will normally only pick up what is a few feet directly in front of it, so the camera can only be up to seven or eight feet away from a subject to get usable sound. Such a close-up can be fine for simple documentaries or monologues to post on YouTube. But otherwise, whoever is doing the sound should use mikes that are separate from the camera or part of a separate sound recording unit.

The two types of mikes that can be hooked up to the camera or a separate recording device are lavalier (or "lav" for short) mikes or shotgun mikes. The lavalier mikes are the small clip-on mikes that are often used in talk shows. You clip on this small mike, which is about two inches long and looks something like a tiny cigar, so it is a few inches from the person's mouth. Then it transmits what the person is saying wirelessly to the camera.

By contrast, a shotgun mike is placed on a boom that hovers near the actors. It picks up whatever one or more people in a scene are saying in about a 45-degree angle from the mike to about eight to ten feet. Then the sound is transmitted by a cable to the camera's input. Commonly each camera has two channels for sound so it can pick up sound from one or two mikes.

Usually any mike works best in a quiet environment with limited or no background noises. Accordingly, turn off any devices that make noise in your shooting location, unless you want them to add to the ambience of the setting, such as the quiet hum of a heater.

If there are any sounds that will be distracting, turn them off if you can or use another location. Some sounds to avoid include:

- Air conditioners and loud heaters
- Noisy refrigerators
- Construction in the area
- Heavy traffic

When you check out a location for filming, listen for the noises inside and outside where you plan to shoot to decide if those will work for the film.

Also, be careful about the wind in outdoor shooting. If there is only a light wind, you may be able to compensate with a protective covering around the mike—often called a "dead rat" because it is soft and furry like a rat. But if it's a very windy day, the wind may be too strong and loud to shoot the scene, unless you can get the mikes very close to the actors, or unless you can put the mike in an enclosed casing and put the protective covering around that. You can purchase this casing in a store specializing in audio equipment.

While experienced sound professionals will be very aware of these considerations, on a low-budget shoot, you will often work with people who are new to the field and inexperienced. So check that they are aware of these considerations, and during the shoot listen in to the audio to double-check on the quality of the sound they are getting. If it's not good, they have to adjust the mikes, or you may need to find another location.

Power Strips and Extension Cables for the Cameras, Lighting, or Sound Equipment

Other miscellaneous items you need for the shoot include power strips, surge protectors, and extension cables. In some cases, the crew members handling the cameras, lighting, or sound will bring some or all of these items, but not always, so check in advance to know who is bringing what so you can determine what you need to bring yourself or find someone else to bring it. The key items to have on hand are:

- **Power strips or surge protectors.** These typically have five to seven three-prong outlets for plugs. While it is ideal to plug in the lights and other equipment that are the heaviest power users directly into the wall, a power strip or surge protector is the next best thing.
- **Extension cables.** Use very heavy three-prong connections, which typically are about 1/8" to ¼" in diameter. Don't use standard extension cords because they aren't strong enough, especially for the lights, and might burn up and blow a fuse.

Getting the Supplies You Need

Other needed supplies, which you will sometimes supply if others don't plan to bring them, include the following.

SD Cards or Mini-DV Tapes for Video Recording

Whether you need SD cards or mini-DV tapes depends on the cameras being used. Many of the new HD cameras use SD cards, though some offer a mini-DV option. The older standard definition (SD) cameras generally use mini-DV tapes. There is talk that the mini-DV tapes will be going the way of other phased-out technologies, but for now they are still quite popular. Many filmmakers also prefer them, since the video is recorded on the tape in a linear fashion, whereas the video is recorded on SD cards as individual video files, which are labeled by number as they are recorded, such as .001, .002, .003, and so on. This labeling can create a problem when the files are downloaded onto a hard drive or computer to clear the tape, because it can be confusing to know which videos were taken when unless the files are put in folders to indicate the location or day when the clips were taken. For instance, after four days of shooting, you can end up with four files labeled .001, .001(1), .001(2), and .001(3). So it can be difficult to know which is which or to explain to an editor how to connect the files to the scenes and takes in the Scene Log.

As the producer, you will generally be responsible for getting the SD cards or mini-DV tapes or reimbursing whoever provides them. Commonly the SD cards, which come in 2GB, 4GB, 8GB, and larger sizes, cost from $8 to $20, while the mini-DVs, which usually come in thirty-, sixty-, and ninety-minute formats, cost from $3 to $10, depending on their size and where you get them. The amount of time you can film on the SD cards for each GB depends on the resolution of the video, so it's a good idea to check this out on your camera by recording some test footage. To be on the safe side, it's better to get the cards with the most memory that can be used in your camera.

Also, get the highest quality brands, such as a SanDisk SD card or Sony mini-DV, to get the best quality video. Check with your DP, camera person, or the store selling the SD cards or mini-DVs to see what they recommend.

SD Cards, CD Disks, or DVD Discs for Audio Recording

When the camera person is recording the sound on the camera, any audio will be recorded on the SD cards or mini-DV tapes, so you don't need additional cards or tapes for this.

If the sound is being recorded separately, you will use SD cards, CDs, or DVD discs, depending on the separate sound equipment used. Again, get the highest quality SD cards or discs, such as from Sony or Verbatim. Professionals generally advise against using Maxwell CDs or DVDs, since this is a mass market brand not up to professional quality.

A Slate (Clapboard) or Cards and Chalk or Pens for Recording Shots

You need a slate, or clapboard, which looks like a small blackboard or whiteboard with a bar that makes a sound like a loud clap when it is pulled down to designate the scenes and shots and the number of takes. The slate will also include information about the production, including the name of the director, camera operator, and the date.

You can either write this directly on the slate or a piece of tape you can remove after the shoot.

Whoever is slating the scene does this by holding the slate in front of the camera and bringing down the bar to make a sharp clap so the director can keep track of what has been shot and indicate what are the best takes. Then the editor can use this information to select the scenes to include in the film.

You can use a standard-size slate, which is about 12" wide and 12" high, or a mini-slate, sold as a toy, which is about 7" x 7" high. While most filmmakers use the standard-size slate, the mini-slate is good for marking scenes in small areas, such as if you are filming inside a car.

The most common slate is the black one, which is marked by chalk and is a little less expensive—about $60–$70, whereas the white one, which is marked with an erasable pen or markers, is about $80–$90. Less expensive ones are also available online for about $15–$20 for the larger size, $10–$15 for the smaller size, plus postage and handling. Get whichever one you prefer. Generally these are available through stores catering to the filmmaking industry. If you can't find one in your area, locate a store through an online search and buy it there.

If you don't have a slate, you can use 8 ½" x 11" sheets of paper to record the same information as you would on a slate. But instead of erasing the information on a board after each take, you write down the information on a sheet of paper, one for each take. It's best to use cover or index stock for these slate cards and preprint them with the name of the production, the producer, and the words "scene," "shot," and "take" so these don't have to be rewritten each time. Then during the production, the PA, script supervisor, or whoever else is tracking the shots can write in the scene, shot, and take numbers with a marking pen and hold them up like a slate in front of the camera and then clap their hands.

Here is an example of a slate card used in a production. Since it would normally be printed on a 8 ½" x 11" card in landscape layout, the type is a little smaller than on an actual card. The "scene" section can be used to make in any notes on the card about the shot. Or you can simply write "SCENE 1," "SCENE 2," and so on, on a series of cards and hold those up for each scene.

PRODUCTION: BEHIND THE SCENES DATE: 4/18/10
SCENE NO:_____   TAKE: 1 2. 3 4

SCENE:

Scene Log for Recording Each Scene and Take

The scene log, which is commonly kept by the PA or script supervisor, is used to write down each scene, shot, and take, as noted on the slate, and commonly the same person who slates the shot will record this, or one PA will slate the shot while the other records this on the scene log. Print up a few scene log pages so there are enough to record all the scenes, shots, and takes for the day.

While the scene log forms on big shoots can become quite complex, with plenty of space for notes to record the director's comments about each scene, shot, or take and preferences about which take to use, I developed a simpler form that I have found sufficient for a low-budget shoot. Here's an example of this.

SCENE LOG FORM

Project_____   Date_____

Scene Number	Take Number	Scene Location and Description

Masking, Electrical, or Gaffers Tape

Masking, electrical, or gaffers tape might be needed during the shoot for taping up signs, adjusting clothing, taping gels and filters to lights, and the like. Gaffers tape is ideal if you can find it, since that's what the people involved with lighting, called "gaffers," use.

This tape might also be used to mark the equipment supplied by different people so everyone gets back their own equipment when they pack up. These markings are especially important when different people bring the same cameras or similar equipment, such as tripods, lights, and camera cases that look very much alike.

To get gaffers tape, you may have to go to a store that sells supplies for filmmakers or order online. As an alternative, you might use electrical or masking tape. But don't use duct tape or any very sticky tape, because such tape can be hard to get off and can damage your furniture or walls.

Pens for Marking the SD Cards or Mini-DV Tape, Taking Notes, and Signing Release Forms

Have a half dozen or more pens on hand for miscellaneous purposes, such as:

- Writing on the SD cards or the mini-DV tape labels during the shoot to indicate what has been or will be recorded
- Signing the cast and crew release forms
- Keeping the equipment and scene log forms
- Making notes about how things are going on the set
- Making a to-do list as things come up during the shoot
- Making labels to identify what equipment belongs to whom

Highlighter Pens for Marking Scripts

Get some colored highlighter pens, which might be useful for various purposes, such as by actors marking their parts in a script.

Equipment Log for Noting What Equipment Has Been Brought by Whom for the Shoot

Use an equipment log to keep track of who brought what. You can keep a master list for all of the equipment on the set (or assign a PA to do this), or ask each person who has brought equipment to keep their own list.

If you are keeping a master list, note the person supplying that equipment in parenthesis or add an extra column to indicate this. Here's an example of a simple equipment form I have used.

EQUIPMENT LIST

Project_____   Date_____

Equipment	Number of Items	Owner

Release Forms for the Actors and Crew

You need a release from the actors or anyone else who appears on screen allowing you to use their image. Since you may be taking photos or creating behind-the-scenes videos, prepare release forms to be signed by crew members too.

These release forms can also be helpful for keeping track of everyone on the shoot so you can send them e-mails, mail them copies of DVDs, or call them about something. While some people like to put everything in their mobile phone, PDA, or iPad, I like to have a complete record of the shoot in a binder, which includes those forms.

Some filmmakers also include a liability waiver, although I haven't done so for most shoots, since these have been all-volunteer shoots we were doing as a team to get clips for our portfolios and help us get gigs in the future. So I felt a liability waiver would sound overly legalistic for what seemed more like a fun endeavor for everyone.

But now I have added a waiver for many shoots on the recommendation of associates involved with various film projects to protect myself in case someone should get hurt or has a property loss during filming, although no problem ever occurred before. However, while writing this book, I heard about an associate who was filming a short on some country railroad tracks, and a half dozen actors and crew members got scratched up from stray railroad ties, thistles, and falls on the rocky ground. Though no one sued him for damages, the incident was a wake-up call that I should include a liability waiver on my forms too.

Decide for yourself if you want to take the risk, or add a brief liability waiver, releasing you from any damages caused by anyone or anything on the set that is not due to your negligence or an intentional act. Check over this situation with a lawyer if still unsure.

Here's a copy of a release form I have used on over a dozen shoots, and a second one that includes a liability release. I simply adapt the form to include the name of the particular project, such as in the following example for *The Engagement*. Note that the form includes the benefits the actor will get in participating in the short, such as a copy of the short on a disk or online and permission to post it on his or her website or otherwise use the video for promotional purposes. Thus, the actor knows, from the release, how he or she will gain from doing the video, which provides a written statement of these benefits in return for the actor signing the release and providing his or her complete contact information. The second release, for *The Deal* and *The Consultation*, is the same, except for the addition of a one-sentence liability release.

I would recommend putting this release form on your own letterhead so it looks more official, though you can type up a simple release form on any kind of paper.

CHANGEMAKERS PRODUCTIONS

6114 La Salle, #358 . Oakland, CA 94611

(510) 339-1625; Fax: (510) 339-1626

changemakersproductions@yahoo.com

www.changemakersproductions.com

ACTOR/PERFORMER/CREW AGREEMENT FOR
SHORT FILM—ENGAGEMENT

This is to indicate that you have my permission to use my image or video I have filmed for a short video/film, *Engagement*, you are producing. I understand that you will be posting this on various social media and video sharing sites like YouTube, as well as on your own and other websites, to pitch the short for future projects, as well as entering it into film festivals. I also understand you will be showing this to prospective clients for making short films, trailers, features, and other production work, and I will receive credit for my role or participation in the project.

I further understand that I will be free to post the *Engagement* short on my own website or share it individually with others, once I have been advised in writing that it is released. I may also be free to post it on other websites, subject to the approval of CHANGEMAKERS PRODUCTIONS, so as not to interfere with CHANGEMAKERS PRODUCTIONS' own postings. I will also be considered for the commercial production if the short is picked up by a network, studio, independent producer, production company, or Internet channel, though any decision will be up to the company producing any commercial production

---

      Signed   Date

NAME: _____

ADDRESS: _____

CITY:_____STATE:_____ZIP:_____

PHONE:_____FAX:_____

E-MAIL: _____

WEBSITE _____

CHANGEMAKERS PRODUCTIONS

6114 La Salle, #358 . Oakland, CA 94611

(510) 339-1625; Fax: (510) 339-1626

changemakersproductions@yahoo.com

www.changemakersproductions.com

ACTOR/PERFORMER/CREW AGREEMENT FOR
THE DEAL and THE CONSULTATION

This is to indicate that you have my permission to use my image or video I have filmed for a short video/film, *The Deal* and *The Consultation*, you are producing. I understand that you will be posting this on various social media and video sharing sites like YouTube, as well as on your own and other websites, to pitch the short for future projects, as well as entering it into film festivals. I also understand you will be showing this to prospective clients for making short films, trailers, features, and other production work, and I will receive credit for my role or participation in the project.

I further understand that I will be free to post the NAME OF VIDEO short on my own website or share it individually with others, once I have been advised in writing that it is released. I may be free to post it on other websites, subject to the approval of CHANGEMAKERS PRODUCTIONS, so as not to interfere with CHANGEMAKERS PRODUCTIONS' own postings. I will be considered for the commercial production if the short is picked up a network, studio, independent producer, production company, or Internet channel, though any decision will be up to the company producing any commercial production. I also waive all rights or claims I may have against your organization and/or any of its affiliates, subsidiaries, or assignees other than as stated in this agreement.

> Signed   Date
>
> NAME: _____
> ADDRESS: _____
> CITY:_____STATE:____ZIP:_____
> PHONE:_____ FAX:_____
> E-MAIL: _____
> WEBSITE _____

Clipboards or Binders

Have three or four clipboards or binders available for the shoot. Use one for each of these purposes, although you can combine some forms on the same clipboard or binder if the same person is handling the forms.

- Cast and crew release forms.
- Equipment checklist.
- Scene log form.
- Master copy of the scene breakdowns.

Three-Ring or Other Binder for Keeping a Complete Record of the Shoot

Finally, it is helpful to collect all of your information for a shoot into a binder, rather than keeping it in separate files. Create sections separated by colored paper or tabs for the major areas of the shoot. These sections might be:

- Correspondence about the shoot with cast, crew members, and others
- Release forms signed or to be signed
- Scene log forms
- Equipment log forms
- Printouts of prospective cast members
- Photos and resumes of cast members you plan to audition or collect at the audition
- Photos and resumes of the cast members who are cast
- Information and photos about possible venues
- Final reading script
- Scene breakdowns—sequentially and in the order of shots
- Other information for the project

EQUIPMENT AND SUPPLIES NEEDED FOR FILM SHOOT

Name of Film			Date of Shoot:

Chapter 11

Planning Your Budget

Creating a budget can help you plan what funds you need for the shoot and indicate where you might reduce expenses, if necessary.

If this is an all-volunteer short with donated equipment, you can generally figure on the following expenses as a minimum:

Mini-DV tapes or SD cards	$20–$30
Food/water for the cast and crew	$30–$60
Misc. supplies (pens, paper, tape, etc.)	$20–$30
Printing (release forms, scripts, etc.)	$5–$10
DVDs for copies of rough cuts/final cuts	$5–$10
Total:	$80–$140

Thus, you can create a short for as little as $80 to $140, if you don't need to rent any equipment or pay any salaries to actors or crew members.

However, I would recommend figuring on some additional expenses to facilitate completing your film. First and foremost, unless you are editing your own film, plan to pay the editor, since it commonly takes an editor ten to twenty hours and sometimes more to edit a short film, and editing is a specialized skill that takes extensive training and experience to do a good job.

Depending on where you are, the length of the raw footage, and the experience of the editor, budget $200 to $500 for this. While the amount is low for editors, who generally earn about $25–$60 an hour, many experienced editors will be willing to do the edit for less for a low-budget film when they are between projects. Generally in the LA area, you can expect to spend a little bit more since there are so many experienced editors and film projects seeking editors there—for instance, what may cost about $200–$300 someplace else, would be about $500 in LA. While some editors who are new at editing and want to build a portfolio to get paying clients will edit for free, you can get better and faster results if you pay the editor.

By the same token, you might find new producers, directors, and videographers who can take a script you have written and complete a short for you for under $250. For example, I worked with a number of newcomers when I was in LA who created a dozen music videos and book trailers for $200–$240 for themselves and $40 for the actors.

Still another optional expense that is worth paying for is the music. While free music is available from various sources—from friends and associates to the Internet, to have more choices you can license royalty-free music from various sources, as will be described in chapter 17, "Getting the Music." Figure on about $10–$60 for getting low-cost original music.

You can use the form on the following page to help you work out a simple budget.

BUDGET FOR FILM			
Name of Project:		Date:	
Item	Expected Cost Low High	Actual Cost	Cost of Selected Items

Chapter 12

Communicating with Your Cast and Crew

Good communication is critical to making sure that everyone shows up for the shoot and knows what to do. It starts when you ask people to audition for the cast or participate as a crew member. When you invite people to join the production, you have to be clear about what they will be doing and if they might play an additional role, such as inviting an actor to both play a small role and help out as a PA.

After you choose someone for a role, you need to not only confirm this with them verbally but also by e-mail. Later you have to follow up with reminders or reconfirmations to make sure they don't forget that they agreed to participate on a particular day and let them know where and when to come, how long to be there for their role, and if there are any time or script changes. You also need to be clear that they need to let you know at any time if they can't make it. This way, you can find a replacement if necessary or even rework the script or shots planned to compensate for their inability to come, versus cancelling the shoot. Or if someone is wavering, you might be able to let them know how important they are to the shoot to convince them to stay.

By using these various strategies, I've been very fortunate on almost all of my shoots. In virtually all cases, people have shown up for casting sessions and on the set. When people haven't been able to make casting sessions, they have told me by phone or e-mail. And in only a few cases did an actor or crew member have to cancel within a few days of the shoot, and in each case, they let me know, so I was able to find a replacement. There was only one time when I didn't know until shortly before the shoot that two PAs couldn't come—one due to a last-minute job, the other because of a family emergency, and at least they called the night before to let me know.

Sending Out Group E-Mails

When you send out e-mails to multiple people on your production team, I have found it preferable to not let everyone know everyone else's e-mail address. Besides the privacy consideration of sharing the e-mail address of one person with someone else, there is the strategic consideration of staying the central organizer or coordinator of the project. You don't want people in the group individually contacting others without your involvement and potentially discussing other projects that could interfere with your shoot. Once they meet one another and exchange numbers and e-mails on the set, that's fine. But before then, I recommend keeping yourself as the center of communication.

To this end, in sending group e-mails, I address everyone "Hi, all," and I send the e-mail to myself, using the Blind Copy field (bcc) to send an e-mail to everyone without others seeing their e-mail addresses.

Sending an Initial Audition Confirmation Letter

If you are inviting someone to an audition after they have responded to a posting on a casting service, on Craigslist, film group, or other call for actors, a good way to reply is with a letter in which you send additional information on the film, along with your audition arrangements. This letter should also describe your plans for filming, your audition address and directions, and a copy of the script. Even if you have spoken to the actor about the audition on the phone, it is good to send a letter to confirm all the details, as well as send the script—to make it more likely that the actor will take your project seriously and show up. You can later adapt this letter to other projects.

As an example, here's an initial audition confirmation letter for *Zoo Do*. I have left out my address and directions.

ZOO DO AUDITION CONFIRMATION LETTER

Thanks for your interest in participating in *Zoo Do* for Saturday, May 8. This is a five- to seven-minute short about a meek guy who works in IT and an uptight woman with an oppressive boss who separately go to the zoo. There they experience a growing freedom and power as they see the different animals. Then they meet each other and become more powerful at their respective offices. We'll be working with the Berkeley Community Media on this project, which will be aired first on BETV in Berkeley, then entered in festivals, posted on YouTube and other video sharing sites, and you'll get a copy for your portfolio, which you can post on your own website. It's an all-volunteer shoot, except for a small payment to the editor.

The plan is to shoot at the zoo on May 8 from 10 a.m. to 1:45 p.m. with no sound and two to four handheld cameras—one or two cameras following each actor; and from 2:30 p.m. to 4:30 p.m. at the offices using my house in Oakland.

My address and directions for the auditions (and the shoot on May 8) is _____.

I'm sending along a copy of the script and timeline for the shoot. I have you down for an audition on _____. Can you bring a headshot and resume? Please also reconfirm that this time and date is correct.

Sending an Audition Reconfirmation Letter

After you set up the audition, usually by phone, send an initial audition confirmation. This letter will help to make sure the person comes, calls or e-mails you to reschedule, or lets you know if he or she can't make it. Then send one or two follow-ups, one about seven to ten days before the shoot, the other one to two days before it, to remind the actor to show up or to let you know if there are any problems preventing him from doing the film. Each time include your address and directions to be sure the actor has this.

Keep a copy of this letter in a Word, .rtf, or .txt document on your computer so you can easily adapt it in auditioning for other projects.

Here's an example of an audition confirmation letter.

ZOO DO AUDITION RECONFIRMATION

I just wanted to reconfirm that I have you down for an audition on Sunday, May 2, at _____ p.m. You should have already received a copy of the script. Can you bring a headshot and resume?

If you don't already have them, my address and directions for the auditions (and the shoot on May 8 except for the scenes at the zoo) is_____.

I'll look forward to seeing you then. Please let me know of any changes.

When you reconfirm again, you can use essentially the same letter. Just state you are sending this to reconfirm the audition. For example, when I sent a follow-up, I simply added the word "again" in *italics*, "I just wanted to reconfirm *again* that I . . ."

Sending a "Thanks but No Thanks" Letter

If you decide not to cast someone for the project, it's a nice courtesy to send a "thank you but no thanks" letter, which keeps the door open for future projects. Another plus is that if you have a last-minute cancellation by an actor, an actor you originally turned down might be more receptive to filling in at the last minute.

For example, here's an example of a letter I sent after the auditions for *Zoo Do*. I simply changed the name for each person who auditioned.

ZOO DO AFTER-AUDITION NO-THANKS LETTER

Dear *******:

Thank you so much for coming in for an audition for *Zoo Do*. I wanted to let you know that we did cast someone else for the part, but I will be putting together another short film shoot in June or July, and I hope to be in touch with you about that then.

Welcoming the Cast or Crew Member by Phone or Letter

When anyone agrees to participate, or even if they tentatively say yes, in addition to making an agreement on the phone or through an e-mail exchange, send a confirming welcome letter. You can create a template for this, so you just have to change the details indicating what role a person is taking on for this production.

Ideally first call a new cast or crew member to let them know you would like them to join the project and are glad they want to do so. Then you can briefly tell them other information on the phone about the shoot, such as which part they will play and when and where to be for the shoot.

I find this initial phone welcome approach preferable, because I can get the cast or crew member's confirmation immediately on the phone. Then I send a follow-up letter in the next day or two with the details of the shoot in an e-mail attachment, in which I list them and the other cast and crew members, indicate the times of the shoot, include directions for where we will meet, ask for any corrections in how they are listed, and any other pertinent details. The advantage of this approach is it shows the actors and crew members how the project has been coming together and their role in it. Later this list can be used to create the credits list for the editor, which has been corrected by everyone listed.

After this phone conversation, it's ideal to send a welcome letter in which you say how glad you are that the person will be joining you on the cast or crew for your short _____ (mention it by name), and that they will be_____ (indicate the role they will be taking in the production). Include the date when you will be doing the shoot, the time you expect them to arrive, and the approximate time you expect the shoot to end. You might include a timeline for the shoot if you know this, which can be helpful to let anyone arriving during the shoot know what time to arrive. Conclude by saying you welcome them and hope to see them on the shoot, and ask them to send back a confirmation.

You can also use this welcome letter to indicate what other needs you might have for the shoot, in case anyone knows someone, such as extras for a scene or someone with another camera.

For example, here's an example of a follow-up welcome letter I sent out to the cast and crew after welcoming them on the phone to the shoot.

WELCOME TO *ZOO DO* LETTER

I'm so glad that you will be participating in *Zoo Do* on May 10, and you will be (playing the role of_____/joining the crew as_____). We'll be doing the shoot starting at 9 a.m. for the crew members, and 10 a.m. for the cast, and we expect the shoot to end at around 3:30–4 p.m. I'm including a copy of the approximate timeline. I'll look forward to seeing you on the shoot, and please reconfirm that you have received this e-mail and will be joining us for the shoot.

The following timeline is based on the map of the Oakland Zoo. There is about a five- to ten-minute walk between locations, and we'll spend about fifteen to twenty minutes filming in each location. If animals aren't outside, we can substitute other nearby animals. If we can stay on schedule at the zoo, we plan to leave by 1 p.m. and do the indoor shots in the afternoon.

9:00–9:45 A.M.—Crew sets up for shoot of offices in my house: _____. And here are the directions:_____

9:45–10:00 A.M.—Crew/others drive to zoo from my house.

10:00 A.M. —Melinda/Jackson and crew with handheld cameras meet at zoo, meet in front of gate or go through gate (I'll get a family membership and cover costs for everyone).

10:15–10:30 A.M.—Melinda sees flamingos, Jackson sees toucans in the bird aviary.

10:40–10:55 A.M.—Melinda sees meerkats, Jackson sees hyenas.

11:05–11:20 A.M.—Melinda sees gazelles, Jackson sees elephants.

11:30–11:45 A.M.—Melinda sees tigers, Jackson sees lions.

11:55 A.M.–12:10 P.M.—Melinda sees chimpanzees, changes outfit; Jackson sees baboons, changes outfit; both meet by squirrel monkeys.

12:20–12:40 P.M.—Melinda and Jackson take zoo's sky ride together over the zoo.

12:50–1:00 P.M.—Leave zoo, return to house for office shots.

1:30–2:30 P.M.—Crew does additional set up, lunch.

2:30–4:00 P.M.—Shooting opening and closing office scenes in house; bosses will dress the same; Melinda and Jackson will dress differently to reflect changes in character after trip to zoo.

Sending Additional Reconfirmation and Update Letters

To make sure everyone is still on board when there is more than a week between making casting and crew arrangements, it helps to send occasional updates, along with your current cast and crew list to make sure you have the correct titles and the names spelled correctly.

Here's an example of a cast and crew update I sent out for *Zoo Do*. I included an attachment with the details about the cast, crew, and shoot. Or instead of an attachment, you can copy and paste this information to an e-mail. As with other e-mails to the group, I sent it to myself and included everyone else's e-mails in the bcc field. If you have a new cast or crew member, you can include a welcome to them as part of this update.

CAST AND CREW UPDATE FOR *ZOO DO*

Hi, All . . .

And welcome new cast members. Here's an update on the *Zoo Do* shoot, which is scheduled for May 15. Please check to see if I have you listed correctly, since I'll use this for the credits. Also, we could still use one or two people with handheld cameras that look like tourist cameras to join us at the zoo. I'll be posting this announcement in various places and feel free to post this or contact people you know as well.

More details and a revised script with expanded roles for Melinda's two bosses, co-worker, and Melinda will follow tomorrow.

Here's a copy of the attachment listing the current cast and crew I included with the update. Later, as I added other cast and crew members, I sent out additional updates. When there were revisions of the script, I sent those out too. Since I had already arranged for an editor, I included that in the cast and crew list. I have used initials for the names of the cast members to protect their privacy in this book, although you'll see their names in the credits on the short.

ATTACHMENT WITH CAST AND CREW UPDATE
FOR *ZOO DO*

Here's the current cast and crew list. I revised the first scene of the script, so Melinda now has two bosses and one co-worker. I'm still looking for one or two more people with small SD or HD cameras to come to the zoo, so ideally there will be two cameras for each actor and one person to take B-roll.

We'll do advance set up at 9 a.m. at my house, shoot at the zoo from 10 a.m. to 1 p.m.; do additional setup for the crew from 1:30 p.m. to 2:30 p.m., with actors for the indoor shooting only arriving at 2 p.m., and should finish shooting about 4 p.m. I'll cover the costs for the zoo passes (I'll probably get a family membership) and pick up the mini-DVs when I pick up the cameras at the Berkeley Community Media on Friday night. If you are using SD cards, I can either get you a SD card to use or I can copy the file from your card. Let me know what you need.

Here's the cast and crew list so far, plus times and locations for shooting. Can you correct how you are listed, and if you are bringing a camera, fill in the type and recording format if not listed so I can let the editor know and have the right kind of mini-DV tape or SD cards. I'll put together short bios later once the film is edited and I start entering it in festivals, posting on the web, and sending out PR. (I have used initials for the names of the actors and crew members.)

Cast:
Zoo and Office (arrive at 9:40 a.m. at my house for ride or 10 a.m. at the zoo; let me know which)

      Melinda—AA (Zoo and Office)

      Jackson—KRB (Zoo and Office)

Office Only (arrive at 2 p.m. at my house)

      CEO—AS (Office)

      Melinda's Boss—SH (Office)

      Melinda's Co-Worker—MMG (Office)

      Jackson's Boss—GF (Office)

Crew:
Zoo and Office (arrive at 9 a.m. at my house to set up)

      SC, Videographer; Zoo and Office, SD Camcorder; SD Card—Sony PD 170

      RS, Videographer, Zoo and Office, Camcorder, DP for Office Shots, Lighting, HD Camcorder, SD Card, Sony PD 170

LS, Videographer, Zoo and Office, HD Camera; SD Camera—Canon XL2—Mini-DV

CLB, PA/Script Supervisor

LW, PA/Still Photography

GGS, Writer/Director, Producer, Still Photography

Zoo Only (meet at 10 a.m. at zoo)

SS, Videographer, Zoo, SD Camera—Mini-DV

Office Only (meet at 1:30 p.m. at my house for additional setup)

DL, Videographer, Office, SD Camera—Panasonic DVX-B—Mini-DV

JW, Videographer, Office, SD Camera—Mini-DV

SC, Editor

Sending Out Further Updates

To make sure everyone is still on board and remembers the plans for the shoot, I usually send out one or two update letters with further details on the shoot. This serves as a further reminder so anyone who discovers at the last minute that they can't make it can let me know. For example, here's a letter I sent out two days before the *Zoo Do* shoot on May 8. I attached the latest credits list.

CAST AND CREW UPDATE FOR *ZOO DO*—May 6, 2010

Here's the updated cast and crew list. We'll do advance setup at 9 a.m. at my house, shoot at the zoo from 10 a.m. to 1 p.m.; do additional setup for the crew from 1:30 p.m. to 2:30 p.m., with actors for the indoor shooting only arriving at 2 p.m. Phone:_____; Cell:_____.

We'll be setting up Jackson's office downstairs, Melinda's office upstairs, and we may need until 4:30 p.m. to get some additional angles with an extra take or two. I have gotten an SD/HC memory card reader, so if you are using SD cards, I can copy the file from your card. I have gotten three extra 4G SD cards. I would estimate about forty-five minutes to an hour shooting time per camera at the zoo.

Here's the cast and crew list so far, plus times and locations for shooting. The only change is that we will have four cameras for the indoor shoot—possibly two in each location—or we'll have a third camera location. Again, if you haven't already done so, can you correct how you are listed, and if you are bringing a camera, fill in the type and recording format if not listed so I can have the right kind of mini-DV tapes or SD cards. I'll put together short bios later once the film is edited and I start entering it in festivals, posting on the web, and sending out PR.

Other Communications

In sum, from the beginning of the casting process to the day of the shoot—and afterward, stay in touch with your actors and crew to keep people apprised of developments and make sure they are still on board.

One reason many volunteer projects fall apart, apart from the lure of other jobs, illness, and last-minute family emergencies, is because of communication breakdowns. People forget and make other plans; they have said yes, but think the project is uncertain and they have only given a tentative or conditional yes; they get another paying job; and so on. One way to reduce the risk that people won't show up for the shoot is to communicate regularly to show this project is moving forward, trigger their memory, and refresh their commitment to participate.

As other situations develop, send out communications about that too, and generally respond back in the same medium the person used to contact you. For instance, if the person calls to tell you they may have a family emergency, discuss it with them on the phone. If they leave a message on your phone, call them back to find out what they want to discuss.

If they send you an e-mail, reply by e-mail. Consider the way you respond as a form of mirroring, in which one person mirrors the other person's voice, movements, and way of speaking to increase rapport. The way the person takes the initiative to contact you also suggests their preferred or more frequently checked mode of communication, so by responding in kind, you are more likely to get a quicker and more positive response from them.

For example, when one woman scheduled to be the lead in a shoot for *The Deal* and *The Consultation* e-mailed me to say she had an unexpected family gathering the day of the shoot and she hoped to be there, I wrote her back to say how important she would be for the shoot and how much the director liked her work in a previous film shoot for *Peace Out*. I also offered a possible compromise arrangement, in which we might shoot *The Deal* with her and shoot *The Consultation* with another actor. Ultimately, she responded to my e-mail by saying she could work it out to do both.

Here are examples of our series of e-mails, starting with my follow-up e-mail to reconfirm the shoot and provide an update to everyone.

My Follow-Up E-Mail
Eleven Days Before the Shoot on Sept. 18 (Sept. 7)

Hi, All . . .

We had our meeting today for the crew and saw the rough edit for *Peace Out*, which will be finished in a few days. It looks great and you were all terrific. I'll let you know as soon as it gets posted on You-Tube, and I maybe able to have copies on DVDs for everyone on the 18. I'm glad you can all be in our shoot for the 18.

I wanted to let you know our plans for the day. We'll start at 9 a.m. again, start setting up the lights and cameras and rehearse downstairs from about 9:30 to 10:30 a.m., and shoot *The Deal* from 10:30 a.m. to 12:30 p.m. The plan is to shoot in adjacent rooms upstairs with two cameras, with one scene in the kitchen, and the last scene will be in different parts of the living room. So we think it should go fast.

Then we'll have lunch from about 12:30 to 1 p.m.; rehearse from about 1 to 2 p.m. while we're setting up the cameras in the lower level, and shoot *The Consultation* down there, with two cameras in different parts of the lower level. We're hoping to shoot from 2 to 4 p.m.

Some more suggestions on what to wear will follow next week. Please wear something different from what you wore for *Peace Out*, and plan on wearing a different thing for each of the shorts.

I believe you all have copies of the scripts, but if you need me to send them again, let me know.

An E-Mail from One of the Actresses
Ten Days Before the Shoot (Sept. 8)

I know this is short notice but I was just (literally just now) informed of a family function with out of town family members on the 18th. I can make it work if absolutely need be, but if you feel comfortable with calling in another actress I'm absolutely fine with that. It's incredibly unfortunate because it was a joy to work with you all on *Peace Out* but I haven't seen this part of my family for many years. Like I said I can absolutely make it work if I have to, but if you can call in another actress please feel free to do so at this time. I'm so sorry to be a complete inconvenience. Let me know what you think and again I'm so sorry.

My E-Mail Response That Same Day (Sept. 8)

I don't have another actress in mind now. You really did such a great job on *Peace Out*, and I know Steffi really liked working with you and it's great to be able to have the whole team together again for the shoot. Would you be able to make the morning shoot for *The Deal*, which should end about 12:30 or 1 p.m., if it would be very difficult for you to do both?

Gini

An E-Mail Response from the Actress the Next Day (Sept. 9)

No worries Gini :) I'll make it work for both shoots. Sorry to worry you. I just wanted to see if I could make it work. I'll be there. Thanks for responding so quickly.

My E-Mail Response Confirming That I Was Glad
the Actress Could Still Be in the Shoot (Sept. 9)

Thanks so much for letting me know. Glad you'll be able to do both shoots.

In sum, be ready to respond quickly as necessary by phone or e-mail to deal with any issues that may come up for the cast or crew before the shoot. Then try to work things out so everyone can come as expected.

If you find that someone needs a ride to get there, see if a cast or crew member can pick them up for the shoot—either at their home or at a local bus or train stop. Or if necessary, arrange to pick up the person yourself at a nearby bus or train stop, if they can arrive early, so you are back at the location to begin the shoot at least fifteen minutes early so you can greet any early arrivals or respond to any phone calls about the shoot. Consider your role a little like a travel agent helping to smooth the arrangements for a client's trip.

PART II

Production

Chapter 13

Participating in a Shoot

If you have done your preproduction preparation well, you should have everything you need to set up the day or night before the shoot. This will help your shoot go smoothly so you aren't rushing around getting everything ready at the last minute.

Once everything is prepared, if you are just acting as the writer and producer, you can mostly relax, help out if needed (such as assisting the PAs with slating and arranging the lunch), and let the team you assembled take the lead in shooting the film. Or if you are directing too, you will guide the shooting for the day, working with the DP, camera operators, and others.

Following are the major things to do to make the shoot go well.

Preparing for the Shoot—The Day Before

The day or night before the shoot, have everything ready for when people arrive. Depending on the shoot, you should have the following set up:

- Confirmations from the crew and cast members so you know that everyone you expect plans to be there.
- The food already purchased so you have it ready for the cast and crew when they arrive and for lunch. A good time to buy everything is the night before so that any fruit and salad fixings will be fresh.
- Any equipment you are providing (as you may have already indicated on the equipment and supplies setup form).
- Any supplies you are providing (as you may have already indicated on the equipment and supplies setup form).
- Any props you are providing.
- Any clipboards and forms, including the equipment log, scene log, and cast and crew release forms.
- Copies of the script with order-of-shots breakdowns for crew and actors who don't bring their copy or don't have the latest updates.
- A camera and film if you plan to take behind-the-scenes photos.
- Your cell phone for communicating with others in the field.
- Anything else needed for the shoot.

Coordinating Rides

In some cases, cast or crew members will need a ride to get to the location of the shoot, as well as get home afterward. In that case, see if anyone else on the shoot can pick up those who need rides on the way, possibly at a bus or train stop that's convenient to get to. You might also send out an e-mail to everyone in the group to ask if anyone can make the pickup, and if so, share the contact information with whoever is giving the ride and whoever is getting picked up so they can coordinate the arrangements together. Then follow up yourself with whoever needs a ride to make sure everything is arranged.

In the event you can't find someone to pick up the cast or crew members, arrange to do the pickup yourself. Ideally those needing rides can get to a nearby bus or train stop a half hour, or more if needed, before the time for everyone else to be at the start location so you can get back in time yourself. You or someone else from the crew should be at the location fifteen minutes early, in case there are early arrivals.

If the person needing the ride can't make the pickup time or experiences a delay on the way (such as getting to the wrong station and having to wait for a train), you may be able to get away or send someone else who has arrived to make a late pickup, since in the first hour or so, everyone is still setting up the equipment or participating in rehearsals.

Usually you can work out these arrangements so everyone is on the set as planned, though be ready to adjust if there are unexpected problems, such as when a crew or cast member can't make it. For example, combine two smaller parts into one, or have a crew member take over the missing crew member's tasks.

Fortunately I have found that most people needing a ride will be very conscientious and even get to the pickup spot a few minutes early to be sure to get their ride.

Getting Started—The Beginning of the Shoot

Arrive at the location where everyone is meeting about five to ten minutes before the scheduled arrival time in case anyone arrives early. Have your cell phone or phone at the location easily accessible in case anyone calls to get directions, usually because they have left them at home or have gotten lost in trying to follow their GPS or Google Maps rather than your directions.

Bring whatever equipment, supplies, food, and water you are responsible for with you and set it out so it is ready as the crew and cast arrive. Typically the crew members will arrive a half hour to an hour earlier than the cast, unless you (or the director if not you) wants the actors to arrive early to rehearse while the crew sets up.

Generally the crew members handling the equipment will know what to do, using either their own equipment or the equipment you have gotten for them. The DP will direct them, and they will begin setting up the cameras, lights, and sound equipment, along with moving any furniture out of the way or into position.

The PA or PAs will usually need some direction since many are new to being on a set, so let them know what to do. Some of the tasks to assign to one or more PAs are the following:

- Give a PA a clipboard with the equipment log form to record the equipment the crew is using and who owns what.
- Give a PA the slate with chalk or a marking pen (or use scene-take cards if you don't have a slate). Also, give a PA the scene log form for recording takes.
- Give a PA the release forms to get signatures and contact information for cast and crew members.
- Ask a PA to help the crew set up equipment, as needed.
- Ask a PA to help set up the food.
- Ask a PA to pick up a cast or crew member from a nearby bus or train stop, if someone else isn't available to pick them up.

Once the actors start arriving, make them feel welcome. Offer them coffee or water. Introduce them to other cast members, though some may need no introductions since they know each other from previous shoots. Let them know the crew is setting up the shoot now and give them an estimate of about how long the wait will be until they are needed on the set.

If you have timed out the scenes well, including the setup time needed, and the crew is efficient in getting everything set up, the crew will start filming at about the time planned.

Rehearsing the Actors

On most short shoots I have been on, there is no separate rehearsal time for the actors. Typically the actors have informally gone over their lines in scenes with each other to help remember their lines and determine how to say them. In many cases, the actors will not have done any rehearsals on their own before coming to the set, so this is their first time to practice and learn their lines.

If you are handling other logistics to help make the shoot run smoothly and are the director, you will not have time to rehearse the actors yourself. So just give the actors some general guidelines about how to prepare, and let the actors rehearse however they want while the crew is getting ready. For instance, tell them to go through a reading of their lines and then create a scene in which they act out these lines.

If you have a director who wants to conduct a rehearsal, particularly one with theatrical training, allow an hour or two for rehearsing with the actors while the crew sets up. If the crew finishes setting up before the actors are ready, the crew can wait. For example, that happened on the shoot for *Peace Out*. The director began rehearsing with the actors at 9:30 a.m. until 11:30 a.m. while the crew set up—and the crew needed this extra time since they had to rearrange some furniture, take some photos off the walls, and cover up the TV and stereo equipment to avoid reflections.

If you have previous experience directing actors, having a rehearsal can be a good idea to help the actors warm up and try out different ways of playing a scene so you can choose which approach works best. A good way to start is to ask the actors to describe their acting experience, and you can give some highlights of your background working with actors in films or the theater.

For example, to rehearse for *Peace Out*, the director took the actors to a basement room while the crew set up in the living room. Then, sitting across from the actors, she described her background in learning the Meisner approach to acting and talked about her plans for the rehearsal. After the actors briefly introduced themselves, she asked them to first read the parts, and after that she asked them to read their lines again with more intensity and emotion. Next she asked them to stand and go over their parts without reading them, and as necessary fed them their lines. After a few more run-throughs so the actors could practice their lines, she asked them to add some action and suggested how they might first sit and then stand to interact with each other.

In short, the director gradually built the actors up from reading to acting out their lines. In general, the actors stuck closely to the written script, shaping the lines slightly to their own style. After nearly two hours, the director felt the actors were ready, and she led them upstairs to where the crew was almost finished setting up.

In other cases, with no special rehearsals, the actors usually had a few minutes before each scene to rehearse while positioned wherever they would be in the scene. Then as best they could, they recalled or improvised their lines as they played the scene.

Shooting Each Scene

Ideally if you are working with the DP and sometimes with a director, if you aren't directing yourself, you will have already decided on the shooting order for the scenes and will follow the determined order. Yet expect possible changes—from minor dialogue changes to changes in the plot and action, and changes in the order of shots.

For example, if an actor has to leave early or is only in a few scenes and would like those to be shot first, you may need to change the order of shots to accommodate this person. Or you might have to make adjustments because of the weather, such as if there is a slight rain; in which case, it is better to shoot the indoor scenes first until the weather clears up, rather than start with the outdoor scenes as planned.

Following the Order of Shots

Baring exigencies requiring changes in the shooting order, it is best to follow the shooting order you have already worked out, which will help you stay on time. Then if you have estimated the time needed to shoot each scene well, you will be on time and close to it. That's what happened on most of my shoots—at most they were only a half hour or an hour longer than the time planned, and in a couple of cases we even finished early.

But the one time a DP decided to completely rearrange a schedule, everything went horribly wrong, and we not only didn't finish the shoot, but I brought in another DP and we had to reshoot the short from scratch.

What went wrong is that the DP wanted to shoot the scenes of a couple talking and arguing in a car with a green screen, rather than following them in a car or shooting from the backseat as they drove. This way the DP and his assistants could take pickup shots of what they passed while driving on the freeway and city streets to edit in later. Originally we planned to shoot several other scenes of the couple arriving at a gas station, convenience store, and house in the suburbs first. The plan was for them to walk out of their car in each location, and I had estimated about thirty minutes for each scene, plus another ten minutes to go from location to location, and afterward we would return to my house, where a green screen would be set up around the car. Then we would shoot some voice-overs, break for lunch, and do the green screen shots—for a total of about four hours of shoot-ing—two in the car and two in the other locations.

However, just before we were about to leave to shoot the three outside location shots, the DP announced that he wanted to shoot the four minutes of green screen shots first, since it would take some time to set up the green screen and he wanted to get those out of the way. So I led the actors back into the living room to wait while he finished setting up the green screen. The only problem is that it took three hours, not two, to set up the green screen, and after we shot a few scenes in overcast lighting, the sun came out, so the DP had to readjust the green screen while the actors waited in the car. Then after a few more shots, the green screen had to be readjusted again, because by now the early afternoon sun was in the west, and as it continued to move in the sky, the green screen required further readjustments. So instead of being on the side of the car, the screen was moved in front of it, and when that didn't work out well, the car was turned around in the driveway. Meanwhile, the actors were becoming hot and irritable because the scenes were taking so long to shoot.

Eventually we couldn't even finish the four minutes of green screen shots, because after six hours of shooting, resulting in dozens of takes to capture about three out of four minutes of dialogue, the audio disk was full and there was no time to download it into the computer, which the DP could have done during lunch had we stuck to the original schedule. So while the DP got some good shots, the shoot was a total bust because the film was only half done. And subsequently the new DP preferred not to use any shots from that day, because it would be too hard to match the green screen shots with shots taken by a car mount on another car.

The Steps for Shooting Each Scene

Generally shooting a scene follows this sequence.

- The DP or director decides which scene to shoot.
- Whoever is slating and logging the scene, usually a PA or script supervisor, marks the slate or scene cards with this information and writes down the number of the scene from the shooting script. For example, if this is scene 5 in this script, it will be designated as scene 5; if this is the first in a series of shots for this scene, it will be recorded as scene 5a. Then each take for that shot will be noted. The first will be take 1, the next take 2, and so on.
- Once the slate is ready, the director or DP will say, "Speed" or "Cameras ready?," after which each camera operator will start the camera and indicate being ready by saying, "Camera one rolling" and "Camera two rolling."
- If someone is separately handling the sound, he or she will indicate that the sound is now being recorded by saying, "Sound rolling."
- The slater will stand in front of each camera to show the slate or scene card, and afterward the slater will pull down the bar to make

a loud clap, which is used in editing to synchronize the sound and images coming from the different cameras and sound sources.

- The slater will quickly move off the set.
- Once the slater is out of camera view, the director will call "Action."
- The actors will wait three to five seconds, then start to act.
- At the end of the scene, the director will allow three to five seconds, then call "Cut" to end the scene.
- The slater or script supervisor will note the just-completed take on the scene log form and make any notes about it, such as if the director or DP says this is the best take, or that the end of the take is good but the first part isn't, so the editor might combine the end of one take with the beginning of another.

Different directors, DPs, and crew members may use different variations of what they say, such as whether they say, "Camera one ready" instead of "Camera one rolling." But essentially they are following this sequence of actions for each take.

In some cases, if there is a break in the action, such as when an actor forgets a line or a loud passing truck rumbles by, the director or DP will ask the actors to keep going or repeat the scene from the beginning or an earlier point in the scene while the cameras and sound continue to roll. In that case, the slater won't announce another take, and the editor will figure out that the scene continued in the editing room.

Also, a director or DP might ask the actors to repeat a scene two or three times, one after the other, without stopping to set up another take, and the slater or script supervisor will duly note this on the scene log sheet.

Directing the Shoot

If you are the director, your main job is working with the actors, giving them the cues for "action" or "cut," and possibly looking through the camera eyepiece or monitor for the cameras to check the framing of a shot. But if you have a good DP, you can leave the decision about the look of the film to him or her. That's what I have usually done, since I have felt most comfortable with the writing, producing, and casting of the short and letting someone else handle most of the functions of the director. But if you prefer, you can take a more controlling role in checking on the framing of the shots.

In working with the actors, let them know which scene or scenes you will be shooting so they are prepared. Also, whoever is directing, along with the DP, should block out the scene so the that actors will know where they will be sitting, standing, or moving during the scene and can play out the scene dramatically and stay in the camera frame. If necessary, put tape on the floor to indicate where an actor should be at the beginning, during, or end of the scene. The tape is called a "mark," and that's what actors mean when they talk about "hitting their mark" during a performance.

Commonly actors on a low-budget short will first rehearse their scene the day of the shoot, although there usually are rehearsals before this day in feature productions, and sometimes low-budget directors will want some advance rehearsal time. But generally figure on doing one or two run-throughs with the actors before the crew starts shooting the scene.

In these run-throughs, many actors will improvise based on the gist of the written dialogue, because they can't fully remember their lines in the short time available for rehearsals and haven't taken the time to learn their lines before the shoot. As long as the actors are giving a good performance, it's best to let them continue improvising the scene. But if they are sufficiently off track or if their performance is becoming wordy because they are adding other lines, remind them to keep their lines shorter as in the original script, and most actors will do so. Alternatively if you let them continue to improvise extra dialogue, the editor can cut the extraneous lines from the scene.

Once the actors appear to be ready, let the crew know so they can get into position for the scene. Then let the actors know that you will now start filming, and do so.

If an actor flubs a line, he or she may know to continue with the scene since an editor can cut out any flubs in the editing room. If the actor goes on, let the scene continue until the end before calling "Cut." But if an actor not only flubs a line but seems distracted, announce a "Cut" and ask the actors to start from the top. Usually the director determines whether to go on or "Cut." It is a personal preference whether to restart any scene after a call to "Cut," or whether to go on without slating an additional take. In other words, if an actor flubs a scene, the four options are:

1. Start again from just before the flub and slate it as a new take.
2. Start again from just before the flub without slating.
3. Take the scene again from the top and slate it as a new take.
4. Take the scene again from the top without slating.

After you have been shooting for a while, if the actors or crew seem to be getting tired, call for a short five- to ten-minute break. Or if it is around lunchtime when everyone seems to be tiring, this might be a good time to call for a lunch break.

If you are following your shooting script, it can be easy to determine where you are in the script and cross off the shots you have already gotten. But if the order has been changed, mark the scenes that have already been shot on your script so you can look for shots you still need to get.

Toward the end of the shoot, check with the DP (or with the director if not you) to see if the crew has taken all of the necessary shots and what else is still needed. For example, you may still need some additional pickup shots, which don't have any dialogue, such as shots around a room, house, or building where the film takes place. If any actors need to be in these shots, be sure the crew takes them before the actors leave. If they aren't needed, a DP or camera person can take the pickup shots after the actors leave or on another day if you are running late.

Finally, once you have gotten all the scenes you need with the actors, you can let them know the shoot is over for the day by calling "It's a wrap."

Getting It All in One Day

Ideally you will have all the necessary shots, apart from any remaining pickup or B-roll shots, after shooting for one day, since it can be hard to get the actors to come on another day that is convenient for everyone due to scheduling conflicts. Or an actor may not want to take time out of a busy schedule for another day on a volunteer project after originally agreeing to participate in a one-day shoot. I know how hard, or even impossible, it may be to set up an extra day, because after the disastrous green screen shoot described earlier, it was hard to match up schedules. One of the actors had to leave on a vacation for two weeks, and after she returned, she was ill for three weeks. Then after she recovered, the new DP I brought in for the project had to put any shooting on hold for several weeks due to a family emergency. It took about eight months to finally reschedule the shoot at a time when everyone could make it.

Thus, toward the end of the shoot, if it looks like it will run past the scheduled end time, let the actors and crew know and see if everyone can stay for an extra hour or two. Commonly the actors and crew will want to see the film completed, so they are willing to stay, even if they have to juggle their own schedule to change an appointment or be a little late for an event or meeting.

If you can't finish everything and have a few scenes left to shoot, consider if it is possible to adapt the script to cut down on the remaining scenes, so you can complete the shoot in one day.

In short, do all you can to make the film a one-day shoot, since otherwise, you may not be able to shoot with the same actors again, and you may have to start again from scratch, or even table the film for a time until you can put the same or another cast and crew together.

Making Suggestions During the Shoot

Whether you are directing the short or not, as the producer, you can and should make suggestions to the DP to keep everything on track and avoid any errors you notice in framing a shot. Sometimes the DPs and other crew members don't notice these things since they are busy with other details, so they will welcome such suggestions. In particular, some things to pay attention to are:

Backgrounds. Sometimes extraneous things end up in a shot and can ruin it. Things to be careful of include: pictures under glass, which can cause a reflection, or decorations and bric-a-brac that are out of place with the character or scene being filmed. For example, in *Zoo Do*, there were plastic kids' toys on a table behind the head of the CEO, who was supposed to look very serious as he spoke about company layoffs, so we couldn't use the shot.

Timing. If you are getting seriously behind schedule because the DP is spending too much time on a shot, let the DP know, because if too much time is spent on setups, you may not be able to complete the short in one day, which may mean never. If the DP doesn't pay attention to your initial warning, assert your authority as the producer (and as the director if you are doing that too). For example, in the green screen disaster, the DP spent over three hours trying to set up a green screen and two more hours trying to adjust it, though not very successfully, which meant not getting nearly half the shots planned for the day. Though I warned the DP about the time problem, I failed to follow-through to stop the timing train wreck, so I had to start again with another DP, who also became the director.

Continuity. This means keeping the setting the same from one take or scene to another. It also means making sure the actors are properly positioned or wear the same clothing or accessories in a series of takes or shots so the editing can be cut smoothly together. Commonly the script supervisor will pay attention to continuity and let the DP and actors know when something is off. However, you should pay attention to this too so you can make suggestions about continuity, if the DP, script supervisor, or others miss something. For example, if a scene starts with an actor picking up a cup to take a drink and putting it down, the cup should be in the same position at the beginning of each scene.

Noises. If there is an especially loud noise, like a passing jet or motorcycle roar during a scene, let the DP know, if he or she hasn't noticed, since the noise may require shooting the scene again, or at least continuing shooting from where the noise occurred.

Playbacks after a shot. Once the shooting has been going on for a while, playbacks after each shot aren't necessary and should be avoided since they will slow the shoot down. The DP and camera and sound people will normally be able to tell if things are being recorded by the monitors on the camera and audio equipment. However, after the first few scenes, there should be a check that everything is recording successfully and there aren't any equipment problems, such as an unusual hum in the background or overexposed lighting, requiring adjustments or tracking down the source of the problem. For instance, on *The Consultation*, after shooting the first scene, the DP discovered an odd buzzing sound, and at first, everyone thought there was some room noise or the sound level had been set to high. But after further checking, including listening to one tape on another camera, the DP checked the mike and cable and discovered that the problem was a faulty ground on the shotgun mike. So instead of using it on a boom, I had to assist by holding the mike in a certain way to ground it in order to eliminate the buzz. Had we not checked, we would have ended up with unusable footage at the end of the day.

Taking a Break for Lunch or Dinner

Generally plan on having a lunch or dinner break for about a half hour during a natural break in shooting or if the actors and crew seem to be getting tired after several hours of shooting. Commonly a lunch or dinner break will be for about a half hour, with lunch any time from about 11:30 a.m. to 1:30 p.m. and dinner between about 6:00 to 7:30 p.m., if you expect to shoot into the evening. You can also take occasional five- to ten-minute breaks to give everyone a chance to relax between scenes. A good time to do this is if you have to stop shooting for a short time to set up another scene.

If you are having lunch or dinner on the set, arrange to have everything you need on hand, unless you are having a lunch or dinner order delivered or you expect everyone to pick up some food at a local deli, fast food place, or grocery. If the actors or crew do have to buy their food anywhere, plan to reimburse them since normally the producer covers these expenses.

If you plan a meal on the set, set everything out a few minutes before the crew and cast break for lunch or dinner, and usually you can get a PA or two to help you. It's easiest if you serve everything buffet style so everyone can pick up their cups and utensils and make their own salads and sandwiches. To that end, set everything out on plates or in bowls so everyone can serve themselves. If possible, set up chairs in the kitchen or dining room area so people can eat there rather than scattering around the set.

If you are having an order delivered, ask people what they want from the menu before the shoot begins, and ask the restaurant or deli to deliver your order at a certain time or be ready to make the delivery after you call to request it. About a half hour before you expect to break for lunch or dinner, call to reconfirm the delivery time.

Alternatively if there are nearby restaurants, you can go with the cast and crew, ask them to order what they want, and then pay for everyone or ask people to keep the receipts for reimbursement. Still another approach is to give each cast and crew member a stipend, such as $5 to $10, to pay for their own lunch or dinner.

To reduce the time required to clean up, have some garbage bags in which people can discard everything. At the end of the shoot, you can finish any remaining cleanup, and generally a PA or two or other crew members will help.

Once the lunch or dinner break is over, announce this to let everyone know that it's time to resume the shoot.

At the End of the Shoot

Once the shoot ends, there are a few last things to do:

- Thank the cast and crew for their participation.
- Before the actors leave, make sure you have their signed release forms with their contact information.
- Let the actors and other crew members know when you will send them videos or have the edited short posted.
- Check that the PA handling the equipment checklist will check off the listed equipment as it is packed up.
- Get the mini-DVs or SD cards for any film that has been shot to take to the editor, unless the DP will be editing the film and will take this.
- Be available to help the crew pack up as needed.
- Coordinate the cleanup efforts, usually with the help of the PAs and other crew members, to put everything back the way it was. Thus, any furniture or decorations that have been moved should be put back in place.
- If there has been any property damage, note it so that you, your insurance company, or the owner's insurance company can take care of this later. In the long run, it's best to take responsibility for any damages, even if caused by a cast or crew member, since as the producer, this is your shoot. You may be able to get reimbursed by

whoever caused the damage later. But since this is a volunteer or low-pay shoot, it's most appropriate if you, as the producer, take responsibility for any problems during the shoot.

Once everything is packed and cleaned up and everyone leaves the set, you can relax. The shoot is over, and hopefully you got all the needed footage for the next phase of the production process—working with the editor and then promoting your finished film.

Having a Wrap Party

In some cases, you or others in the crew might have a wrap party after the shoot. But normally everyone in the cast and crew is tired and just wants to get home.

Thus, if you want to hold a wrap party to celebrate the shoot, the best time is after there is an edited short. Then rather than just organizing a cast and crew party, you might have a larger party, where the cast and crew members invite their family, significant others, and friends. Or make it an even larger event, where you invite members of the film and business community, and even the press. I'll discuss these different options in Part IV: Promoting Your Film.

Chapter 14

Taking Behind-the-Scenes Photos and Videos

It's ideal if you or someone on the crew can take behind-the-scenes photos or videos of the shoot. You can use the still photos to show highlights of the story and photos of the crew in action. Then even before the video is edited, you can use these photos to show off what you have done and build interest, such as by posting them on your website or on Facebook.

Generally only still cameras are used for taking these behind-the-scenes photos, though sometimes a video camera set on photo mode to take still shots can be used, or an editor can turn any shots from a video into a still photo, though these are usually lower resolution and are grainier than photos taken by a still camera.

Occasionally a video camera might be used to create a behind-the-scenes short about shooting the short. But normally no one does this, since the video cameras on the set are used for shooting the short.

Just about any kind of still camera is fine for taking shots during the shoot, though you'll get better quality with an SLR (standard lens reflex) digital or film camera since you can see through the lens and have a choice of what lens to use. But some photographers use the small point-and-shoot cameras and even mobile phone cameras, which are fine if you mainly want to post the photos on the web, since these kinds of cameras take lower resolution photos and on the web photos are normally a 72 DPI resolution. But if you plan to use these photos in a portfolio, include them in a book, or blow them up for an exhibit, it is better to begin with higher resolution shots from an SLR digital or film camera (usually 300–500 DPI).

For indoor shooting, use a flash, unless the scene is already well lit by the lights on the set.

If you take the photos yourself, don't just post everything. Rather selectively choose the best shots and crop them to make them look even better to highlight scenes from the short and tell the story of the shoot. You can then post these photos on your website, Facebook page, or create a bound portfolio of these photos. Perhaps add some captions to create a story. If you can include the names of the people in the shoot, you will increase the chances of people seeing these posts since the photos will show up when someone puts in that person's name in a search engine. If someone else takes photos, ask them to send you JPEGs, so you can post them or print them out.

Generally the actors and crew members don't bring still cameras to these shoots since the actors are focused on acting and the crew members on shooting the scene. But sometimes PAs—and on occasion actors and crew members who are also photographers—will bring their cameras to take photos when not shooting the film. Or at times you might find a professional photographer who would like to come to take photos during the shoot, commonly to add to their own portfolio.

Whoever is taking photos, here are some general guidelines to keep in mind.

- Don't take photos while the cameras are rolling. The click of the camera will be picked up by the audio, and if you use a flash, this will be appear on the video.

- Don't slow down the shoot by asking the actors to restage a scene so you can take a photo.
- Take your photos of the actors or the crew members during rehearsals or between takes.
- Get some photos of the main scenes in the shoot so you can tell a story of what happens in the short.
- Get some photos of the crew members doing the major tasks for the shoot, such as setting up the lighting and doing camera checks before shooting a scene.
- Take a few shots of everyone in the crew posing together. If possible, get one of the PAs or someone not in the shoot to take a group picture with you in it.
- Post the photos on a website, Facebook, or other online destination within a day or two to show the cast, crew members, and others as soon as possible. This posting will help give everyone who participated in the shoot a feeling of accomplishment and excitement about the shoot since it will usually be a few weeks, or even months, before the short is edited. Also, you can use this advance posting to show others scenes from your short-in-progress to let them know what you are doing.

Chapter 15

Winging It

Sometimes when you try to set up a shoot, particularly if you try to get permissions, everything seems to go wrong. Or you find that everything seems to be falling apart the day before or the day of the shoot. For example:

- You call about getting permits, such as to shoot at a city or county park, and find you can't get them or they are much too expensive.
- You call or send e-mails to get permission to film at a local business, but no one returns your calls or e-mails.
- You get the run-around in getting permission, since the store clerk refers you to his manager, and the manager says he has to get approval from an owner, but he can't reach the owner or the owner is a franchisee who has to get permission from the corporate legal department.
- You think you have everything set up for a shoot, but a few days before the shoot, the manager who gave you permission says you now have to pay for the company's lost business during the shoot since the company can't assist other customers while you are there

for twenty to thirty minutes, though you are willing to film between customers—and the amount requested is so large it is ludicrous.

- You believe a company owner is eager to appear in your film, but then he has a change of heart, claiming the message might be confusing to potential customers—even if that's not the case.

In short, just about anything you might think of could jeopardize the shoot, despite your best-laid plans. Well, don't despair. That unexpected last-minute emergency is often the nature of low-budget filmmaking. But you can take various actions to save your shoot. You just have to think creatively, hope for the best, and be ready with innocuous explanations in case you face interference from the powers that be.

Dealing with the Permit Problem

At times you won't be able to get a permit in time for your shoot, or it will be far too expensive. In some places, such as some heavily patrolled areas of LA and Santa Monica, you can't do much if you can't get a permit, because if you try to shoot without one, you will quickly be shut down. That's what occurred when I co-produced and wrote a TV pilot called *Meet and Compete*, which was filmed in Santa Monica. Initially while our crew had been able to film without a permit for about an hour on the Santa Monica beach without anyone bothering us since it was an overcast day and few people were around, including any beach patrols. But as soon as the crew began setting up a tripod to film near the Santa Monica Third Street Promenade, a security guard appeared within seconds, saying "Shut it down." In such cases, you have to find another place to film.

However, many places that require permits are often not well patrolled, particularly in today's economy with budget cuts. So if you go with a limited crew and use a smaller video camera that looks like one a tourist might use, you may be able to shoot without any interference. Or if anyone asks, you might be able to get a pass if you say this is a student film. Alternatively if you are asked to move on a one-day shoot, it can be relatively easy to do so and continue to film somewhere else, since you don't have to match location shots from a shoot on a previous day.

For example, I've been on several shoots where we used city streets and parks in San Francisco. Though we were supposed to get permits from the SF Traffic Department for filming on city streets or from the state or federal park departments for filming in the parks, we grabbed a few shots without a permit, and no one asked what we were doing or tried to stop us.

So if permits are a hassle or too expensive, maybe you can take your chances and shoot without getting one, and be ready to give an explanation so you can stay or move on.

Can't Get No Permission

What if you get the permission run-around, no response, or a change of heart? Possibly it may turn out that you don't need that permission after all—or you can try the student film explanation and quickly move on if that doesn't work. You don't want to risk going onto someone's private property or into a home without an approval, since you are trespassing and can get in serious trouble if a homeowner thinks you and your cast and crew might be burglars. But if you hope to shoot on private property that's open to the public, such as a gas station or shopping mall, you may find it's easier to go and shoot there than deal with the bureaucracy of trying to get permission. Just don't include any company names and brands when you film, since that's trademark infringement unless you get approval.

For example, we pulled off a great on-the-fly shoot for *Massage Wash*, in which four actors took turns going through a car wash on a massage table. At first, I repeatedly tried to go through channels to get permission to shoot at several gas stations with car washes. I even had help from the massage company owner who knew one of the managers, and I wrote up a description of how the car wash company could use the short video for promotional purposes to publicize their business. But that approach didn't sway anyone, nor did my offer to pay for the time that we used the car wash like regular customers, except that we didn't want any water when the massage table went through the car wash. One manager said no; another said he had to get the owner's approval and never called back; a third told me to call the corporation's customer service line at an 800 number, but I never heard back from them either.

Then after I thought everything was finally arranged with one manager, everything fell apart when I called to confirm two days before the shoot once I knew the weather forecast indicated good weather for that day. Rather than calling me weeks before, the manager now told me that when he spoke to the owner, the owner said he needed to get a payment from me for their lost business, and since they could process one car a minute on a normally busy day, he wanted $700 for a half hour. Needless to say, that was about seven times the budget for the entire shoot, and I turned him down.

But as it turned out, we didn't need anyone's permission, and we shot the whole video in about two hours at three car washes, which I found within a mile of each other on two main streets in West Oakland—on Broadway and on Telegraph. At the first car wash, the manager wasn't there, and the half dozen car wash attendants who detailed the car didn't speak English. So we just filmed away as we sent each of the actors to go over and talk to them like interested customers. At the second car wash, a pay-at-a-machine tunnel was located at the far end of the gas station, where the sole clerk at the convenience store couldn't see us. We set up a massage table there between two cars and took shots of the masseuse greeting a customer. Since a customer at the station wanted to get a car wash, we let her go through, and then I put my car, which badly needed a wash, through the tunnel while the videographer filmed my car getting washed by the dangling foam and rubber buffers.

Finally, at a self-service car wash with four bays, I put my car in the last bay, away from the vision of the location supervisor, who sat in a pickup truck at the other end of the car wash. After I got his help buying eight tokens for ten minutes and he returned to his truck, we set up the massage table and spent about twenty minutes as each actor got a massage from the actress playing the masseuse and from two actors wearing red windbreakers to look like detail men. During each massage, the three actors stroked the other actor with large sponges and squeegees obtained at a local variety store. So without getting permissions from anyone, we were able to complete our film.

Using Private but Public Land and Facilities

Sometimes you will find great locations that are on private property, but you can easily get in by slipping in or walking around a gate. Unless the area is marked by repeated "No Trespassing" signs, you can probably use the location without any problem—and if necessary, try the student film excuse.

For example, in shooting *Heads Up*, I found the perfect location for a spooky woods scene about four blocks from my house. It was at the end of a residential street, and a long metal gate with a chain lock on it spread across the entrance to the path. But one could easily crawl through the upper and lower metal bars or pass beside one of the posts that was next to the side of a hill. The path led to a PG&E substation for the area, and a narrowing path led from that through a densely wooded area alongside the freeway. Though the freeway noises would have to be replaced with dialogue recorded elsewhere, the woods had a perfect mysterious quality, so we decided to chance using the location and the shoot went off without a hitch. Not even one official appeared on the path. Instead the path was used by a number of neighbors to walk their dogs, and occasionally a neighbor would stroll by with a dog, and a few joggers passed us as well.

You may find a number of such "private" locations in your area, which are ideal, since they have little public traffic compared to shooting in a clearly marked public area, such as a local park. But while such locations are private, they are often used by the public, so you generally don't have to worry about being shut down during the shoot.

Faking and Fudging It

If you can't use the real thing for a location or a prop, sometimes you can make something look like it is for real with a little creative planning. For example, you can start a scene with a wide shot from someplace else, such as a stock video or photo of a landscape or city street. Then you can use medium shots or close-ups to make it look like the actors are really there. Or use some decorations and props to simulate the real thing.

For example, in filming *Heads Up*, apart from a few shots of people walking along a path in the woods by the freeway, we shot the rest of the video in my small backyard, using medium shots and close-ups so a few trees looked like they were part of the woods. In another case, for the trailer for *The New Child*, we used a trowel and Australian bush hat to look like an archaeologist's dig. We also used a few bottles to turn a corner of my garage into a mad scientist's laboratory.

Dealing with a Contributor's Change of Heart

Suppose someone contributing to your film, such as a local business owner bringing an essential prop or providing a special location, has a change of heart and doesn't want to participate any longer? This is where diplomacy comes in. Use it to help you figure out the reasons for the change, discover how you might deal with the person's concerns, or work around their decision to no longer participate. One solution is to persuade them there is no problem; another is to find a substitute actor or an alternate location, or perhaps borrow the needed equipment they were going to bring from them.

That's what happened with *Massage Wash*. Originally the idea was inspired by a one-on-one meeting I had with a massage studio owner who is a member of a business group I belong to. At the meeting, designed for members to get to know each other better, as we talked about different massage techniques, I suddenly thought it might be funny to do a massage at a car wash, and the idea for the film was born. At first the owner was very excited at the idea of using the video to promote her business. She even contacted the owner of several gas stations with a car wash since she knew him personally. Though he was hard to contact and eventually said no, she was still excitedly on board and was delighted when I told her I had found a car wash where the manager would turn off the water—though he later asked for $700 for the loss of business, and we had to scramble to find another place.

Then three days before the shoot, at our business group meeting, the owner, who had just returned from a week's vacation, told me she had concerns about the shoot. As she explained, many people she spoke to thought the video might be giving a confusing message about her business—because in the real world, people are naked during a massage, not fully dressed as they would be in the video, and she didn't feel comfortable not using oils since they are part of a regular massage too. Somehow the humor of combining a massage and a car wash no longer seemed funny to her.

Sometimes the key in such a situation is using diplomacy to show the person that things aren't what they think or adapting the video script to present them in a different way. But here the massage business owner's mind was already made up: she didn't want to create the film to promote her business and no longer want to appear in it. One easy fix was to select an actor to play her non-actor role as a masseuse in the film, which I easily arranged, since I was auditioning actors for other parts, and I asked one of them to play her part.

But the big problem was the equipment the owner would be bringing to the shoot—a large massage table, which would be both hard to find at such late notice and very expensive—about $150 to $250. But fortunately the owner felt so guilty about pulling out at the last minute that when I asked her where I could buy a massage table, she said I could borrow hers for the weekend, and she showed me how to open and set it up. So the problem was quickly solved—and not only did we have a table, but having all actors made the shoot go even more smoothly since we didn't have to be concerned about the studio owner liking the way her business was being presented.

Likewise, if you are in a situation where someone with needed equipment pulls out of participating, maybe you can quickly find an alternative, such as finding an actor to play their part and borrowing or renting their equipment for the shoot.

Learning the Art of Strategic Delay

The art of strategic delay can come in handy, if you are filming someplace where you don't have permission to be, such as in a shopping mall or in the common area of an apartment complex where a tenant has invited you to film, but the manager discovers you there and says no. In such cases, it might be possible to delay for a short time so you can get a few last needed shots, rather than leaving right away.

A good way to do this is to have the writer, producer, director, or one or two crew members or actors not in the scene being filmed talk to the person who wants everyone to stop filming. This way, one person or a few people can explain what the group is doing and try to persuade the owner, manager, security guard, or whoever is trying to stop you to let you continue. Or even if they continue to say no, you can buy time with your explanation so the crew can finish shooting the scene. And as long as you don't have anything identifiable for that property, that approach will often work. If not, the worse that can usually happen is you have to cut short the scene and pack up and go.

For example, delay worked perfectly as a strategy when I was living in a large apartment complex in LA and a director and film crew were filming a few scenes from one of my scripts, *Unbalanced*. Although this was a feature-length film, the strategy will work for filming any type of project. At one time, I had asked the building manager about filming a few scenes at the swimming pool, and she had explained that we would need the permission from corporate headquarters to film there, and to get that approval we would have to obtain liability insurance before we applied. Besides the daunting application process, the insurance would be hard to get since we had no company structure, and it would be expensive—over $500—even if we could get it. But the manager said it would be fine to film in my apartment or on a terrace shared with a neighbor.

So we decided to forget about filming at the pool, which was frequently used during the day, and instead decided to set up some scenes on a few secluded terraces and picnic areas on the two top floors that were little used during the day when people were at work. Though the manager had been referring to shooting on my own terrace, I had access to these other areas as a tenant, so we decided to chance it.

Once the crew arrived, I let them in through a side entrance, and for the next hour or so, we shot several scenes in three different locations, and everything went fine. Finally, it was time to shoot the last scene, which the set designer dressed up to look like a fancy restaurant, and as the camera rolled, three actors began having a conversation. Then it turned into an argument, and one actor picked up another and took her kicking and screaming from the restaurant. Unfortunately, a couple of tenants who were home in nearby apartments heard the kicking and screaming. One of the tenants peered out to see what was going on, and one of the actresses, an attractive young blonde in her 20s, went over to him and was able to persuade him not to call the management, explaining that we were doing a student film, and that seemed to satisfy him. He wished us good luck and returned to his apartment while the crew continued filming the scene.

However, another tenant also heard what was going on and called to complain, so about ten minutes later, the manager, who had turned down the pool request, appeared, and she angrily asked everyone to stop filming and leave. Otherwise, she threatened to call the police. At this, I, as the writer and tenant, along with the director, went over to her to explain the situation and ask her to let us stay. Meanwhile, as we talked to her, the crew kept on filming. When she again threatened: "I want you packed up and gone or else," two crew members acted like they were going to start packing up their equipment. So she left, believing the filming was over.

But as soon as she was on the elevator, the filming continued, and this time the director and I took the elevator down to her ground-floor office. As we entered, she was holding the phone as if she were about to call the police, though even if she did, it was unlikely they would show up for at least a half hour since the police would probably consider our filming a low priority crime, if indeed it was a crime, since this was a common area of the building to which I had access as a tenant. Still, to keep her from calling, we began talking to her again about the project, and she put down the phone. Mostly we explained how we had gotten permission from one tenant and that this was a student project, saying whatever we could think of to keep her talking to us. And the strategy worked. We kept the conversation going for another ten minutes, and when she finally insisted on going back upstairs to check if the filming had in fact ceased, the cast and crew had just finished the scene and had started to pack up. So by delaying, we were able to get in about twenty more minutes of filming time—enough to finish the scene.

Likewise, if you find yourself in a situation where you are not officially supposed to be filming, as long as you are not actually being stopped by a police officer or other law enforcement official, try to delay long enough—say, about ten to thirty minutes—to finish the scene.

PART III

Post-production

Chapter 16

Working with an Editor

In some cases, the DP or director you bring into the project may want to edit the film. But usually you will arrange for a separate editor. While you may find some editors who will work on a volunteer basis, especially those who are in film school or have just learned some editing skills, paying an editor a small amount—say, $20 to $50 an hour or $100 to $500 for a short project—is generally well worth it since editing is a special skill that takes weeks to learn and months to do well. So if you pay the editor, you will get the work done better and faster.

Commonly volunteers will only be available to work on weekends or evenings since they have other jobs and may take vacations or go on other trips during your project. So instead of weeks, it can take months to edit your short.

While I have been in all-volunteer competitions, such as the 48-Hour Film Project and one-day shoots organized by local film groups, like Movie Making Around the Bay Area, where editors complete shorts in a day to a few weeks, generally super-fast editing projects are the exception. So usually I have paid the editor a small amount.

What to Pay an Editor

What to pay an editor depends on a number of factors:

- The editor's experience
- The length in minutes of the original raw footage
- The length in minutes of the final video
- The amount of cutting involved
- How quickly you need the finished edit
- How much an editor likes the subject of your film

While an experienced editor will normally ask for more per hour or project than an inexperienced editor, an experienced editor can work much more quickly, which will keep costs down. If an editor is hungry for new work or can fit your video in between other projects, that can lead an experienced editor to cut the costs for you too. And if an editor especially likes your project, that can also lead an editor to charge less.

So everything is negotiable. If you have a budget for editing (i.e., $300 for a five- to six-minute short), the editor can decide if he or she can work with that—or may ask if you can spend a little more (say, $500, when you have offered $300). If you can afford it, it can be worth it to pay an additional amount to get an experienced editor to take on your project.

Finding Editors

There are numerous ways to find prospective editors:

- Do a Google search or go to a special search engine like local.com, where you can find editors in a particular area. Just put in "film editors" and your city.
- Check with local film schools and training centers.
- Join film groups on LinkedIn and Facebook and announce that you are looking for an editor.

- Contact local groups involved with the film industry, such as film Meetup groups or film groups like the United Filmmakers Association, Movie Making Around the Bay Area, Women in Film, and Film Independent, which have chapters around the U.S.
- Check in a film industry directory for your area, such as the Reel Directory in the San Francisco Bay Area.
- Put an announcement under "gigs" or "jobs" on Craigslist in your area.
- Get a referral from an actor or crew member on your film.

When you place your announcement or first contact an editor from a directory, indicate the range of your budget based on experience and other factors, so you won't spend time reviewing the work or interviewing editors who want much more. For example, clearly state that you have a $200–$500 budget for editing a six- to seven-minute video from about two hours of film for an inspirational self-help project. That will help narrow the field to prospective editors who like the idea of the project and are willing to work for that amount.

Selecting an Editor

Once you announce that you are looking for an editor, you may get dozens of responses. To help you choose, ask the editors to send you a DVD with their work or send a link to some projects they have done. Typically editors will have samples on their website, YouTube, or Vimeo, making it easy to quickly review the work of different editors. Though some editors have DVDs, generally they only put them out at film events for prospective clients and don't expect to mail them to anyone. Instead they commonly refer people to their video links online to keep down their job hunting expenses.

As you review the videos, make notes on who you do and don't like and why. One approach to narrowing down the field is to keep a list or e-mail file of everyone who has expressed interest in editing your video. Next, rate their work on a scale of 0 to 5 (from no interest to great work). Then pare your list down to the top four to six editors whose work you like the best and plan to interview them.

While you might work with an editor outside your area, ideally find one who is local, which can be easy to do in locations with a thriving film community, such as LA, New York, San Francisco, or Las Vegas. This way, you can meet with the editor from time to time in addition to seeing what they are doing through e-mail attachments and online links.

In choosing an editor, assuming your budget is acceptable, consider not only past work but his or her vision for the project and how well you will work together. Often editors will take the lead from you, seeking your guidance in what to select from the raw footage to complete the finished film, while bringing their own approach to your project. For example, some will tend to edit with a lighter, more humorous touch; others a more serious or darker tone. Some will do a lot of quick cutting; others use longer cuts. Some will tend to choose more of the wide and medium shots; others prefer to emphasize close-ups. Get a sense of their style from discussing your project with the prospective editors, as well as looking at their previous work.

Sometimes an editor will want to interview you and learn about your past work in deciding whether to take on a low-pay project. The editor will want to know what you have done before and what you plan for the completed short, such as entering it in film festivals and posting it on your website and various video sharing sites. If they like what you have done and feel you will proactively promote the film, those are incentives to take on the project since they can add it to their portfolio and gain exposure from your efforts to promote the film.

Editing Formats

Most editors work in Final Cut Pro and have their own setups on a Mac system. The latest version until recently was Final Cut Pro

7.0 (about $1,000); Apple then came out with Final Cut Pro X, a lower-cost version (about $300) with most of the features, though uncompleted projects in 7 can't be imported into X. Final Cut Pro 7.0 was taken off the market but brought back after some controversy from editors. The final verdict isn't in, and many editors have both versions, or one of the 6.0 versions, which are fine.

The most expensive system that some editors have is AVID, which costs about $2,000. It's used by a great many top pros, so if someone uses AVID, they are likely to be a top-notch editor. However, you are less likely to find an editor using this for a low-budget short, and if so, it may be difficult to find a replacement editor who can use what the first editor has done if you have to change editors mid-course.

That's what happened with the *Meet and Compete* TV game-show project. My co-producer found a volunteer editor who did a rough cut on AVID for part of the video, which was then intended to be a twenty-eight-minute pilot featuring a sample episode from the proposed series. But after the editor got involved with other projects and couldn't finish the video, it was difficult to find another editor to polish up his rough cut. So eventually, after nearly a year of searching, we decided to start again from the raw footage and create a five-minute sizzle reel to sell the concept. And this time, the editor planned to edit the project in Final Cut Pro.

Entering into an Agreement

You can have an informal or formal agreement, depending on the preferences of you and the editor. If possible, keep your original footage and only give the editor a copy so you can easily turn everything over to a replacement editor if things don't work out with the first. However, if you do develop a long-term relationship with an editor you trust, then it might be fine to give the editor the original footage, such as when you don't have your own equipment to make a copy of it (say, if you only have a PC and the footage can only be read on a Mac).

Having an Informal Agreement

An informal verbal agreement can be fine when you know the editor, have worked together before, or have mutual associates. In such an agreement, state that you will pay the editor X in return for editing Y, and include a date when you foresee the editing being finished. Or if it's a volunteer effort, verbally agree that the editor will edit the video at no charge and will aim to complete it by a certain date.

However, even if you have a verbal agreement, it is a good idea to put your understanding in an e-mail or letter you fax to the editor. This way, it is clear what you believe you have agreed to and what you expect, and if that's not what the editor understood, he or she can correct it.

Even though you may agree on a date to get the completed video, be prepared for possible delays, since in working with volunteer or low-pay editors delays may occur for various reasons, including that the editor needs more time to do the edit since he or she is relatively new at editing. If the process drags on too long, you can find another editor and start again.

Still, despite the possibility of a delay, these informal arrangements can work well when you have a limited budget. I have produced over a dozen short videos this way.

Having a Formal Agreement

A formal agreement with an editor is a good idea when you haven't worked together before and don't have any mutual associates. Such an agreement should include the length of the completed project, the format it is to be delivered in, the cost of additional copies, and other details. As an example, here's a copy of a contract that my co-producer for the *Meet and Compete* sizzle reel drafted for an editor, with the names of the editor and producer deleted for confidentiality.

CONTRACT OF ACCEPTANCE

NAME OF EDITOR

EDITOR

Project: "Meet & Compete" (estimated TRT 3 —
5min) Producer: NAME OF PRODUCER (PHONE
NUMBER)
Acquisition format: DVCAM
Final delivery format: DVD & Quicktime
Number of copies to be delivered: 1 standard definition
DVD Scope of work (highlight all that apply):

Picture edit   *Sound design*   *Sound mix*   *Title effects*   *Credit roll*   *Color Correction*   *DVD menu*

I, NAME OF PRODUCER, agree to pay NAME OF EDITOR $ 250 upon delivery of a rough cut (YouTube
link) for the purpose of the above noted work for the Project "Meet & Compete". Balance of payment ($ 250) to
be paid upon delivery of satisfactorily completed Project as agreed by all parties concerned. Payment is to be
made in person, either as cash or check written to "NAME OF EDITOR". Producer is responsible for
additional copies needed beyond initial delivery, or NAME OF EDITOR can provide them for a fee ($5 each
for DVD) with 24 hours notice.

Acquisition of rights and releases for all material (audio and visual) are responsibility of the Producer. NAME
OF EDITOR is not to be held liable for any legal actions taken due to content used in this project.
Low-resolution digital files will be transmitted electronically for approval purposes throughout the duration of
the project. Inherent final quality differences between formats are to be expected and cannot be eliminated
with the provided footage.

If the credits contain individual cards before the roll, "EDITED BY NAME OF EDITOR" is to appear
individually on one of the cards, and it is also to appear in the credit roll.
It is understood by all concerned that this product is intended for completion by October 17, 2010 and once a final
version is agreed upon, this project cannot be re-edited without additional financial obligation to the below
signed person(s).

NAME OF EDITOR will maintain an archival copy of the AVID project file and only the media actually
utilized by the project.

This contract is intended to protect all parties concerned.
I understand and accept these terms by my signature(s).

Producer Name:_____ Signature:_____ Date:___/___/2010

Name of Editor:_____ Signature:_____ Date:___/___/2010

ADDRESS_____

CITY, STATE,_____ ZIP_____

PHONE_____ E-MAIL_____

What the Editor Needs from You

Ask the editor what he or she needs from you.

Generally an editor will need a copy of the raw footage, along with
the final and shooting scripts with breakdowns to follow during the
edit. This raw footage will either be on a mini-DV tape or a SD card,
which can be turned into files the editor can use.

- If the video was shot on mini-DV tape and the editor has a mini-DV deck, he or she can covert the mini-DV into a digital file for the edit, or run the tape from each camera directly into the Final Cut Pro program on the computer.
- If the video was shot with an SD card, the editor just has to copy the files onto his or her computer.

If you can't use the camera that shot the original footage (perhaps because the camera belongs to someone else, was borrowed or rented for the weekend, or is an older camera that is incompatible with the settings on the editor's computer) and the editor doesn't have a mini-DV deck, you or the editor have to arrange for access to one. If you can't get the deck through a local college or community training center, check with a local audio-visual service that does conversions from one video format to another. Look in your phone book or search online under audio-visual services for your community.

Sometimes editors can also work from digital downloads or copies on DVDs, though you may lose some quality from the original edit. However, this loss of quality won't be observable if you primarily plan to post your video online or show it on a TV screen, laptop, or mobile device. The usual files for high-quality videos will be uncompressed .mov or .vob files. Other formats include compressed .mov or .vob files, which are lower resolution, smaller files. Preferably don't give the editor MP4 files, which are highly compressed files.

Also, give the editor a breakdown script with scenes in the regular sequence and in the actual order of shots. If you have written up an order of the shots, but these are changed during the shoot, make a revised order of shots to conform with what was actually shot. Also, give the editor the scene log, if available, which indicates all the scenes, shots, and takes, and should include the DP's or director's notes on which take is preferred and when to combine clips from one take with clips from another.

In the event there will be voice-over narration taken at a later time for a feature short or short doc, give the editor the script for that, along with your suggested shots to accompany the voice-overs. If this is a music video, give the editor a script with the lyrics, along with a description of what shots should go with what lyrics.

While an editor may add his or her creative spin in deciding on cuts, selecting takes, and combining material from different scenes, shots, and takes, as much as possible give the editor your input and that of the director and DP to guide the edit.

Providing Information Credits

Additionally sometime during the edit, give the editor the credits to be used, including any opening credits (such as the name of the film and a film produced by_____, directed by_____, and edited by_____) and the closing credits and contact information.

In writing the credits, the opening credits may include the major players in creating the video—the producer, director, and editor, although often these are left out to get quickly to the title or opening scene of the video. Unless the actors are known, they are not normally included in the opening credits on a short, since you want to quickly get the viewers' attention.

In writing up the closing credits, either start with the cast and crew and then your contact information, or put in your contact information first for viewers who are interested in further work by you or others in the film or who might want to develop the short into a feature film. By putting your contact information first, you up the chances that the viewer will see this since many viewers will stop watching once credits roll. Before or after any contact information, include the cast first and then the crew.

Typically the role of the character or crew member comes first, followed by the name of the person playing that role. Generally list the characters by the order of their importance in the short or in the order of their appearance in it. In listing the crew, list the most important functions first, and if two people are performing the same role, like two PAs, list them alphabetically by last name. Also, include the name of the editor at the end. For example, here are the credits for *Zoo Do*.

CAST AND CREW FOR ZOO DO

Cast:

Melinda—Amelia Avila

Jackson—Kip Rowdy Baldwin

Melinda's Boss—Scarlett Hepworth

Melinda's Co-Worker—Molly M. Gazay

Jackson's Boss—Gregory Frediani

Crew:

Producer, Writer, Director, Still Photography—Gini Graham Scott

Director of Photography—Russell Stewart

Camera, Zoo and Office—Sharon Collins

Camera, Zoo and Office—Lee Stokes

Camera, Zoo—Stephanie Slade

Camera, Office—Dyna Lopez

Script Supervisor/PA—Carolynn Levi-Burton

PA/Still Photography—Laura Wong

PA—Liz Ball

Editor:

Steve Castro

It is also acceptable to include the names of the actors and crew members first and then their role, though this is less common. For instance, my original cast list for the TV pilot *Behind the Scenes with Debbi and Frankie* used this format.

CAST AND CREW FOR BEHIND THE SCENES

Cast:

Debbi DiMaggio—Host

Frankie Joseph—Host

Shelly Costantini—BellaPelle Owner

Janette Licata—Client

Producers:

Debbi DiMaggio

Frankie Joseph

Gini Graham Scott

Crew:

Gini Graham Scott—Director/Writer

Al Casselhoff—Director of Photography

Joey Williams—Production Associate/Videographer

Crystal Chan—Videographer

Carolynn Levi-Burton—PA

Liz Ball—PA

Blake Michael Burton—PA

Matthew Lyn Burton—PA

Gianluca Corinaldesi—Editor/Sound

Makeup: Lia Sabella

Still Photographer: Gini Graham Scott

Getting a Time Schedule of the Editing Process

Ask the editor for a general timeline on editing the project, if you haven't already gotten this info when selecting the editor. This timeline should indicate the following:

- When the editor expects to begin working on the project (since sometimes there can be a delay if the editor has other projects to complete, is starting a new job or school, or for other reasons)
- When you might expect to see some dailies or rough edits
- When the editor might have a finished edit, after you have given your suggestions after seeing the rough cut

While an editor with a tight deadline like a weekend film competition might complete an edit in one or two days, commonly expect about one to two weeks before the editor has a rough edit to show you—more if the editors has other projects or commitments before yours.

After you see some dailies or a rough edit, expect a few days to a week or two for the editor to incorporate your suggestions. If you have still more suggestions, add another few days or a week or two until the editor has the final edit.

Once you approve everything, it will usually take a few days for the editor to give you the video in various final formats.

Reviewing Dailies and Rough Edits

Commonly an editor will show you the edit in progress in the form of rough cut, although occasionally an editor might show you all or some of the raw footage, called dailies. Commonly the editor will send you a file or a link to a video online through a private link on YouTube, Vimeo, or on his or her website.

A reason for seeing the raw footage, or dailies, is so you can give the editor your comments on what to include in the short, before he or she selects takes to use and cuts them together. And some editors like to get this feedback. While you, the DP, or director might have already provided some suggestions based on the shoot, this additional review of the footage might provide some further insights and help to narrow down the footage to be used in the final cut of the short.

In some cases, these dailies might include everything taken at the shoot, including footage taken when the camera began rolling until the director's call to cut. Often the editor will cut out obviously bad takes and extraneous shots when the camera was rolling before the action for each take begins, so it will not be necessary for you to review this clearly unusable footage.

If you do want to see the dailies, ask the editor for them. Otherwise, just ask to see a rough edit, which will speed up the process. I have found it generally unnecessary to see the dailies, since the editor may already have some indication on the scene log sheet, which lists all the takes, and may include which takes the DP and/or director prefer. Or even without a scene log sheet, the editor may be able to tell from the dailies what takes are best to use. Another reason I prefer not to see the dailies, apart from saving time, is that I would rather trust the editor's judgment as to which are the best shots, since the editor will be imagining how the scenes will cut together and will select clips from the dailies to create the rough cut. But if you would like to see the dailies first, let the editor know.

Seeing the dailies also makes sense if you have a clear idea of what you would like to see in the short. If you know the rudiments of editing, you can make subclips so that editor can use them in choosing shots to be included in the short. For example, I did this for *Zoo Don't*, since I had a clear idea of using certain bad shots during the shoot to create a video of what not to do in making a short. As a result, I went through all of the original footage and selected the beginning and out points of the different clips I wanted the editor to draw from in deciding how to cut the video.

In making a rough edit, the editor will put clips from the selected takes in a timeline that corresponds generally to the original sequence of shots, not to the order of filming them. Often the editor will leave a few extra seconds at the beginning and end of each scene so he or she can later cut each scene more precisely. This way, there is more flexibility in doing the final edit as to how much to cut.

Usually the rough edit will include any dialogue and sound effects from the actual filming, but not the music or any sound effects to be added later. It may include the cast and crew credits and contact information if you have already sent this information to the editor, or these credits and contact information can be added later after you review the rough cut.

What to Look for in Reviewing a Rough Cut

In reviewing the rough cut, some considerations are the following. While you may not be able to do any further filming to make any fixes, since it can be hard to set up extra days of filming for a low-budget short, you may be able to figure out workarounds. For instance, you might use a voice-over or titles if the dialogue is hard to hear due to noise or low sound levels.

The questions to ask yourself while reviewing the rough cut are:

- How does the story flow together?
- Are there any places where a few frames or seconds could be cut at the beginning or end of the clip to speed up the story?
- Does the sound level seem consistent throughout, or are there places where the sound is much louder or softer? If so, the editor can smooth this out.
- Is the sound level too low? If so, the editor can increase the level.
- Is there noise in the background? If so, the editor may be able to use another clip, a newly recorded voice-over, or a title to correct for this.
- Are there any shots with obvious mistakes, like a boom in the picture? If so, maybe the editor can cut this section out, or use another take without the error, or zoom in to eliminate the boom.
- Do you like the font the editor has used for the titles? If not, you can suggest using a different font or making the font selected larger or bolder.

- Are the credits there and correct? If not, you can give the editor a corrected copy.
- Do you like having the credits roll by or would you prefer separate screens? If so, let the editor know which format you prefer.
- Are there any changes in the color of different scenes in the film? If so, the editor can color-correct selected scenes so everything matches.
- If the editor has included music, do you like it? How do you feel the music fits the story? If you don't like the music or think it fits, you can ask the editor to change the music or help the editor find music you prefer.
- Is this original music composed for this piece in the public domain, or has the editor gotten the right to use this music (such as by buying royalty-free music)? If there are questions about gaining permission to use the music, get the permission by calling or writing whoever owns the rights or ask the editor to find other music.
- When there are changes in the music from one piece to another, do they flow together well? If there are any awkward breaks, ask the editor to smooth these out.

Getting the Final Edit

After your review and input, the editor will make those changes and resubmit the revised edit, in much the same way that he or she showed you the first rough cut—via a link to the file online, as an attachment, or on a DVD, usually in a compressed lower resolution format.

This revision and review process can go on several times, and generally it will take a couple of days to a week or two each time. Ideally limit this process to one or two reviews, where the editor fixes what he or she can. Otherwise, if you strive too hard for perfection, it can take a very long time to get the video edited, and your costs can go up substantially if you are paying the editor for extra edits. Also, you and the editor can feel increasingly frustrated and burned out by the process.

Thus, after a couple of edits, I recommend ending the process and consider whatever you have gotten as part of the learning process. If you strive too hard for perfection, you may end up having to wait many months to get your short edited or even not get anything completed. I think it is better to have something to show off your script and your ability to put together a team to shoot and edit the film. Then you can use that short to help you get the next project and the next.

Once the edit is finalized, the editor can give you the finished edit in various formats that you can use to show on a DVD player, on your computer, on your website, or on a video sharing site, such as YouTube or Vimeo. Ideally get the original footage back in case you want to use any of the footage in other projects or find another editor to do a different or better edit.

The formats to obtain include:

- A video you can play on a DVD player—usually in a .VOB format
- A video you can upload onto video sharing sites—usually in an MP4, .mov, or .VOB format, and compressed, if necessary, to under 2 GB, which is the limit on most video sharing sites. You can play this with video viewing software on your computer, such as Windows Media Player, Quicktime, Real Player, or Internet Video WinDV.
- A high-resolution video in a .VOB or .mov format, which you can use, if necessary, to make other formats

You should be able to play a video in these formats on a PC or Mac. However, if you get the original footage and it will be edited in Final Cut Pro, copy it onto a Mac or a hard drive formatted for a Mac, since Final Cut Pro is normally used on a Mac system and a PC will not recognize anything formatted for a Mac.

Chapter 17

Getting the Music

Many editors will handle getting the music and submit it for your review before or after adding it to your video. But some editors will ask for help in finding and choosing the music. You can help in various ways.

Finding the Music

Unless you are composing and providing the music yourself, here are some ways to get music for your short.

- Find a musician to compose the music or provide already composed music. Some musicians will compose original music on a volunteer or low-pay basis. Or they may have an archive of music you can use. You can find such musicians through local film community groups or post an ad for a musician under "gigs" on Craigslist.
- Find a source for free or royalty-free music online. A number of sites offer different types of licensing arrangements for music, which you can download usually in MP3 or .wav formats. Some of these sites include:

www.pond5.com
www.royaltyfreemusic.com
www.neosounds.com
www.musicbakery.com
www.beatsuite.com
www.partnersinrhyme.com
www.audiobank.fm
www.royaltyfreemusiclibrary.com
www.premiumbeat.com

Prices start at $20 and up, even as much as $150 for some pieces, with most charging around $20–$40 per song or musical composition. Since so many different services offer music, check them out for yourself online or ask your editor to do so and select some possibilities for you to listen to. For additional links, enter "royalty free music" or "licensing music for film" into a search engine and you'll find dozens of such services listed.

If you select the music providers listed on the first or second page, these are the ones rated highest through the search engines, and commonly they are the most accessed by others looking for music.

Choosing the Type of Music

A good starting point for your music search is describing the genre of music and the kind of effect you want to achieve. For example, do you want lighthearted and lively music for a romantic comedy, otherworldly and spooky music for a horror short, strange and mysterious music for a suspense thriller? Think of the feeling you want to convey for your short as a whole or for different parts of it.

Also, consider the style of music that fits your short. For instance, if your short takes place in the inner city, consider using hip-hop or rock; if it's an avant-garde fantasy, electronic instrumental music might work well; if it's a drama about everyday life, maybe a pop or country sound might be ideal.

In short, the two key considerations in choosing the music for your film are:

- The feeling you want to convey
- The genre of music to convey this feeling

Chapter 18

Getting Additional Graphics and Pickup Videos

In some cases, you might want additional graphics, photos, or videos that don't require any sound or actors (sometimes called pickup or B-roll shots). You can also obtain royalty-free videos from the Internet or from video services. While many editors already have access to such sources, you might help those who don't by obtaining the images or advising the editor on where to find them.

Getting Graphics and Photos

There are a number of sources for free or inexpensive graphics and photos, say, if you want to add in the scenes of a busy city street or a landscape to provide a sense of place. Or you might find images of space, seascapes, mountains, office buildings, animals, just about anything. For example, for my short *Cougar and Cub*, about an older woman who meets younger men, the editor I worked with found some images of cougars and cubs from an online service. In another short, *Heads Up*, which includes images of the Cheshire Cat and the Queen of Hearts from *Alice in Wonderland* and the Headless Horseman from *Rip Van Winkle*, I found public-domain images by putting those names in a search engine. I used the original images from the nineteenth century, not the modern animated cartoon images by Disney, which are definitely not public domain.

You can find images from various sources:

- Click "Images" on the home pages for Google or Yahoo. Some of these will be free images taken by amateurs; others will be copyrighted and you can ask for permission.
- Put in a description of your video subject or the type of image you want in a search engine, and you'll find images from various websites. Then ask the website owner for permission to use that image.
- Buy some graphics software, such as from Hemera Graphics, which include The Big Box of Art with 615,000 images, The Big Box of Art with 1 million images, BizArt, and Photo Objects I, II, and III. Once you buy the software, you can use any of the images for free.
- Use a service that sells photos and graphics, such as:
    www.istockphoto.com
    www.fotolia.com
    www.bigstockphoto.com

You can find images for as little as $1 or $2, which are ideal for a website, though higher resolution images for a video are about $10–$15 an image. You can download them as JPEGs or other popular image formats to insert them into your video.

Getting Video Clips

There are many sources for free or inexpensive video clips, which you can use to make it look like you were filming in different locations or to provide a context for your film, say, by providing a few seconds of city or country scenes. For example, for *Behind the Scenes with Debbi and Frankie*, the editor added in some shots of the countryside around

Northern California to indicate the locations they might go to film additional segments of the show.

The various sources for finding videos include:

- Videographers you meet at local film community events. Ask them if they have some footage of a particular location or subject that you could use.
- Click "Videos" on the home pages for Google or Yahoo and put in the subject of the video you are looking for. Some of these clips will be free videos taken by amateurs; others will be copyrighted by amateurs or pros; in either case, you can ask for permission.
- Briefly describe of the subject of your video or the type of image you want into a search engine, and you'll find videos from various websites. Then ask the website owner for permission to use a video you like.
- Use a service that has videos, photos, or graphics, such as:
  www.istockphoto.com/video
  www.footage.shutterstock.com
  www.freestockfootage.com

While some of the more expensive services charge around $300–$500 for stock footage, these lower priced stock footage sources start at $10–$15 to $25–$50 a clip. The video clips can be downloaded in a variety of formats, from DVCam to BetacamSP to HDCam. Your editor can tell you the preferred format to incorporate these clips into your video.

PART IV

Promoting Your Film

Chapter 19

Showing and Promoting Your Film

Now that your short film is completed, what do you do with it? How do you get it seen? Generally there is no commercial market for short films, so don't expect to make money on your short, unless you are making the film for a paying client. Rather the main reason for making most short films is:

- The experience of making it, including the fun of doing it and what you will learn to bring to your next film.
- To add to your portfolio to show what you can do so you can get clients to hire you to make films for them, or to be hired by an established producer to participate in a feature film or documentary.
- To gain recognition by other filmmakers so you will be invited to participate in other film projects.
- To introduce characters, a story, or a subject for a TV or web series or a full-length feature.

Your reasons for making your video will influence how you show and promote your film after it is completed. Select those approaches to showing and promoting that are most suitable for you.

Show Your Film to Friends and Family Members

If you have mainly made your film for fun and to learn from the experience, you may simply want to show your film to friends and family members in person or through online video sharing sites. For example, bring your film to social gatherings with your friends or family, or let them know where they can see it on YouTube or Facebook. Perhaps have a party where you invite those close to you and include a showing of your film at the party.

If you have other purposes in creating your film, showing it to your friends and family members while pursuing other venues can be a good way to get suggestions and possibly referrals, if they know someone who might be a potential client or has film industry contacts.

Post Your Film on Your Website and Video Sharing Sites

If you have a website, definitely post your video there. You can upload a file directly to your site, or as many people do, embed the code from YouTube or other video sharing site so your video can be viewed from that link. One advantage of using a video sharing link is that when people view your video from that link, this increases the number of people viewing it on the video sharing site, which ups your numbers for that video. In turn, as your numbers go up, that increases your rank on that site, which can lead to your video getting even more views, and at some point, some sources will offer you money for hits. Another advantage of using a link to the video sharing site and not posting your video directly on your own site is that you don't add a large file size to your website. Currently it seems like a safe bet to embed the code from YouTube, since it doesn't seem like YouTube will be dropping any videos anytime soon because it keeps expanding and is backed by its affiliation with Google.

However, in case YouTube or another video sharing site changes the link or removes your video, keep a copy on a DVD or on your computer, just in case you need to upload it to another video sharing site and link to that or upload it directly onto your website.

If you plan to put your film on other video sharing sites besides YouTube, here are the other major sites, in order of popularity.

www.metacafe.com
www.break.com
video.google.com
www.dailymotion.com
video.yahoo.com
www.revver.com
www.vimeo.com
www.vidilife.com
www.stickam.com

These video sharing sites have various rules about the length of your video and how large the file size can be, but generally they will all accept shorts of under ten minutes or under two GB. YouTube, Google, and some of the other sites will accept shorts of under fifteen minutes.

While higher resolution files—around 500,000 MB or more—will have a better appearance when viewed, they take much longer to upload and process—about four to six hours. And they may stall for some viewers if their network for viewing videos isn't fast enough. For instance, a DSL connection through AT&T is only about 100.0 mbps (millibytes per second), whereas a cable connection via Comcast is about five times faster. So it is generally better to upload a more compressed file, such as a MP4, which is about 50,000 MB, since it will be faster to upload as well as smoother to stream for many viewers.

Post or Link to Your Video on Social Media Sites

Besides the video sharing sites, you can post videos or links to them on social media sites, like LinkedIn, Facebook, and Twitter. If you don't already have an account, start one and begin building up connections, variously called contacts, friends, and followers.

After you post the video or link, send a note to your connections on these sites letting them know the video is up there and inviting them to view it, as well as comment. If people like it, invite them to indicate this, such as by giving you a recommendation on LinkedIn or a "like" thumbs-up sign on Facebook. Later you can add any recommendations and favorable comments to your website to show how much people like your work.

Join Film Groups in Your Area and Online

Film groups in your area can be a great way to network with other filmmakers who might be interested in seeing your film and working with you on future projects. Some of these groups might also arrange special events for members, such as a night of short films, and you can submit your film for such a showing.

Check into both the national groups that have local chapters and the grassroots organizations of local filmmakers. You may additionally find many Meetup groups in your area that have film programs and networking events at which they might show your film. For example, some groups in Southern or Northern California include:

- Women in Film (www.wif.org)
- Bay Area Women in Film and Media (www.bawifm.org)
- Film Independent (www.filmindependent.org)
- United Filmmakers Association (ufa.metahelion.com)
- Making Movies Throughout the Bay Area (www.moviemaking-bayarea.com)

- Bay Area Film and TV Connection (www.meetup.com
  /bayareafilmandtvconnection)

Most of these groups have a Facebook page, where they have an interactive community of users and announce upcoming events, which you can sign up to attend. Just put the names of these groups into the Facebook search box to find them; then join the group or indicate you "like" it to become part of the community.

You can also join a variety of film groups on LinkedIn and post announcements and links to your videos in each of these groups. Some of groups I belong to in the film community include these.

Film and Television Professionals
Film TV Professionals
Film Financing Forum
Producers Network
Filmmakers
Hooray for Hollyworld!
Independent Filmmakers and Screenwriters
ThoseInFilms
Media & Entertainment Professionals
Media Professionals Worldwide
Animation, Media & Entertainment
Showbizjobs.com
Associated Producers Worldwide
Film Angels
Media Leaders

Besides getting people to see your video, you can use these postings to invite people to contact you about working with you on future projects or developing your short into a feature film. For more information on how to use LinkedIn to promote your video, read my book *Using LinkedIn to Promote Your Business or Yourself.* It's available on Amazon and multiple e-book platforms.

Create Postcards, Flyers, Bookmarks, or Posters Featuring Your Film

Another approach to getting publicity is creating promotional materials about your film, such as postcards, flyers, bookmarks, or posters, which you can bring with you to networking events and meetings. You can hand them out when you talk to people, put them on tables for people to take, or possibly post them on the walls.

These materials can direct people to go to your website, YouTube link, Facebook page, or other online site to view your video. Or use these promotional materials to promote a screening of your video.

Send E-Mails or Messages to Your Business Associates and Online Contacts

You can send e-mails to people in your database to let them know where to view your video online or at an upcoming event. Or if you have social media connections, you can send them an announcement through LinkedIn, Facebook, Twitter, or other services. While you can post longer messages on LinkedIn or Facebook, any announcement on Twitter is limited to 140 characters or less. However, within this limited space, you can include a link to a website or a page where you have more details about the video or the screening.

Should you have accounts on different services, you can send a mailing to multiple groups at the same time through www.ping.fm, though keep it to 140 characters or less if one of these groups is Twitter. If you have an especially long link to send people to, you can shorten it to a much shorter link through www.tinyurl.com.

Participate in or Put on a Promotional Event for Your Film

Another type of promotion is participating in or organizing an event to showcase your film.

One approach is to see if other people who are planning an event might be interested in including your film in the program. For instance, contact local church groups, singles groups, community groups, and civic service groups about this. If they are doing an event that ties in with the topic of your film, so much the better, since that will be an even better promotional platform. If the event organizers decide to include your film, ask how you might help them promote the program, which will also help you in getting more people to see your video.

Another approach is to put on a promotional event yourself or team up with others to put it on. In planning the event, allow some time before and after the program for networking. A good format is to have a half hour to an hour of networking time before the program, allow ten to fifteen minutes at the end of the program for Q & A, and another half hour to an hour for more networking at the end.

By having plenty of time for networking, you'll have a chance to meet the attendees and talk about your film with them personally. Having this networking time also provides a more involving experience for everyone than just showing a series of films followed by a short Q & A, after which everyone leaves.

As an example of this networking approach, I helped to organize an event for a nonprofit—United Media Productions—where I am one of four board members. Besides sending out press releases to the local print, broadcast, and Internet media, we invited people through personal invitations and announcements to my six Meetup groups involved with films and social trends. The program was scheduled from 7 to 10 p.m., and for the first hour, people were invited to help themselves to a light dinner at an informal buffet and mingle with others. At 8 p.m. we began the program by introducing the board members and the films, along with a guest who was featured in one of the films, and then showed a half dozen different film projects. After the films ended at 8:45 p.m., we invited the audience members to ask questions of any of us for about fifteen minutes. Most of the questions focused on how the films were made and on how we found the interviewees featured in them. Finally, we broke up for more informal networking for about 30 minutes.

Enter Your Video in Short Film Festivals

Another way to get exposure for your film is to look for short film showings and for festivals that have a division for short films.

One way to find festivals to enter is to go to the online clearing house for most festivals—Without a Box (www.withoutabox.com)—and put in "short" in the search field. You will then find about 300 festivals with "short" or "shorts" in the title. Then search through this list to find festivals in your area. Or put in "short film festivals" and the state or location you are interested in, and a number of entries will come up, including larger film festivals that have a division for short films.

Most of these festivals will have entry fees—commonly around $25 to $50—and if your film is selected to be shown, use this opportunity to promote your film. If you win or receive an honorable mention, add that to your promotional material. You may also win a small monetary reward along with a ribbon or statue.

An efficient way to make your entries is through Without a Box since you can pay and in many cases submit your entry online. Just register to open an account as a filmmaker. Then you can enter each festival, and if you are entering multiple festivals, you can get a discount pack giving you discounts of $5 to $15 each time you submit an entry. The discount packs cost $160 for $185 in entries and $400 for $500 in entries.

For example, I have an account under Changemakers Productions, and I can list each of the projects I want to submit. Then, say, I want to enter the Aspen Shortfest in the Drama category, I would pay a $40 entry fee and send in my short on a disk in various formats. In other cases, such as the Beverly Hills Shorts Festival, I can upload a video in various popular formats, such as .mov (Quick Time), .flv (Flash Video), .wmv (Windows Media), or MPEG4 or MP4.

If you submit an entry and your film is accepted, attend if you can. Besides being fun, these festivals offer an opportunity to meet other filmmakers and industry pros at screenings and through informal networking, which can open other doors for you. For instance, you might find a producer who wants to see future submissions by you if he or she likes your short.

Festivals are also a great way to build up accolades for your project if you win something, which you can use in subsequent promotion. However, apart from some small rewards, don't expect to make money on your short. The vast majority don't earn anything. Rather promote it with a focus on building up your portfolio of videos with accolades, making contacts, and getting future projects as a result of people seeing and liking your short.

Participate in Short Film Showings and Events

Another way to promote your film is to contact film groups and others in your area who might be interested in showing your short with other films or activities. Some possibilities include:

- Indie film theaters that sometimes show the work of local filmmakers, including shorts
- Church groups
- Singles groups
- Networking and business groups
- Social groups, including Meetup groups

In most of these cases, don't expect any money for showing your film, especially if these are showings at free events. However, these events can be fun for networking and making contacts.

Contact Potential Clients, Employers, or Producers with Your Film

Finally, consider your short as a calling card or addition to a resume, which you can use to get clients or employers to hire you or producers to invite you to participate in other film projects.

For example, you might show your video—or even better, show a few videos or a trailer with clips from several videos—to prospective clients to demonstrate the kind of work you do. If the viewers like this, they might hire you to write a script or produce and direct a video for their company. To get such a job, it is best to show a video that not only shows off your compelling story as a writer and the high-quality cinematography of the team you have put together as a producer, but also relates to what the company or organization does. For example:

- If you feature a sport in your video, approach a sports shop or company that manufacturers a sports product about doing a promotional video for them.
- If you feature a story set in a corporation, approach local corporations about doing a short narrative video about their company.
- If you feature a story dealing with a social issue, approach community groups about developing a story around one of their issues.
- If you have created a music video, approach some local music groups about doing a video for them.

As an illustration of how this works, I have been creating some videos based on stories with a message that I wrote and produced with a nonprofit group, United Media Productions, devoted to creating a better world. One video, *Peace Out*, features three people trying to put together a peace event, but they have different visions of what it should be like and the argument escalates into pushing, shoving, and slapping, which is edited like a slapstick comedy. Another video, *The Deal,* features a sleazy investment broker trying to take advantage of a writer in a deal, but she turns the tables on him. A third video, *The Consultation,* shows an underhanded insurance broker who is trying to avoid paying a business consultant, but she discovers who he really is. The plan is to approach community groups with the first video and corporations with the other two to write and produce videos for them. In addition, the UMP team plans to use the videos—and others in development—in a series of workshops and seminars where the films are used to generate discussion around a particular topic.

You can also use your video to seek employment from companies doing films for clients to see if they will hire you as a writer, producer, or director. If they like your work, they might hire you on particular projects or as a member of their staff.

Another possibility if there are producers and production companies doing feature films in your area is to use your video to seek a job with them. Or if you are serious and willing to buck the difficult odds, try moving to LA. The competition can be daunting, but with persistence, if you've put together a strong body of work, your short videos might help you break in.

In short—no pun intended—writing and producing, and in some cases directing, your own shorts can be a good way to get started so you have examples of what you can do with a very low budget. Then that can open some doors to writing and producing, and even directing, larger films.

The big door opener is if you can raise the money to produce the film. The shorts you have created can help—but the trick is getting the money if you don't have the family and friends to get you started. And raising money is a job in itself—and the subject for another book.

Chapter 20

Copyrighting and Protecting Your Work

A common question of filmmakers is what to do about copyrighting and protecting your work. In general, formally registering a copyright isn't something you have to worry about with most shorts since there is usually no commercial market for them, and most filmmakers making shorts want to show off their talents, not copy from someone else. Also, your work is automatically protected by a copyright from the date of creation under the Berne Convention.

You can readily show the date when it was created in various ways. For example, you can post it on YouTube or other video sharing sites, send video files to others working on the project, or have dated releases from everyone working on the video. By contrast, when you only have a script or book manuscript, the date of creation can be less clear, unless you send these materials to someone by e-mail or regular certified or registered mail and don't open the envelope until you have to prove the date of creation.

The main reasons to register a copyright for your short or file a registration with the Writers Guild of America for your script are:

• You want to develop the characters into a feature film.

- You have created a script trailer to sell a script.
- You have created a pilot for a TV show or documentary.
- You have a complete script on which the trailer or short was based.

It is generally unnecessary to register your work with the copyright office or the WGA if your main reason for creating the short is to add to your portfolio to show off your skills in writing, producing, or directing short projects in order to get work doing other shorts or being hired on a feature film project.

However, if you do want to register your work, here's what to do.

Getting a Copyright Registration

To register your copyright, get a copyright form from the U.S. government copyright office. Go to the website at www.copyright.gov.

The cost is $35 if you file online, $45 if you mail in your material. Preferably file online since it's much faster and cheaper. You fill out an online form, and then upload certain categories of deposits as an electronic file. The acceptable file types include most video files, including:

- .avi (Audio Video Interleave)
- .mov (QuickTime)
- .mpg, .mpeg, .mp4 (Moving Picture Experts Group)
- .rm, .rv (Real Media File)
- .swf (Adobe Flash, formerly Shockwave Flash)
- .wmv (Windows Media Video)

You can also upload almost any image and text files.

When you file online, you will receive your certificate within six months, sometimes earlier, whereas it may take up to twenty-two months to receive a certificate when you file a paper form. In either case, your registration begins on the date the copyright office receives a completed submission in an acceptable form. However, if you use the mail, there can be a delay in the Copyright Office receiving the mail through the U.S. Postal Service or a private carrier since, as the Copyright Office explains, "All of the mail sent to the Copyright Office is being screened off-site prior to arrival on Capitol Hill. This process can add 3 to 5 days to the delivery time for all mail sent to the Copyright Office."

To register online, go to the Electronic Copyright Office site at https://eco.copyright.gov/eService_enu/start.swe. As a new user, you click to register, then fill in some personal information about yourself. Once you do, you can view a tutorial in PowerPoint on how to register a new claim. Just follow the prompts. When it comes to the type of work, register your screenplay or script for a trailer or TV pilot as a work of the performing arts (PA) for a screenplay, script for a trailer, or TV pilot. If you have created a short, register it as a Motion Picture/Audio Visual (VA) Work.

If you plan to file, do so within three months of completing the work to gain statutory protection under copyright law, which permits certain damages for an infringement. Once you file for your registration and become a copyright owner, an infringer may be liable for your actual damages plus any profits made from the infringement. Or the copyright owner can avoid proving actual damage by electing a statutory damage recovery of $750 to $30,000 or, if the court determines the infringement occurred willfully, you can win up to $150,000 plus attorney fees. The actual amount of the award will be based upon what the court in its discretion considers just. However, if you haven't filed for a registration, you can only get actual damages.

Thus, because of the threat of a high damage claim, a key value of having a registered copyright is that you can better fend off people who might copy your work. But the reality is that you have to file a civil suit to obtain these monetary and other possible damages (such as an injunction against the infringer) if you win. Then even if you win, you still have to collect any judgment you receive. Actually collecting anything can be a very long and expensive process, so realistically, since there is little commercial value in shorts, there is not much likelihood of infringement nor are you likely to suffer any damages. So as a practical matter, in most cases, you don't need to register your copyright.

Registering Your Work with the Writers Guild of America

Another option for protecting your work is registering your complete screenplay or script for a trailer or TV pilot with the Writers Guild of America. You don't have to be a WGA member to register it. The registration lasts for five years if you register with the East Coast branch, ten years with the West Cost branch, and you can renew it. During this registration period, your material is kept on file, in case you need to show it as evidence of infringement.

At one time, if you lived west of the Mississippi, you would register with the WGA West, and if you lived east of the Mississippi, you would register with the WGA East—and the WGA East still makes that distinction. But now you can register with the WGA West office no matter where you live.

Making registration even easier, you can now do it online rather than having to send in your material. However, if you still opt to register by mail, you have to send in a complete unbound loose-leaf copy of your material on standard 8 1/2" x 11" paper, along with a cover sheet with the title and all of the writers' full legal names.

The key difference between the WGA West and East is in the cost and the time the registration lasts. The WGA West cost is $20 for a five-year registration for non-members and $10 for members; the WGA East cost is $22 for non-members for a ten-year registration, $10 if you are already a member, and $17 for students with an ID. Though the length of registration with the WGA East is twice as long and the payment is about the same, most screenwriters register with the WGA West, probably because the film industry is centered in LA.

You can upload any file format, though the preferred formats are ASCII text, PDF (Adobe Acrobat), Microsoft Word files, Final Draft, and Movie Magic Screenwriter 2000.

While WGA registration doesn't provide the statutory protections of copyright in case of infringement, it provides the legal evidence of the date of your authorship when you submit it to agents, managers, or producers, and some industry pros ask that you have either registered your script with the WGA or with the U.S. Copyright Office.

As the WGA West describes it, the reason for registration is to provide preventative measures against plagiarism or unauthorized use of your material. "While someone else may have the same storyline or idea in his or her material, your evidence lies in your presentation of your work. Registering your work does not disallow others from having a similar storyline or theme. Rather, registering your work would potentially discourage others from using your work without your permission."

Thus, although registering your work cannot prevent someone from plagiarizing it, you can produce the registered material and confirm the registration date, which creates legal evidence that you created this work and when you did so.

For more details and to register your script, the website for the WGA West is www.wga.org and the website for the WGA East is www.wgaeast.org.

Chapter 21

The Biggest Mistakes Filmmakers Make

Some of the biggest mistakes filmmakers make have already been alluded to in previous chapters. Here I want to highlight the ones I have noticed the most.

Writing too much detail in the action or narrative section, or discussing what the characters are thinking or feeling. Don't treat the script like a novel. Only describe what will go on the screen and keep these descriptions short—just enough to set the scene, since the director will set up the script based on the chosen location and the available décor and props. Only include the minimal descriptions of a character's feelings to indicate how an actor might show those emotions on screen; don't go into detail about the character's internal processes.

Having the characters say too much, explain past events in detail, or describe what they are doing or plan to do. You want to keep the dialogue natural. But even if some characters might have a lot to say if this was real life, avoid long speeches. Generally keep your dialogue to five lines or less. If someone has a lot to say, break it up with cuts ahead or some kind of action. Also, avoid characters describing at length something that has happened in the past—find a way to show it in action, such as through a flashback—though avoid too many of those since the audience can become lost and confused. Additionally the audience doesn't need detailed explanations about why a character has done or plans to do something. They can usually figure it out by inferring a motive or intention from the action.

Feeling that a "final" script is final. Even if you have gotten feedback and engaged in rewrites based on the comments you have gotten, be open to change, since any script might be revised in the process of filming. Many actors have different ways of reworking the dialogue to make it their own, and you may get other input from the director (if you are not directing the film yourself), from the director of photography, or from others on the set. Even some PAs, especially ones who have gained experience working on other sets or aspire to become a DP or director, may have suggestions. So be open and flexible to change if it seems reasonable and desirable, while keeping any changes within limits, so they don't turn your script into a completely different story. You will often get a better performance from everyone when you are open to some improvisation and changes on the set.

Failing to follow up and confirm arrangements for a shoot. You want to be sure everyone who is expected arrives. This is especially critical for a small shoot, since if a key person doesn't show up at the last minute and can't be replaced—such as your director of photography or a lead actor—you can't shoot your film. That's why it's crucial to follow up with reminders after you have gotten a confirmation to make sure the person remembers and is still on board so you have time to find a replacement if necessary. Thus, send out reconfirmations three times—about seven to ten days, three to four days, and one day before the shoot. These confirmations don't have to be repeats of the same message, which might be seem too heavy-handed. Rather you can combine these reminders with providing additional information, such as sending the latest cast list, a scene breakdown, or providing directions on how to get to the start of the shoot.

Not clarifying who will be doing what on the set. You want to be clear—preferably in advance, or at least on the set—about the different roles people are playing so they understand what they are supposed to do.

Not being prepared to make last-minute changes. You need to be flexible to making revisions to adapt to unexpected events, such as when someone can't come or you can't shoot at an expected location. For example, on most shoots the actors don't take on crew roles. But if someone on the crew, such as a PA or script supervisor, doesn't show up, if you ask, one of the actors not in that scene might help, such as by using the clapboard and logging the scenes or helping to set up a green screen for a shot. Or if you have to shoot in a different location, change the action to suit that new location.

Letting someone else take charge, when you don't like what they are doing. As the producer, your job is to bring together the team and see that everyone is performing their expected roles. If you are also the director, you are in charge of what the actors and crew members do. While the DP is responsible for supervising the technical aspects, including framing the shots, the director normally checks what the DP is doing and can ask the DP to reframe a shot. If you like what everyone is doing, fine, give them free rein to do it. But if not, rein them in, especially the DP, and remind them of your vision for the finished short. Normally those on the set will respect this, since there is a clear hierarchy flowing from the producer to the director to the DP and then to everyone else.

Losing track of the time so you don't complete the shoot that was planned for one or two days. Because of the nature of the low-budget short, it is usually planned to shoot in one or at most two days. If the shoot goes over, it may prove difficult to get the actors or crew back together to complete the film. Thus, besides setting up a shooting schedule with approximate times for each scene, stick to this as much as possible. If the scenes are going over, check with the cast and crew to see if they can stay a little longer to finish the remaining scenes. If not, consider if you can adapt the script or eliminate less important scenes so you can finish in one or two days as planned rather than not finishing the film.

Letting a cast or crew member's ideals of "art" or "perfection" get in the way of completing a shoot. The risk of letting others envision what the film might be is that a cast member may want even more takes than planned to get their part absolutely perfect. Or a director, if other than you, or your DP may be so determined to get the scene right that you go seriously over your time schedule and risk not completing the film. If you see such a problem developing, you have to take back your control. To do so, as appropriate, take the person who is trying to take over aside, or remind the whole group that you need to get the production back on track in order to complete it in the one or two days scheduled, or you may not be able to finish the film. Such a warning will commonly get everyone to be more conscious of the time. But if it doesn't, say, because you have a DP who pulls the "I'm an artist" card, at least you tried. Later, if necessary, you can bring in another DP you can work with to finish the film.

Failing to make sure the actors or crew members have what they need for the shoot. While as a writer, producer, or director you are not responsible for the more technical aspects of the shoot, you want to make sure that everyone has what they need for the shoot and knows what to do. For example, while the actors may expect to bring their own selection of clothing and even some props (such as an engagement ring to show off in a scene), you might send the actors a list of the type of clothing to bring or the special props they need. Similarly, while the DP and camera people generally expect to bring their own cameras, you might make sure they are bringing enough supplies, or that you have extra batteries or extra mini-DV tapes or SD cards for recording the video or audio, if needed, so you don't run out in the middle of filming.

Failing to adapt the shooting schedule in response to last-minute emergencies and no-shows. Unfortunately it happens. Key people don't show up, equipment breakdowns occur, new camera and sound people need extra time to figure out what to do. In the case of such problems, in lieu of cancelling the shoot, you might make some changes to the script or shots so shooting can go on. For example, you might combine the lines of two characters into one. You might set up the scene to be shot with several takes by one camera shooting from different angles rather than having two or three cameras shoot the scene at the same time. You might recruit an actor with a small part to become a PA or change his or her look to play another role. In short, find creative ways to make changes, if possible, to go on with the shoot and get the best shots you can under the changed circumstances.

Working with people who aren't team players. Every film involves people who have to be willing to be guided by whoever is in charge, whether that's the producer, director, or producer/director. If you find that someone is difficult to work with or you hear from others that this person is difficult, it's generally better to find someone else who is easier to work with since you'll have a more comfortable shoot when everyone gets along. Even if someone is great with the camera, sound, or lighting, if someone acts like a "diva" with an inflated sense of his or her own importance, this attitude can quickly undermine morale and make for a tension-filled shoot. So it's preferable to avoid such people. If you feel like you are walking on eggs in working with someone, don't take that walk in the future. Find people who are great to have on the team.

In my own case, I have been on shoots that were successfully concluded despite some technical problems because everyone pulled together to adapt to some issues that came up during the shoot. For instance, while the crew was setting up equipment for one shoot, they discovered that one tripod couldn't be used because the organization that lent us the equipment included the wrong release plate that attaches the camera to the tripod, so the camera didn't fit. But we were still able to do the shoot by resting the camera on a table or taking handheld shots. In another case, when the sound connections on one camera didn't work, we were able to use another camera that was set up to only record sound. So being resourceful saved the shoot.

But in another case, a failure to take control and adapt nearly destroyed a project, until I was able to find another DP and director to take over and shoot at another time. In this case, I had made arrangements with a man who prided himself on being an excellent DP and post-production specialist since he wanted to edit what he shot. We had driven around checking out locations and had gone over the script to indicate what would be shot where. Then I worked out the scene breakdowns, and the night before the shoot, the DP and I went through the order of shooting the scenes, which included distinguishing some shots that would be voice-overs and others that would be shot at selected locations or in front of my house using a green screen. The plan was to shoot the on-location shots first and then do the green screen shots. Though I thought it would make more sense for the DP to be the director, since he had a clear idea of what he wanted and had done green screen shots before, whereas I hadn't, he wanted me to be the director, which meant that I would say "action" and "cut" once he was ready to shoot.

However, some problems soon developed, since the day before the shoot, two of the PAs who were scheduled to come advised me they couldn't make it, and the third PA arrived with her leg in a cast because of an injury a day before on a feature-film set. Then when the DP arrived, he announced that he first wanted to do the green screen shots that involved placing a screen next to a car in my driveway. His idea was to get the green screen shots out of the way since we were already here, so the actors could relax inside the house while he was setting up the green screen with the help of an assistant, who he came with him to assist with the sound. The DP's setup certainly looked impressive. He brought a large monitor so the actors and crew could see the shot setup in advance, and his sound man brought a large mixing board so he could set the levels on all of the mikes.

But more problems quickly developed, because the DP didn't bring the weights that normally hold up the green screen so he had to use bricks and a large ceramic duck from my front yard. Unfortunately a light wind made it even more difficult to keep the green screen standing. Thus, what should have taken about twenty minutes to set up took about three hours, starting at about 9 a.m.

Then more problems developed, since when the DP first set up the green screen, the morning had been overcast. But about noon the sun came out, so the DP had to move the green screen and reflectors to accommodate this. Then once that was set up and the actors recorded their voice-overs and a few scenes in the car, the sun moved, so it was no longer directly overhead and the reflectors had to be adjusted again.

After a few more shots, as the sun moved lower in the western sky, the DP decided that the green screen should be set up in front of the car, and after a few more shots there, he decided the car had to be turned around. Then to make matters even worse, just as we neared the end of the green screen shoot, the audio stopped recording because the disk was full. Unfortunately the DP didn't have another disk. So he would need an hour to download the disk onto his computer and clear it to shoot again. But by now it was too late, because in an hour it would be too dark to shoot. So that ended our shoot for the day.

Under the circumstances, the actors felt bummed because they felt so little had been accomplished, even though they had stayed longer in what turned into a ten-hour day, while the DP felt unappreciated and he sought to blame everyone else for the failed shoot. As he claimed, he didn't get any help from the actors (though he didn't ask), and since he was an "artist," he wanted every shot to be perfect, so I shouldn't have expected to finish the shoot in one day. But if he hadn't changed the order of the shots, hadn't spent so much time on setting up the green screen, and had another disk for the audio, we could have finished all the green screen shots and possibly the scenes in the three other remaining locations.

But as the producer, as well as the director, at least in name, my mistake was in giving up my control to the DP early on rather than standing firm that we stick by the original agreed-upon schedule. Then we would have gotten those shots, and if problems later developed with the green screen, I might have suggested other adjustments, and had the DP been willing to make them, that would have saved the shoot. And if he wasn't, at least everyone wouldn't have spent most of their time waiting for ten hours to set up a shoot in one location.

Fortunately I found the actors receptive to shooting the film on another day, though the schedules were very difficult to work out. Also, I found another DP and director who was eager to work with me on continuing the project, even though we had to start again since he didn't want to use any of the green screen shots, though he might possibly use the audio from the voice-overs. Instead he wanted to shoot any scenes in the car using a camera mount on the front of a car rather than using a green screen, and I drove around with him getting the shots we needed using my car.

I also learned an important principle in this shoot. Every film project, no matter how low budget and small, involves some degree of collaboration, and you need to work with team players who are willing to take direction. If someone proves difficult to work with, don't work with them again, unless you can discuss your concerns with them and you feel confident they understand what to do to be cooperative with you and others on the team in the future. If not, it's not worth the hassle to work with them again.

Chapter 22

Resources and References

Following is a list of books, articles, screenplay software, websites, conferences, training materials, fundraising sites, and film festivals for shorts you may find helpful. Because of the dynamic nature of the Internet, many of these sources are continually changing and this section will be updated from time to time on my website, www.changemakersproductions.com. I also welcome your suggestions for future editions and supplements.

Books

On Writing, Producing, and Directing

Adelman, Kim. *Making It Big in Shorts: The Ultimate Filmmakers Guide to Short Films*, 2nd Edition. Michael Wiese Productions, 2009.

Brown, Robert Latham. *Planning the Low-Budget Film*. Chalk Hill Books, 2006.

Dean, Michael W. *$30 Film School*. Course Technology PTR, 2003.

Garvy, Helen. *Before You Shoot: A Guide to Low-Budget Film and Video Production*. Shire Press, 2007.

Gaspard, John. *Fast, Cheap & Under Control: Lessons from the Greatest Low-Budget Movies of All Time*. Michael Wiese Productions, 2006.

Gaspard, John. *Fast, Cheap & Written That Way: Top Screenwriters on Writing for Low-Budget Movies*. CreateSpace, 2009.

Gilles, D. B. *The Portable Film School: Everything You'd Learn in Film School (Without Ever Going to Class)*. St. Martin's Griffin, 2005.

Kenworthy, Christopher. *Master Shots: 100 Advanced Camera Techniques to Get an Expensive Look on Your Low-Budget Movie*. Michael Wiese Productions, 2009.

Levy, Frederick. *Short Films 101: How to Make a Short Film and Launch Your Filmmaking Career*. Perigee Trade, 2004.

Newton, Dale and John Gaspard. *Digital Filmmaking 101: An Essential Guide to Producing Low-Budget Movies*. Michael Wiese Productions, 2007.

Rea, Peter W. and David K. Irving. *Producing and Directing the Short Film and Video*, 4th Edition. Focal Press, 2010.

Ryan, Maureen. *Producer to Producer: A Step-by-Step Guide to Low-Budget Independent Film Producing*. Michael Wiese Productions, 2010.

Schmidt, Rick. *Extreme DV at Used-Car Prices: How to Write, Direct, Shoot, Edit, and Produce a Digital Video Feature for Less Than $3,000*. Penguin, 2004.

Tomaric, Jason. *The Power Filmmaking Kit: Make Your Professional Movie on a Next-to-Nothing Budget*. Focal Press, 2007.

Thurlow, Clifford. *Making Short Films: The Complete Guide from Script to Screen*, 2nd Edition. Berg Publishers, 2008.

Wales, Lorene. *The People and Process of Film and Video Production: From Low Budget to High Budget*. Allyn & Bacon, 2004.

On Writing the Short Film

Cooper, Patricia and Ken Dancyger. *Writing the Short Film*, 3rd Edition. Focal Press, 2004.

Cowgill, Linda J. *Writing Short Films: Structure and Content for Screenwriters,* 2nd Edition. Lone Eagle, 2005.

Johnson, Claudia H. *Crafting Short Screenplays That Connect,* 3rd Edition. Focal Press, 2009.

Phillips, William H. *Writing Short Scripts.* Syracuse University Press, 1999.

Snyder, Blake: *Save the Cat! The Last Book on Screenwriting You'll Ever Need.* Michael Wiese Productions, 2005.

Articles

Brunton, Colin. "Tip Sheet for Low-Budget Film Scripts." *The Online Communicator Website.* Rich Wilson Creative Services, 1996–2009. Web. Sept. 20, 2010. www.online-communicator.com/scriptip .html.

Kolber, Jerry. "The Right Way to Raise Money for a No-Budget Film." *MovieMaker Magazine.* April 2, 2003. Web Sept. 20, 2010. www.moviemaker.com/directing/article /the_right_way_to_raise_money_for_a_nobudget_film_3212.

Software

Celtx. Screenplay Writing and Editing Software and Other Media Packages. From Celtx. www.celtx.com. Free to download.

Final Draft. Screenwriting Software. From Final Draft, Inc. www .finaldraft.com/products/final-draft. Software that automatically formats scripts to meet industry standards. About $250; $80 for an upgrade.

Hollywood Screenplay. Screenwriting Software and instructional CDs. From Hollywood Screenplay. www.hollywoodscreenplay.com. About $50.

Movie Magic Screenwriter 6. Screenwriting Software. From Write Brothers, Inc. www.screenplay.com/p-29-movie-magic-screenwriter-6.

aspx. Screenwriting software that helps create script outlines with acts, sequences, and scenes. About $180.

Save the Cat! The Last Story Structure Software You'll Ever Need, Version 2.0. Software program for outlining screenplays. www.blakesnyder .com. About $80.

Retailers for Books, Software, and Training Materials

Writers Store, 3510 West Magnolia Blvd., Burbank, CA 91505. Phone: 800-272-8927 or 310-441-5151; Fax: 818-566-8644. www.writers store.com. Has books, software, training programs, and film industry directories, available online or at the store.

Directories and Databases for Film Industry Contacts

Creative Handbook, 10152 Riverside Dr., Toluca Lake, CA 91602, Fax: (818) 752-3220. A production directory offered for free to anyone working in production in the Southern California area; just pay about $10 for delivery. www.creativehandbook.com

Film and TV Connection provides an e-mail query service to contacts in all areas of the film industry, including producers, agents, managers, distributors, sales reps, casting directors, entertainment attorneys, film festivals, and music industry pros. www.filmand tvconnection.com

Hollywood Creative Directory publishes both print and online directories:

- *Blu-Book Production Directory,* which is available as a free PDF download plus a free subscription for one-week online access to all of the other directories. The print cost for each directory, published one to three times a year, is $65–$80; an online subscription is about $20 a month, $200 a year. www.hcdonline.com

- *Hollywood Creative Directory* for producers and production companies
- *Hollywood Distribution Directory* for distributors and sales reps
- *Hollywood Music Industry Directory* for record labels, music publishers, music agents, and managers
- *Hollywood Representation Directory* for agents and managers

Reel Directory, P. O. Box 1910, Boyes Hot Springs, CA 95416. (415) 531-9760. The number-one source for film, video, and multimedia in Northern California, which features working industry professionals. Advertise for $50. Copies are $45 or distributed free through various venues, such as the Northern California Film Commission offices and at many conventions and trade shows. Advertisers also get a free copy. www.reeldirectory.com

Services for Casting Actors

Backstage, 5055 Wilshire Boulevard, Los Angeles, CA 90036. (323) 525-2356; 770 Broadway, 7th floor, New York, NY 10003. (646) 654-5700. www.backstage.com/bso/index.jsp

Bay Area Casting News, P.O. Box 1624, El Granada, CA 94018-1624. (650) 726-5424. bayareacasting.com/directorportal.html

Casting Networks LA, 3250 Wilshire, Suite 1800, Los Angeles, CA 90010. (323) 462-8200. www.lacasting.com

Casting Networks SF, 84 First Street, San Francisco, CA 94105. (415) 896-2228. www.sfcasting.com

Direct Cast, http://www.directcast.com

Now Casting, 2210 W. Olive Avenue, Suite 320, Burbank, CA 91506. (818) 841-7165. www.nowcasting.com

And check for other online casting services in other areas.

Websites for Finding Music

D.A.W.N. (Digital Audio Worldwide Network) Music—Thousands of tracks for $16–$27. www.dawnmusic.com

Freeplay Music—Various types of uses, from $25 for student use to a few hundred for commercial use. www.freeplaymusic.com

Jamendo—Over 270,000 tracks of all genres, download for free or a small payment, depending on how you want to use the music. www.jamendo.com/en

MP34U—Download any song; all songs are legal with the artist's permission. www.mp34u.fm

Music Loops—Thousands of tracks in different genres, most $25–$40, some a little higher. www.musicloops.com

Musopen—Mainly classical instrumental music; sign in to download MP3 files. www.musopen.org

Pond5—Over 5000 tracks; just move your cursor over a track to hear it; individually priced at $2 up; most tracks $10–$25. www.pond5.com

Public Domain 4U—A mix of public domain and free music with the artist's permission. www.publicdomain4u.com

Public Domain Information Project—Music2Use—Thousands of tracks for download at $19 each, or get all tracks in a category for about $25 to $50. www.pdinfo.com/Music-Production-Video.php

Royalty-Free Music—Over 12,000 tracks for download at $59 each, subscriptions available. www.royaltyfreemusic.com

Stock Music.Net—Thousands of tracks, about $30 per track, plus complete collections from about $50 up. www.stockmusic.net

Stock Music Site—About 400,000 tracks, $39.00. www.stockmusic.com

Stock Music Store—Over 10,000 tracks in different genres, about $30 per download, subscriptions available. www.stockmusicstore.com

TheBeatSuite—About 4000 tracks, $60 per download. www.beatsuite.com

For other sources, search online for "public domain music" or "royalty free music."

Funding Sources for Short Film Projects

IndieGoGo. Create a profile and list a variety of creative projects for funding in various categories, including video/web series, films, writing, the performing arts, music, art, education, technology, transmedia. www.indiegogo.com

Kickstarter. Create a profile and list projects for which you are seeking funding, including shorts and feature films. However, you have to set your target to an amount you can realistically achieve. Otherwise, you get nothing. www.kickstarter.com

Film Classes

Berkeley Community Media. Offers classes to members on digital filmmaking, and has a community access TV station for first showing your film. www.betv.org

Digital Media Academy in Emeryville, California. Offers a variety of programs on professional computer training, including digital film production and post-production video and audio editing. Also classes on digital photography, art, and animation. www.digital-mediaacademy.org

From FilmSchools4u.com. *The Starter Course in Filmmaking*. Set of 5 DVDs for directors, actors, cinematographers, and writers that provide information to become a better filmmaker. About $350. www.filmschools4u.com/index.htm

From NoBudgetFilmMaking.com. No-Budget FilmMaking Ultra-Pack: The Ultimate Film Training Kit. Training pack that includes screenplay software and guidebooks to make a film on a low or no budget. About $50. www.nobudgetfilmmaking.com

Hollywood Film Institute's *DVD Film School with Dov S-S Simens*. Freshman year focuses on screenwriting, independent filmmaking, low-budget agreements, and preproduction. Sophomore year deals with directing and hooting your movie. Junior year on marketing and selling your moving. Senior year on financing and distributing your movie. Set includes sixteen one-hour tapes and workbooks. About $300–$400. Also, two-day classes in major cities, including Los Angeles, San Francisco, New York, Chicago, Atlanta, and London. www.webfilmschool.com

Los Angeles Film School. Offers intensive training in film in the heart of Hollywood. Has an associate of science in film degree. www.lafilm.edu

Mark & Jeanne Simon's. TV Pitch School: The TV Show Creator's Complete Toolkit. Course 1: TV Development; Course 2: TV Packaging; Course 3: TV Power Pitches. About $4,000. www.sellyourtvconceptnow.com

No Budget Film School. The school offers four weekend classes on micro-budget filmmaking in Los Angeles held at Raleigh Studios' Chaplin Theater. www.nobudgetfilmschool.com

San Francisco Film Society. Film Craft and Film Studies. Offers classes on screenwriting, business skills, documentary, production, and film studies. Also has screenings and sponsors the SF International Film Festival. www.sffs.org

San Francisco School of Digital Filmmaking. Workshops on writing, producing, directing, shooting, and editing indie and short films. www.sfdigifilm.com/home.html

School of Motion Picture and Television, Academy of Art University in San Francisco. Offers BFAs and MFAs in film. www.academyart.edu/film-school/index.html

For other film schools and classes, do an online search in your area.

Organizations

American Film Institute
2021 N. Western Avenue
Los Angeles, CA 90027-1657
Phone: 323-856-7600
Fax: 323-467-4578
AFI is a national institute providing leadership in screen education
   and the recognition and celebration of excellence in the art of film,
   television, and digital media.
www.afi.com

Bay Area Women in Film and Media
3288 21st Street, #72
San Francisco, CA 94110
415-273-9820
www.bawifm.org

Berkeley Community Media
2239 Martin Luther King Jr. Way
Berkeley, CA 94704
Phone: 510-848-2288
www.betv.org

California Film Institute
1001 Lootens Place, Suite 220
San Rafael, CA 94901
Main Office Phone: 415-383-5256
Main Office Fax: 415-383-8606
Sponsors the Mill Valley Film Festival and has filmmaking workshops
   and screenings.
www.cafilm.org

Film Independent
9911 West Pico Blvd., 11th Floor
Los Angeles, CA 90035
Phone: 310-432-1200
www.FilmIndependent.org

Film and TV Organizations List
List of major film organizations worldwide
www.masterguide.com/globalmedia/

Filmmakers Alliance
Los Angeles, CA
Has assorted screenings, events, and partnerships with others in the
    film industry. Assistance with financing and fundraising, distribu-
    tion and marketing, competitions, etc., for members.
www.filmmakersalliance.org/Home.html

The Independent
Independent Media Publications
PO Box 391620
Cambridge, MA 02139
877-513-7400
A publication focused on independent film.
http://www.aivf.org

Independent Film and Television Alliance
Members in twenty-two countries, which includes independent pro-
    duction and distribution companies, sales agents, TV companies,
    studio-affiliated companies, and film financing organizations. Puts
    on the largest motion picture trade show in the world: the Ameri-
    can Film Market.
www.ifta-online.org

International Documentary Association
1201 West 5th Street, Suite M270
Los Angeles, CA 90017 USA
213-534-3600
www.documentary.org

International Movie Database
A major source for film credentials and resumes in the film industry.
    Includes boards for sharing information, discussions of films, mes-
    sages. Also industry news, lists, ratings, and more.
www.imdb.com

Movie Making Throughout the Bay
An organization that has monthly events that bring together writers,
    producers, directors, actors, and others to create a film in one day.
    Also has occasional networking events, producer challenges, and
    other activities. Primarily promotes activities through Facebook.
www.moviemakingbayarea.com

Planet Indie: Independent Film Directory
Lists over 800 indie websites
www.planetindie.com/organizations

United Filmmakers Association
An organization that has monthly mixers, producer meetings, and
    other activities in the Bay Area, Sacramento, and other cities. Pro-
    motes many activities through Facebook.
www.ufa.metahelion.com

Without a Box: The World's Largest Independent Film Community
Features over 5,000 film festivals and offers online submittals for over
    800 festivals, assistance with promoting your films in IMDB, selling
    DVDs and video on demand through Amazon.
www.withoutabox.com

Women in Film
6100 Wilshire Blvd., Suite 710
Los Angeles, CA 90048
323-935-2211
www.wif.org

Writers Guild of America, West
An organization of over 12,000 produced screenwriters, who have
   at least twenty-four units of film industry credits, and a registry
   service to register scripts for five years for $20.
7000 West Third Street
Los Angeles, CA 90048
323-951-4000, 800-548-4532
www.wga.org

Film Conferences, Trade Shows, Expos, and Festivals

American Film Market
10850 Wilshire Bvd., 9th floor
Los Angeles, CA 90024
310-248-6105
An annual event in Santa Monica with over 350 exhibitors from
   around the world, primarily distributors and sales reps, held in
   early November. Showings of new films. Great for networking and
   making contacts. About $700 for full event, $300 last four days,
   plus day passes.
www.afma.com

Creative Screenwriting Expo
6404 Hollywood Blvd., Suite 415
Los Angeles, CA 90028
888-556-6274 or 323-957-1405

Sponsored by *Creative Screenwriting* magazine, the expo features speakers, workshops, networking events, film pitches, screenings, competitions, and more. Held in late October in LA.
www.screenwritingexpo.com

Documentary Films.Net
846 New York Street
Lawrence, KS 66044
Provides a listing of festivals and events featuring documentary films, and has a directory of documentary films.
festivals.documentaryfilms.net

Film Conferences, Trade Shows, and Festivals Around the World
A directory of events, including forty-eight in the United States
www.world-design-directory.com/events/film.wdd

Future of Film Summit
Produced by Digital Wire and Variety, and held at the London West Hollywood.
310-855-0033
www.lafilmconference.com

Great American Pitchfest and Screenwriting Conference
Twilight Pictures Inc.
12400 Ventura Blvd. #735
Studio City, CA 91604
877-255-2528
Features pitches of TV shows and movie scripts to producers and agents, development executives, managers, and other industry professionals. Held in June in Burbank. Prices range from about $250 to $650 for the whole event.
www.pitchfest.com

LA Shorts Fest
Los Angeles, CA
Held in July at the Laemmle Theater on Sunset. Features shorts from
    all over the world.
lashortsfest.com

Los Angeles Independent Film Festival
9911 W. Pico Blvd.
Los Angeles, CA 90035
310-937 7770
Held each June for about a week in Westwood. Features newly re-
    leased independent films, networking events.
www.lafilmfest.com

WESTDOC Conference
West Coast Documentary and Reality Conference
3000 Olympic Blvd.
Santa Monica, CA 90404
310-616-5084
Features speakers, networking, and pitching. Held in September in
    Santa Monica.
www.thewestdoc.com

For other conferences, check online for film events in your area.

Film Festivals

Following are some major short films festivals. For details, look up
each festival and others on Without a Box (www.withoutabox.com).
In some cases, you can enter online. Many big film festivals also include short films. Besides the big festivals listed, many other film
festivals include a division for shorts.

Major Film Festivals with Short Films

AFI Fest (Los Angeles, California) (includes a division for short films)

Austin Film Festival (Austin, Texas) (includes a division for short films)

Cannes Independent Film Festival (Cannes, France) (includes a division for short films)

Festival de Cannes (Paris, France) (includes a division for short films)

Los Angeles Film Festival (includes a division for narrative shorts)

Marche du Film, Festival of Cannes (Paris, France)

Mill Valley Film Festival (includes a division for short films)

New York City International Film Festival (includes a division for short films)

San Francisco International Film Festival (includes a division for short films)

Short Film Corner—Festival de Cannes (Paris, France)

Sundance Film Festival, Park City, Utah (includes a division for short films)

Tribeca Film Festival, New York, NY (includes a division for short films)

Festivals for Short Films

Action/Cut Short Films Festival (Studio City, California)

Aspen Shorts Fest

Atlantic City Short Film Festival

Best Shorts Festival (La Jolla, California)

Beverly Hills Shorts Festival

Carnival of Darkness Short Film Festival (Toluca Lake, California)

Chicago International REEL Shorts Festival

Chicago Short Film Brigade

Dam Short Film Festival (Boulder City, Nevada)

Directors Circle Festival of Shorts (Erie, Pennsylvania)

Edgemar Short Film Festival (Santa Monica, California)

FirstGlance Feature and Short Film Competition (Tarzana, California)

Flickerfest International Short Film Festival (New South Wales, Australia)

Gangrene Film Festival of Comedy Shorts (Kaysville, Utah)

GIAA Festival of Short Films and Videos (New York City)

Giggleshorts International Comedy Short Film Festival (Ontario, Canada)

Hero Fest—My Hero Short Film Festival (Laguna Beach, California)

High Deserts Shorts International Film Festival (Pahrump, Nevada)

HollyShorts Film Festival (Marina Del Rey, California)

In the Bin Short Film Festival (Currumbin, Australia)

Indie Short Film Festival (Fort Lauderdale, Florida)

IndieProducer Short Film Festival (Sherman Oaks, California)

International Narrative Shorts Film Festival (Chico, California)

The Iron Mule Short Comedy Screening Series (New York City)

KaleidoShorts Film Festival (London, UK)

KINOFILM, Manchester International Short Film Festival (Manchester, UK)

LA Comedy Shorts Film Festival and Screenplay Competition (Santa Monica, California)

Lakeshorts International Short Film Festival (Ontario, Canada)

Light Up Earth Short Film Competition (Bruce, Australia)

London Short Film Festival

Miami Short Film Festival

Movie Script Short Contest: The Golden Brad Awards (Burbank, California)

NBC Universal Short Cuts Film Festival (University City, California)

New York City Short Film Festival

NexTV Web Series and Short Film Competition (Culver City, California)

NYC Downtown Short Film Festival

Open APPerture Short Film Festival (Boone, North Carolina)

Palm Springs International ShortFest (Palm Springs, California)

SF Shorts: San Francisco International Festival of Short Films

San Jose Short Film Festival (San Jose, California)

Science Fiction & Fantasy Short Film Festival (Seattle, Washington)

Short Attention Span Digital Video Festival (San Luis Obispo, California)

Short Toronto Indie Film Festival (STIFF) (Toronto, Canada)

Shorts Film Festival (South Australia, Australia)

SHORTSNONSTOP Online Film Festival (Toronto, Canada)

Sunnyside Shorts Film Festival (New York City)

Super Shorts International Film Festival (London, UK)

Taos Shortz Film Fest (Taos, New Mexico)

Very Short Movies Festival (Winter Park, Florida)

West Chester International Short Film Festival (West Chester, Pennsylvania)

Women's Film Institute Shorts Tour (San Francisco, California)

Yourindiefilm.com Online Short Film Festival (Vancouver, BC)

Appendix A
Example of Doing a Sequential Scene Breakdown

Here is the complete script for *The Consultation*, with all of the scene breakdowns and suggested shots that the director or DP might use in the shoot.

THE CONSULTATION
by Gini Graham Scott

SCENE BREAKDOWN—SEQUENTIALLY

FADE IN:
1. LOCATION: INT. ANDREA'S OFFICE—DAY (WS)
ACTORS: Andrea, Burt
SPECIAL PROPS: Printout, Paper, Notebook, Chairs
ANDREA, 30s, a marketing consultant, meets with BURT, 40s, an insurance broker.

1a. CLOSE-IN SHOT OF ANDREA (MS)
Andrea flips through a printout.

ANDREA
I do have some suggestions after looking through the
material about your project.

1b. CLOSE-IN SHOT OF BURT (MS)

BURT
Good. And I want to assure you, we'll be paying you.

1c. MEDIUM SHOT OF ANDREA AND BURT (2S)

Andrea whips out a blank sheet of paper.

ANDREA
Thanks. So now if I can get your credit card number.

BURT hesitates, then reluctantly gives it to her.

BURT
Okay. Here it is.

1d. CLOSE-IN SHOT OF ANDREA AND WHAT SHE'S WRIT-
ING (CU)
Andrea begins to write.
Minutes later, Andrea finishes writing and looks at Burt.

ANDREA
Now let me give you my suggestions.

1e. CLOSE-IN SHOT OF BURT (CU)

BURT

Good. I want you to give me the good, the bad, and the ugly. We have a lot riding on this—millions.

1f: MEDIUM SHOT OF ANDREA AND BURT (MS)
Andrea flips through the book as she talks.

ANDREA

Okay. First, I want to understand what you want me to do since you already have a proposal and writer for this.

BURT

Yeah. Now what we need is a publishing consultant to discuss our strategy.

1g. CLOSE-IN SHOT OF ANDREA (CU)

ANDREA

Okay. My first suggestion is why spend $15,000 a month for a PR firm? Most PR firms charge only $3,000 to $5,000 a month.

1h. CLOSE-IN SHOT OF BURT (CU)

BURT

Good point. But this is a top-drawer firm, which represents million-dollar companies and politicians.

1i. CLOSE-IN SHOT OF ANDREA (CU)

ANDREA

Well, my second suggestion is to publish the book yourself since you'll make much more and can publish

in months. With a traditional publisher, you only get a
small percentage of sales. And you have a target market,
insurance agents you can reach yourself.

1j. MEDIUM-SHOT OF BURT AND ANDREA (2S)

BURT
Sounds right.

ANDREA
And I'd also suggest . . .

(Cut ahead)

So now I've got some questions for you.

BURT
Sure. Go ahead.

1k: CLOSE-IN SHOT OF ANDREA (CU)

ANDREA
Well, what about . . . ?

(Cut ahead)

Now my next step is to read the proposal closely and do
a further analysis. And since you're using a credit card,
I'll charge you after I do the work.

1l: CLOSE-IN SHOT OF BURT (CU)

BURT

Good. Let's call this an hour. And since you agreed to give us an extra hour, it'll be five hours total, but charge us for four. So a total of $600. Right?

1m: CLOSE-IN SHOT OF ANDREA (CU)

ANDREA
(Reluctantly)
Yeah. Agreed.

1n: MEDIUM SHOT OF BURT AND ANDREA (2S)

BURT
Good. Well, I'm sure we'll enjoy working together. We're looking for a long-term relationship. You do good by us, and we'll be back to you with more business.

ANDREA
Thanks.

1o: LONG SHOT OF BURT AND ANDREA (WS)
Burt shakes her hand and heads out the door.

2. LOCATION: ANDREA'S OFFICE—LATER THAT NIGHT
ACTORS: Andrea
SPECIAL PROPS: Credit Card Machine, Paper or Bill with Order Information

2a. LONG SHOT OF ANDREA (WS)
Andrea picks up the paper with Burt's credit card information and clicks some buttons on her credit card machine.

2b. A CLOSE-UP OF CREDIT CARD MACHINE (CU)
A close-in shows $175.00.

2c. A MEDIUM SHOT OF ANDREA (MS)
She clicks some more buttons.

2d. A CLOSE-UP OF THE CREDIT CARD MACHINE (CU)
A tape prints out the sale.

3: LOCATION: INT. ANDREA'S BEDROOM—THE NEXT MORNING (LS)
ACTORS: Andrea, Burt
SPECIAL PROPS: Phone, Bed or Couch
A ringing phone wakes Andrea. She picks it up groggily.

3a. CLOSE-UP OF ANDREA (CU)

> ANDREA
> Hello.

It is Burt on the line. Use split screen or voice-over.

> BURT (V.O. or split screen)
> (Angrily)
> Andrea, I had to call. What's the meaning of charging me? You said you would charge me after you did the work.

3b. MEDIUM SHOT OF ANDREA (MU)
Andrea sits up in bed, trying to wake herself up.

> ANDREA
> But I did. For the hour we talked.

BURT (V.O. or split screen)
No, we were just talking about what you'd do.

3c. CLOSE-UP SHOT OF ANDREA (CU)

ANDREA
But I gave you suggestions.

BURT (V.O. or split screen)
And you asked a lot of questions about things that are in
the proposal. Look, $600 is a lot of money to me . . . us.

ANDREA
But you're thinking of paying the PR people $15,000 a
month.

BURT (V.O. or split screen)
So? It doesn't matter. I'm a businessman. $600 is $600.
And I have to be sure I'm getting what I'm paying for.

3d. MEDIUM SHOT OF ANDREA (MS)

ANDREA
Why, sure. After I review your material, I'll give you a
detailed analysis.

BURT (V.O. or split screen)
So what do you mean by that? I need a thirty-five- to
forty-page report I can show my investors. It has to be
slick, polished, on your letterhead.

ANDREA

Huh? I was proposing to write my analysis in two, three
hours, after an hour or two to review your material.
There's no way I can write that much.

BURT (V.O. or split screen)

Well, what if I made it $800? Can you write it for that?
Look, I'm a fair guy, but I gotta be sure I'm getting what
I'm paying for. You gotta give me something good, or it's
of no value to me.

3e. CLOSE-UP SHOT OF ANDREA (CU)
Andrea is shocked speechless.

BURT (CONT'D)

So are you gonna do it? Look, you do me good on this,
and there'll be plenty more business down the pike. I'll
treat you right.

ANDREA

Well, I . . . er . . .

BURT

Look, you think about it. Or you can return my money.

Andrea hangs up, unsure what to do.

4. INT. ANDREA'S HALL/LIVING ROOM—THE NEXT MORN-
ING (WS)
ACTORS: Andrea, Barbara, Tim
SPECIAL PROPS: Couch or chairs
BARBARA, 30s, and TIM, 30s, are seated in the couch or chairs. Cut
ahead for snippets of their comments.

4a. WIDE SHOT OF ANDREA, TIM, BARBARA (WS)

ANDREA
Thanks for coming. I can't believe how much this client expects for so little. I kept hoping to make things work, but he keeps asking for more or wants a refund.

TIM
I think you should keep the money. He's paying for your time.

BARBARA
It's crazy what he's asking you to do in two to three hours. I can't even type thirty-five pages in that time, much less write it.

TIM
Try offering him half back. Then if he doesn't bite, you can always give him a refund.

BARBARA
Offer to split the difference. Or if he doesn't agree, let him take it up with merchant services, and you'll win.

ANDREA
Hmmmm . . .

4b. CLOSE-UP SHOT OF BARBARA (CU)
Barbara looks thoughtful.

BARBARA
No, wait. I just changed my mind in thinking it over. You don't want this guy in your life. Just give him back his money and be done with it.

4c. MEDIUM SHOT OF ANDREA, BARBARA, AND TIM (MS)

ANDREA
Hey, thanks for the advice.

5. INT. ANDREA'S OFFICE—A FEW MINUTES LATER (SAME AS SCENE 2)
ACTORS: Andrea, Burt
SPECIAL PROPS: Computer, Printout of Letter, Printer

5a. MEDIUM SHOT OF ANDREA (MS)
Andrea turns to the computer and writes.

5b. CLOSE-UP SHOT OF ANDREA (CU)
Andrea reads aloud.

ANDREA
Dear Burt . . . I made my charges very clear, and that's why I got your credit card information and charged it.

Andrea looks thoughtful, trying to find the right words.

ANDREA (CONT'D)
But in the spirit of resolving this amicably, I'm willing to return half of what I charged or as a good will gesture, put in another hour at no charge to review your material and give you my suggestions.

5c. CLOSE-IN OF COMPUTER (CU)
Andrea clicks and sends the letter.

5d. MEDIUM SHOT OF ANDREA (MS)
Later, Andrea is at her computer looking at a long two-page letter.

5e. CLOSE-UP ON LETTER (CU)
A few phrases jump out at her, read by Burt.

> BURT (V.O.)
> That's ludicrous . . . We were just having a preliminary
> conversation . . . I have investors to answer to . . . I'm
> only gonna pay for the completion of satisfactory work.
> Kapish!

5f. MEDIUM SHOT OF ANDREA (MS)
Andrea leans back, stunned.

5g. CLOSE-UP ON LETTER (CU)
Andrea continues reading.

> BURT (V.O.) (CONT'D)
> I had planned to use you for other ventures, because this
> project can be worth millions.

5h. CLOSE IN ON ANDREA FOR REACTION (CU)

> BURT (V.O.) (CONT'D)
> But if you're gonna penny-pinch me over $175, there's
> no deal. So do the job for $800, or refund my money.

5i. MEDIUM SHOT OF ANDREA ON PHONE (MS)
Andrea calls Barbara, shown by a split screen.

ANDREA
... So I don't know what to do.

BARBARA (V.O.)
Look, he's got to be nuts. Who spends so much time
and energy on a $175 charge? And what do you know
about Burt? He sounds like a sociopath. Or maybe a
phony. So check him out.

5j. MEDIUM SHOT OF ANDREA AT THE COMPUTER (MS)
While on the phone, Andrea goes on her computer.

5k. CLOSE-UP OF WEBSITE ON SCREEN (CU)
Andrea pulls up Burt's website, which features a luxury building.

ANDREA (V.O.)
Well, he's got a great-looking website. And a great office
building.

BARBARA (V.O.)
Oh, so what's his address?

5l. CLOSE-UP OF CONTACTS PAGE ON WEBSITE
Andrea clicks the contact page. It shows an LA address.

ANDREA (V.O.)
It's in LA.

BARBARA (V.O.)
Now check that out on Google Maps.

5m. CLOSE-UP OF GOOGLE MAPS QUERY SCREEN (CU)
Andrea clicks on Google Maps and puts in the address.

5n. CLOSE-UP OF GOOGLE MAP OF LA STREET (CU)
The screen shows an outlying dumpy area of LA.

> ANDREA (V.O.)
> Oh, wow! What a dive!

> BARBARA (V.O.)
> What did I tell you? He's a phony blowing smoke, and
> there is no million-dollar project.

5o. CLOSE-UP OF ANDREA (CU)

> ANDREA
> Then I won't answer him at all. I've got all the e-mails
> I need to show Merchant Services I earned the money
> fair and square.

> BARBARA (V.O.)
> Exactly! And I'm sure Burt doesn't want anyone to
> know what you know now.

> ANDREA
> No, I'm sure he doesn't.

5p. MEDIUM SHOT OF ANDREA (MS)
Andrea hangs up the phone. She looks at the Google map and prints
it out.

5q. CLOSE-UP OF MAP PRINTING OUT (CU)

5r. CLOSE-UP OF ANDREA (CU)
Andrea looks pleased watching the map print out.

5s. MEDIUM SHOT OF ANDREA (MS)
The phone rings. Andrea turns toward it.

5t. CLOSE-UP OF ANDREA (CU)
Andrea sees on the caller ID that it is Burt.

5u. CLOSE-UP OF CALLER ID (XCU)

5v. MEDIUM SHOT OF ANDREA (MS)
Andrea turns away as she lets it ring.

Appendix B

Example of Turning a Sequential Scene Breakdown into an Ordered Scene Breakdown

Here is the complete script for *The Engagement*, with the scenes first numbered in sequence and then moved around based on one approach to ordering the actual shoot of the scenes. The editor can go by the numbers to reassemble the scenes in the appropriate order.

In this case, instead of doing shot breakdowns for each scene, each shot is designated as a another scene since much of the video was being shot with a green screen, suggesting a car moving from one place to another. The first half provides a sequential scene breakdown; the second half provides a breakdown based on the order of shooting discussed with the director. The scenes are not further broken down into shots since this was left up to the DP.

THE ENGAGEMENT
by Gini Graham Scott
SCENE BREAKDOWN—SEQUENTIALLY

1. LOCATION: EXT. FREEWAY OAKLAND LEADING TO BAY BRIDGE—DAY
ACTORS: None

SPECIAL PROPS: None

A pan shows cars driving toward the toll booth.

2. LOCATION: EXT. CITY STREET NEAR FREEWAY RAMP IN EAST BAY—DAY

GREEN SCREEN—SHOOT ON AMY DRIVE

ACTORS: Sam and Mary Beth

SPECIAL PROPS: Ordinary Sedan

DRESS: Casual weekend wear for professionals

ACTION: SAM, 30s, is driving with MARY BETH, 30s, toward San Francisco. They are both dressed casually, as business professionals might on a day off. Sam stops at a light.

3. LOCATION: EXT. INTERIOR OF CAR—DAY

GREEN SCREEN—SHOOT ON AMY DRIVE

ACTORS: Mary Beth

SPECIAL PROPS: Engagement Ring

Mary Beth holds up her hand to admire her ring.

        MARY BETH

        It's so nice. I can't wait to show it off at the party.

4. LOCATION: EXT. INTERIOR OF CAR—DAY

GREEN SCREEN—SHOOT ON AMY DRIVE

ACTORS: Mary Beth and Sam

Mary Beth leans over and plants a kiss on Sam's cheek.

        MARY BETH

        And finally after two years.

Sam looks up at the light, trying to concentrate on the road and listen to Mary Beth.

SAM
Yeah, it'll be nice to finally announce it.

5. LOCATION: ENTRANCE TO FREEWAY RAMP—DAY
The light changes and Sam heads onto the freeway ramp.

6. LOCATION: EXT. FREEWAY IN OAKLAND HEADING TO
THE BAY BRIDGE—DAY
A long shot shows cars on the freeway.
ACTORS: Mary Beth and Sam—Doing Voice-Overs

MARY BETH (V.O.)
(A little shrewish)
Yes. Mom and Daddy will be so pleased. And I'm sure
you'll enjoy working for Daddy. So much better than the
crappy jobs you've had for the past year.

SAM (V.O.)
I know. But it's been so hard being a writer.

7. LOCATION: EXT: INTERIOR OF CAR—DAY
GREEN SCREEN—SHOOT ON AMY DRIVE
ACTORS: Mary Beth and Sam
SPECIAL PROPS: Engagement Ring
Mary Beth waves her hand around, looking at her ring, as Sam drives.

MARY BETH
But Daddy to the rescue.

SAM
Yeah, I guess.

8. LOCATION: TOLL BOOTH ENTRY TO THE BAY BRIDGE—DAY

A shot shows the toll booth ahead.

9. LOCATION: EXT. INTERIOR OF CAR—DAY
GREEN SCREEN—SHOOT ON AMY DRIVE
ACTORS: Sam
Sam looks up.

10. LOCATION: EXT. TOLL BOOTH ENTRY TO BAY BRIDGE—DAY

Another shot shows Sam's view of toll booth ahead.

11. LOCATION: EXT. INTERIOR OF CAR—DAY
GREEN SCREEN—SHOOT ON AMY DRIVE
ACTORS: Sam and Mary Beth
Sam looks ahead, annoyed.

> SAM
> (Half aloud)
> Oh, shit.

Mary Beth looks up.

> MARY BETH
> What's wrong?

> SAM
> Ummm . . . I'm on the wrong road. I don't want to go to
> San Francisco. Damn. And I can't back up.

12. LOCATION: EXT. INTERIOR OF CAR—DAY

GREEN SCREEN—SHOOT ON AMY DRIVE
ACTORS: Sam
Close-in of Sam, grudging, grabs his wallet to pay.

13. LOCATION: EXT. TOLL BOOTH ENTRY TO THE BAY
BRIDGE—DAY
A close-in of the car shot suggests Sam is at the toll booth.
ACTORS: Mary Beth and Sam—Doing Voice-Overs

> MARY BETH (V.O.)
> (Annoyed)
> Geez. How could you end up here?

> SAM (V.O.)
> Don't worry. I'll just turn around.

14. LOCATION: EXT. ROAD IN OAKLAND
Cutaway shows a sign that says: "Rough Road Ahead"

15. LOCATION: EXT. CITY STREET—DAY
ACTORS: Mary Beth and Sam—Doing Voice-Overs
Sam is driving on a city street.

> MARY BETH (V.O.)
> Now we'll be late. If only you hadn't missed the turnoff.

> SAM (V.O.)
> Well, I was talking to you. I got distracted.

> MARY BETH (V.O.)
> Oh, so it's my fault! Anyway, you know how I hate being
> late.

16. LOCATION: EXT. CITY STREET—DAY

Cutaway shows massive traffic jam or car crash on the road Sam didn't take.

17. LOCATION: EXT. INTERIOR OF CAR—A FEW MINUTES LATER

GREEN SCREEN—SHOOT ON AMY DRIVE

ACTORS: Sam and Mary Beth

As Sam drives, he notices the gauge is almost empty.

> SAM
> Oh, gotta get gas. Tank's almost empty.

18. LOCATION: EXT. INTERIOR OF CAR—A FEW MINUTES LATER

GREEN SCREEN—SHOOT ON AMY DRIVE

SPECIAL PROPS: Almost-Empty Gas Gauge

A close-in shows the almost-empty gas gauge.

19. LOCATION: EXT. INTERIOR OF CAR—A FEW MINUTES LATER

GREEN SCREEN—SHOOT ON AMY DRIVE

> MARY BETH
> Oh, what now? You should have remembered to fill the tank. We'll be so late.

Sam reaches over and squeezes her hand.

> SAM
> Don't worry. It'll be just a few minutes.

20. LOCATION: EXT. GAS STATION—A FEW MINUTES LATER
Passing traffic suggests this is a busy downtown gas station.

21. LOCATION: EXT. GAS STATION—A FEW MINUTES LATER
ACTORS: Sam, Station Attendant, Mary Beth
SPECIAL PROPS: Air Gauge, Low Tire
Sam is by a pump, starting to pump gas, when the STATION AT-TENDANT comes over to him.

>STATION ATTENDANT
>Hey, did you know your tire looks really low?

Close-in shows a low tire.
Mary Beth peeks her head out of the car.

>MARY BETH
>Oh no. We're in a rush.

>STATION ATTENDANT
>Oh, it'll just take a minute. Good thing you stopped, or
>you could have had a blowout.

As the station attendant pumps air into the tire, Mary Beth glares at Sam.

>SAM
>Hey, what can I do? I gotta put air in it.

22. LOCATION: EXT. SUBURBAN STREETS—A LITTLE LATER
GREEN SCREEN—AMY DRIVE
ACTORS: Sam and Mary Beth—Doing Voice-Overs

Sam drives up and down the street.

> SAM (V.O.)
> I'm sorry, but I lost the address. It's been months since
> we've been here.

> MARY BETH (V.O.)
> Geez. I can't believe it. Can't you do anything right?

> SAM (V.O.)
> Well, maybe you'll recognize it from the street view. At
> least we're close.

23. LOCATION: EXT. SUBURBAN STREETS—A LITTLE LATER
GREEN SCREEN—AMY DRIVE
ACTORS: Mary Beth
SPECIAL PROPS: Purse, PDA

> MARY BETH
> Yeah, sure.

Mary Beth pulls out her PDA and checks a map of the area.

24. LOCATION: EXT. SUBURBAN STREETS—A LITTLE LATER
GREEN SCREEN—AMY DRIVE
SPECIAL PROPS: PDA
Close-in on PDA.

25. LOCATION: EXT. HOUSE IN SUBURBS—STILL LATER
ACTORS: Sam and Mary Beth
Sam and Mary Beth pull up across the street from the house.

26. LOCATION: INT. CAR ON SUBURBAN STREETS—MO-
MENTS LATER

GREEN SCREEN—AMY DRIVE
ACTORS: Sam and Mary Beth
Sam looks toward the house.

> SAM
> Well, we're finally here.

> MARY BETH
> Yeah, thanks to my PDA and my e-mail.

27. LOCATION: EXT. HOUSE IN SUBURBS—STILL LATER
ACTORS: Sam and Mary Beth
Sam and Mary Beth walk toward the house, when Mary Beth stops.

> MARY BETH
> You know, we're so late and I'm so bummed out now, I
> don't even feel like going in.

> SAM
> But our friends, our announcement.

> BETH
> Look, I'm sorry. But I'm not in a party mood anymore.
> Okay?

Sam turns to head back to the car.

> SAM
> Sure. If that's what you want.

Sam and Mary Beth walk to the car.

28. LOCATION: EXT: CITY STREET—LATER
GREEN SCREEN—SHOOT ON AMY DRIVE

ACTORS: Sam and Mary Beth
Sam and Mary are driving home.

29. LOCATION: EXT: CITY STREET—LATER
GREEN SCREEN—SHOOT ON AMY DRIVE
ACTORS: Sam
Sam looks ahead dreamily.

30. LOCATION: EXT: CITY STREET—LATER
GREEN SCREEN—SHOOT ON AMY DRIVE
ACTORS: Sam—Doing Voice-Over
Sam passes a freeway entrance sign at 27th or 52nd Street, which have
a jumble of signs. He realizes he missed the entrance.

> SAM (V.O.)
> Oh, sorry. I missed the turnoff again. But I'll turn
> around at the next street.

31. LOCATION: EXT: CITY STREET—LATER
GREEN SCREEN—SHOOT ON AMY DRIVE
ACTORS: Mary Beth and Sam
Mary Beth turns and glares at Sam.

> MARY BETH
> Yeah, you do that.

32. LOCATION: EXT: CITY STREET—LATER
GREEN SCREEN—SHOOT ON AMY DRIVE
ACTORS: Mary Beth and Sam—Doing Voice-Overs
As Sam drives, Mary Beth is becoming more agitated.

> MARY BETH (V.O.)
> You know, I'm feeling so pissed right now. I thought things would change. But you can't seem to do anything right. How can you work for Daddy? He needs someone he can count on.

> SAM (V.O.)
> Hey, come on. I'm sorry. Please relax. We could stop for ice cream. Like old times.

33. LOCATION: EXT. CONVENIENCE STORE—MINUTES LATER
ACTORS: Sam and Mary Beth
SPECIAL PROPS: "Closed" Sign
Sam pulls into the store lot, but a sign says "Closed."

34. LOCATION: EXT. INTERIOR OF CAR—MOMENTS LATER
GREEN SCREEN—SHOOT ON AMY DRIVE
ACTORS: Mary Beth and Sam
SPECIAL PROP: Engagement Ring
Mary Beth reaches down to her ring.

> MARY BETH
> Look. I'm sorry. Just leave me here, and I'll call a taxi to pick me up.

Mary Beth takes off her ring.

> MARY BETH (CONT'D)
> I can't take this anymore. Ever since we started out, so many wrong turns. And now this. You don't seem to know what you're doing.

Mary Beth hands Sam her ring.

> MARY BETH (CONT'D)
> So take this back. If you can't do anything right, I don't
> want to end up doing the wrong thing either.

Sam looks surprised.

35. LOCATION: EXT. CONVENIENCE STORE—MOMENTS
LATER
ACTORS: Mary Beth and Sam
SPECIAL PROPS: Cell Phone, Engagement Ring
Mary Beth gets out, leaving the door open, and pulls out her cell
phone. Sam looks stunned.

> SAM
> Yeah, okay.

Sam looks at the ring, dazed, as Mary Beth walks around the corner
with her phone.

36. LOCATION: EXT. CONVENIENCE STORE—MOMENTS
LATER
ACTORS: Sam, Young Woman
SPECIAL PROPS: Wild Flowers, Cell Phone
Suddenly, a knock on the car door. Sam looks up to see an attractive
YOUNG WOMAN, late 20s, with long, flowing hair in a loose-fitting
dress. She holds some flowers.

> YOUNG WOMAN
> Hi! I'm sorry to bother you. But I took the wrong turn
> and my car ran out of gas. And this store is closed and
> my cell phone died.

Sam looks at her, obviously attracted and intrigued.

> YOUNG WOMAN
> So can you give me a lift?

Sam perks up and smiles broadly.

> SAM
> Sure. Anywhere you want.

The young woman gets in.

37. LOCATION: EXT. FREEWAY—A LITTLE LATER
GREEN SCREEN—SHOOT ON AMY DRIVE
ACTORS: Sam
Sam is driving on the freeway.

38. LOCATION: EXT. FREEWAY—A LITTLE LATER
Sam passes a sign with an uplifting message, such as "Happy Valley Road" or "Pleasant Valley Road."

SCENE BREAKDOWN—SHOOTING SCHEDULE

CITY STREETS, GAS STATION, CONVENIENCE STORE—10:30 A.M.–12:30 P.M.

15. LOCATION: EXT. CITY STREET—DAY
ACTORS: Mary Beth and Sam—Doing Voice-Overs
Sam is driving on a city street.

> MARY BETH (V.O.)
> Now we'll be late. If only you hadn't missed the turnoff.

SAM (V.O.)
Well, I was talking to you. I got distracted.

MARY BETH (V.O.)
Oh, so it's my fault! Anyway, you know how I hate being
late.

20. LOCATION: EXT. GAS STATION—A FEW MINUTES LATER

Passing traffic suggests this is a busy downtown gas station.

21. LOCATION: EXT. GAS STATION—A FEW MINUTES LATER

ACTORS: Sam, Station Attendant, Mary Beth
SPECIAL PROPS: Air Gauge, Low Tire
Sam is by a pump, starting to pump gas, when the STATION AT-
TENDANT comes over to him.

STATION ATTENDANT
Hey, did you know your tire looks really low?

Close-in shows a low tire.
Mary Beth peeks her head out of the car.

MARY BETH
Oh no. We're in a rush.

STATION ATTENDANT
Oh, it'll just take a minute. Good thing you stopped, or
you could have had a blowout.

As the station attendant pumps air into the tire, Mary Beth glares
at Sam.

SAM
Hey, what can I do? I gotta put air in it.

33. LOCATION: EXT. CONVENIENCE STORE—MINUTES LATER
ACTORS: Sam and Mary Beth
SPECIAL PROPS: "Closed" Sign
Sam pulls into the store lot, but a sign says "Closed."

35. LOCATION: EXT. CONVENIENCE STORE—MOMENTS LATER
ACTORS: Mary Beth and Sam
SPECIAL PROPS: Cell Phone, Engagement Ring
Mary Beth gets out, leaving the door open, and pulls out her cell phone. Sam looks stunned.

SAM
Yeah, okay.

Sam looks at the ring, dazed, as Mary Beth walks around the corner with her phone.

36. LOCATION: EXT. CONVENIENCE STORE—MOMENTS LATER
ACTORS: Sam, Young Woman
SPECIAL PROPS: Wild Flowers, Cell Phone
Suddenly, a knock on the car door. Sam looks up to see an attractive YOUNG WOMAN, late 20s, with long, flowing hair in a loose-fitting dress. She holds some flowers.

YOUNG WOMAN
Hi! I'm sorry to bother you. But I took the wrong turn and my car ran out of gas. And this store is closed and my cell phone died.

Sam looks at her, obviously attracted and intrigued.

YOUNG WOMAN
So can you give me a lift?

Sam perks up and smiles broadly.

SAM
Sure. Anywhere you want.

The young woman gets in.

LUNCH AT AMY DRIVE—12:30–1:00 P.M.
SHOOTING VOICE-OVERS AND GREEN SCREEN SHOTS IN CAR—AMY DRIVE—1:00 P.M.–4:30 P.M.

6. LOCATION: EXT. FREEWAY IN OAKLAND HEADING TO THE BAY BRIDGE—DAY (VOICE-OVERS WITH GREEN SCREEN SHOTS)
A long shot shows cars on the freeway.
ACTORS: Mary Beth and Sam—Doing Voice-Overs

MARY BETH (V.O.)
(A little shrewish)
Yes. Mom and Daddy will be so pleased. And I'm sure you'll enjoy working for Dad. So much better than the crappy jobs you've had for the past year.

SAM (V.O.)
I know. But it's been so hard being a writer.

13. LOCATION: EXT. TOLL BOOTH ENTRY TO THE BAY BRIDGE—DAY (VOICE-OVERS WITH GREEN SCREEN SHOTS)

A close-in of the car shot suggests Sam is at the toll booth.
ACTORS: Mary Beth and Sam—Doing Voice-Overs

MARY BETH (V.O.)
(Annoyed)
Geez. How could you end up here?

SAM (V.O.)
Don't worry. I'll just turn around.

2. LOCATION: EXT. CITY STREET NEAR FREEWAY RAMP IN EAST BAY—DAY

GREEN SCREEN—SHOOT ON AMY DRIVE
ACTORS: Sam and Mary Beth
SPECIAL PROPS: Ordinary Sedan
DRESS: Casual Weekend Wear for Professionals
SAM, 30s, is driving with MARY BETH, 30s, toward San Francisco. They are both dressed casually, as business professionals might on a day off. Sam stops at a light.

3. LOCATION: EXT. INTERIOR OF CAR—DAY

GREEN SCREEN—SHOOT ON AMY DRIVE
ACTORS: Mary Beth
SPECIAL PROPS: Engagement Ring
Mary Beth holds up her hand to admire her ring.

> MARY BETH
> It's so nice. I can't wait to show it off at the party.

4. LOCATION: EXT. INTERIOR OF CAR—DAY
GREEN SCREEN—SHOOT ON AMY DRIVE
ACTORS: Mary Beth and Sam
Mary Beth leans over and plants a kiss on Sam's cheek.

> MARY BETH
> And finally after two years.

Sam looks up at the light, trying to concentrate on the road and listen
to Mary Beth.

> SAM
> Yeah, it'll be nice to finally announce it.

7. LOCATION: EXT: INTERIOR OF CAR—DAY
GREEN SCREEN—SHOOT ON AMY DRIVE
ACTORS: Mary Beth and Sam
SPECIAL PROPS: Engagement Ring
Mary Beth waves her hand around, looking at her ring, as Sam drives.

> MARY BETH
> But Daddy to the rescue.

> SAM
> Yeah, I guess.

9. LOCATION: EXT. INTERIOR OF CAR—DAY
GREEN SCREEN—SHOOT ON AMY DRIVE
ACTORS: Sam
Sam looks up.

11. LOCATION: EXT. INTERIOR OF CAR DAY
GREEN SCREEN—SHOOT ON AMY DRIVE
ACTORS: Sam and Mary Beth
Sam looks ahead, annoyed.

> SAM
> (Half aloud)
> Oh, shit.

Mary Beth looks up.

> MARY BETH
> What's wrong?

> SAM
> Ummm . . . I'm on the wrong road. I don't want to go to
> San Francisco. Damn. And I can't back up.

12. LOCATION: EXT. INTERIOR OF CAR DAY
GREEN SCREEN—SHOOT ON AMY DRIVE
ACTORS: Sam
Close-in of Sam, grudging, grabs his wallet to pay.

17. LOCATION: EXT. INTERIOR OF CAR—A FEW MINUTES
LATER
GREEN SCREEN—SHOOT ON AMY DRIVE
ACTORS: Sam and Mary Beth
As Sam drives, he notices the gauge is almost empty.

> SAM
> Oh, gotta get gas. Tank's almost empty.

18. LOCATION: EXT. INTERIOR OF CAR—A FEW MINUTES
LATER
GREEN SCREEN—SHOOT ON AMY DRIVE
SPECIAL PROPS: Almost-Empty Gas Gauge
A close-in shows the almost empty gas gauge.

19. LOCATION: EXT. INTERIOR OF CAR—A FEW MINUTES
LATER
GREEN SCREEN—SHOOT ON AMY DRIVE

> MARY BETH
> Oh, what now? You should have remembered to fill the
> tank. We'll be so late.

Sam reaches over and squeezes her hand.

> SAM
> Don't worry. It'll be just a few minutes.

22. LOCATION: EXT. SUBURBAN STREETS—A LITTLE LATER
GREEN SCREEN—AMY DRIVE
ACTORS: Sam and Mary Beth—Doing Voice-Overs
Sam drives up and down the street.

> SAM (V.O.)
> I'm sorry, but I lost the address. It's been months since
> we've been here.

> MARY BETH (V.O.)
> Geez. I can't believe it. Can't you do anything right?

> SAM (V.O.)
> Well, maybe you'll recognize it from the street view. At
> least we're close.

23. LOCATION: EXT. SUBURBAN STREETS—A LITTLE LATER
GREEN SCREEN—AMY DRIVE
ACTORS: Mary Beth
SPECIAL PROPS: Purse, PDA

> MARY BETH
> Yeah, sure.

Mary Beth pulls out her PDA and checks a map of the area.

24. LOCATION: EXT. SUBURBAN STREETS—A LITTLE LATER
GREEN SCREEN—AMY DRIVE
SPECIAL PROPS: PDA
Close-in on PDA.

26. LOCATION: INT. CAR ON SUBURBAN STREETS—MO-
MENTS LATER
GREEN SCREEN—AMY DRIVE
ACTORS: Sam and Mary Beth
Sam looks toward the house.

> SAM
> Well, we're finally here.

> MARY BETH
> Yeah, thanks to my PDA and my e-mail.

28. LOCATION: EXT: CITY STREET—LATER
GREEN SCREEN—SHOOT ON AMY DRIVE
ACTORS: Sam and Mary Beth
Sam and Mary are driving home.

29. LOCATION: EXT: CITY STREET—LATER
GREEN SCREEN—SHOOT ON AMY DRIVE

ACTORS: Sam
Sam looks ahead dreamily.

30. LOCATION: EXT: CITY STREET—LATER
GREEN SCREEN—SHOOT ON AMY DRIVE
ACTORS: Sam—Doing Voice-Over
Sam passes a freeway entrance sign at 27th or 52nd Street, which have a jumble of signs. He realizes he missed the entrance.

> SAM (V.O.)
> Oh, sorry. I missed the turnoff again. But I'll turn around at the next street.

31. LOCATION: EXT: CITY STREET—LATER
GREEN SCREEN—SHOOT ON AMY DRIVE
ACTORS: Mary Beth and Sam
Mary Beth turns and glares at Sam.

> MARY BETH
> Yeah, you do that.

32. LOCATION: EXT: CITY STREET—LATER
GREEN SCREEN—SHOOT ON AMY DRIVE
ACTORS: Mary Beth and Sam—Doing Voice-Overs
As Sam drives, Mary Beth is becoming more agitated.

> MARY BETH (V.O.)
> You know, I'm feeling so pissed right now. I thought things would change. But you can't seem to do anything right. How can you work for Daddy? He needs someone he can count on.

> SAM (V.O.)
> Hey, come on. I'm sorry. Please relax. We could stop for
> ice cream. Like old times.

34. LOCATION: EXT. INTERIOR OF CAR—MOMENTS LATER
GREEN SCREEN—SHOOT ON AMY DRIVE
ACTORS: Mary Beth and Sam
SPECIAL PROP: Engagement Ring
Mary Beth reaches down to her ring.

> MARY BETH
> Look. I'm sorry. Just leave me here, and I'll call a taxi to
> pick me up.

Mary Beth takes off her ring.

> MARY BETH (CONT'D)
> I can't take this anymore. Ever since we started out, so
> many wrong turns. And now this. You don't seem to
> know what you're doing.

Mary Beth hands Sam her ring.

> MARY BETH (CONT'D)
> So take this back. If you can't do anything right, I don't
> want to end up doing the wrong thing either.

Sam looks surprised.

37. LOCATION: EXT. FREEWAY—A LITTLE LATER
GREEN SCREEN—SHOOT ON AMY DRIVE
ACTORS: Sam
Sam is driving on the freeway.

SHOOTING SHOTS IN SUBURBS—4:30 P.M.–5:30 PM.

25. LOCATION: EXT. HOUSE IN SUBURBS—STILL LATER
ACTORS: Sam and Mary Beth
Sam and Mary Beth pull up in across the street from the house.

27. LOCATION: EXT. HOUSE IN SUBURBS—STILL LATER
ACTORS: Sam and Mary Beth
Sam and Mary Beth walk toward the house, when Mary Beth stops.

> MARY BETH
> You know, we're so late and I'm so bummed out now, I
> don't even feel like going in.

> SAM
> But our friends, our announcement.

> BETH
> Look, I'm sorry. But I'm not in a party mood anymore.
> Okay?

Sam turns to head back to the car.

> SAM
> Sure. If that's what you want.

Sam and Mary Beth walk to the car.

SHOOTING FREEWAY AND TOLL BOOTH AREA—B-ROLL—
ANOTHER DAY
FREEWAY AND TOLL BOOTH AREA—10:00 A.M.–11:30 A.M.

1. LOCATION: EXT. FREEWAY OAKLAND LEADING TO BAY
BRIDGE—DAY

ACTORS: None
SPECIAL PROPS: None
A pan shows cars driving toward the toll booth.

5. LOCATION: ENTRANCE TO FREEWAY RAMP—DAY
The light changes and Sam heads onto the freeway ramp.

8. LOCATION: TOLL BOOTH ENTRY TO THE BAY BRIDGE—DAY
A shot shows the toll booth ahead.

10. LOCATION: EXT. TOLL BOOTH ENTRY TO BAY BRIDGE—DAY
Another shot shows Sam's view of toll booth ahead.

13. LOCATION: EXT. TOLL BOOTH ENTRY TO THE BAY BRIDGE—DAY (VOICE-OVERS WITH GREEN SCREEN SHOTS)
A close-in of the car shot suggests Sam is at the toll booth.
ACTORS: Mary Beth and Sam—Doing Voice-Overs

> MARY BETH (V.O.)
> (Annoyed)
> Geez. How could you end up here?

> SAM (V.O.)
> Don't worry. I'll just turn around.

14. LOCATION: EXT. ROAD IN OAKLAND
Cut away shows a sign that says: "Rough Road Ahead."

16. LOCATION: EXT. CITY STREET—DAY
Cutaway shows massive traffic jam or car crash on the road Sam didn't take.

38. LOCATION: EXT. FREEWAY—A LITTLE LATER
Sam passes a sign with an uplifting message, such as "Happy Valley Road" or "Pleasant Valley Road."

39. CITY AND SUBURBAN SHOTS OF WHAT CAR IS PASSING DURING GREEN SCREEN SHOTS.

Appendix C
Adding a Shot List
to a Scene Breakdown

Sometimes when you do a scene breakdown, you might want to add in camera shots, or the director or DP may give you a list of shots. This shot list can be developed from the original script or from the scene breakdown, either in sequence or in the order of shots. You need to incorporate that in with the action and dialog, so it is clear to everyone what shots occur when.

A shot list will look something like this, and will indicate what is in the shot and the type of shot—such as wide shot, medium shot, or close-up. It can be easily created using a table in Word or another word-processing program, such as this example from *The Engagement*.

SHOT LIST   Page 1

Production Title: The Engagement		Date: 2/12/2011	
SHOT #	SCENE #	TYPE OF SHOT	DESCRIPTION
1	1	Car Ext.	Shot of traffic approaching the toll booths.
2	1	2 shot in car	Two shot from driver's side window.

3	1	2 shot	OTS from backseat showing actors silhouette with stop light framed in center of windshield.
4	1	OTS	OTS shot from backseat cross angle showing side profile with rack focus from face to ring.
5	1		All dialogue shot from four angles: (1) Ext. car from driver's side focused on passenger. (2) External car from passenger side focused on driver. (3) Backseat cross shot OTS shooting driver. (4) Backseat OTS shooting passenger.
6	1	Car Ext.	Close shot of toll booths ahead.
7	1	OTS	Cross shot OTS from backseat of Sam at toll booth.
8	1		Shot of "Rough Road Ahead" sign.
9	1		Shot of traffic jam.
10	1	OTS	Shot from back seat over Sam's shoulder showing that the gas tank is almost empty.
11	2	Wide	Shot of car pulling into gas station.
12	2	Medium	Sam getting out of car and starting to pump gas.
13	2	Medium	Reverse angle of station attendant coming up to Sam.
14	2	One	Mary Beth poking her head out of car.
15	2	Close-up	Station attendant.
16	2	Close-up	Sam
17	2	OTS	Cross shot from backseat of Mary Beth getting out PDA.
18	2	Ext. car	From driver's side Mary Beth using PDA.
19	3	Wide shot	Car pulling into driveway.
20	3	Two	Sam and Mary Beth walking toward house.
21	3	Two	Sam and Mary Beth walking back toward car.
22	4	Wide shot	Car pulling into convenience store.
23	4	Close-up	Mary Beth reaching for ring.
24	4	Med. two	Mary Beth hands Sam the ring.
25	4	One	Mary Beth getting out of the car and pulling out her cell phone.

26	4	Close-up	Hands pulling cell phone out of purse.
27	4	Car Ext.	Shot of Sam sitting in driver's seat. Out-of-focus knock on the passenger side window. Rack focus to young woman.
28	4	Close-up	Young woman asking for a ride.
29	4	Medium shot	Sam from young woman's POV.
30	4	Medium	Shot of young woman getting into the car.
31	4	Wide	Car driving away.
32	4	Close-up	Shot of "Happy Valley" road sign.

Normally, the shot list should follow the order of the scenes in the original script or the scene breakdown, and if the scenes have been numbered, it should use that numbering system so it is clear what shots correspond to what scenes. If not, adjust the numbering to create that correspondence.

For example, here's how I incorporated the above shot list in a scene breakdown I had previously done for a green screen version of *The Engagement*, though I adapted it to film the same script using a car mount. First, I used the sequential order of shots, as indicated in the following. I used bold type to indicate where I had changed a number from the original so the director would know this, or in a few cases, I added some additional shots for the scene.

Incorporating the Shots in a Sequential Scene Breakdown

THE ENGAGEMENT

SCENE BREAKDOWN—SEQUENTIALLY WITH SHOT L1.
LOCATION: EXT. FREEWAY OAKLAND LEADING TO BAY
BRIDGE—DAY

ACTORS: None

SPECIAL PROPS: None

A pan shows cars driving toward the toll booth.

1	1	Car Ext.	Shot of traffic approaching the toll booths.

2. LOCATION: EXT. CITY STREET NEAR FREEWAY RAMP IN EAST BAY—DAY

ACTORS: Sam and Mary Beth

SPECIAL PROPS: Ordinary Sedan

DRESS: Casual Weekend Wear for Professionals

SAM, 30s, is driving with MARY BETH, 30s, toward San Francisco. They are both dressed casually, as business professionals might on a day off.

Sam stops at a light.

2	1	2 shot in car	Two shot from driver's side window.
3	1	2 shot	OTS from backseat showing actors silhouette with stop light framed in center of windshield.

3. LOCATION: EXT. INTERIOR OF CAR—DAY

ACTORS: Mary Beth

SPECIAL PROPS: Engagement Ring

Mary Beth holds up her hand to admire her ring.

> MARY BETH
>
> It's so nice. I can't wait to show it off at the party.

4	1	OTS	OTS shot from backseat cross angle showing side profile with rack focus from face to ring.

4. LOCATION: EXT. INTERIOR OF CAR—DAY

ACTORS: Mary Beth and Sam

Mary Beth leans over and plants a kiss on Sam's cheek.

> MARY BETH
> And finally after two years.

Sam looks up at the light, trying to concentrate on the road and listen to Mary Beth.

> SAM
> Yeah, it'll be nice to finally announce it.

5. LOCATION: ENTRANCE TO FREEWAY RAMP—DAY
The light changes and Sam heads onto the freeway ramp.

5	1	1	All dialogue shot from four angles: (1) Ext. car from driver's side focused on passenger. (2) External car from passenger side focused on driver. (3) Backseat cross shot OTS shooting driver. (4) Backseat OTS shooting passenger.

6. LOCATION: EXT. FREEWAY IN OAKLAND HEADING TO THE BAY BRIDGE—DAY
A long shot shows cars on the freeway.
ACTORS: Mary Beth and Sam—Doing Voice-Overs

> MARY BETH (V.O.)
> (A little shrewish)
> Yes. Mom and Daddy will be so pleased. And I'm sure you'll enjoy working for Dad. So much better than the crappy jobs you've had for the past year.

SAM (V.O.)

I know. But it's been so hard being a writer.

6	1	Car Ext.	Close shot of toll booths ahead.

7. LOCATION: EXT: INTERIOR OF CAR—DAY

ACTORS: Mary Beth and Sam

SPECIAL PROPS: Engagement Ring

Mary Beth waves her hand around, looking at her ring, as Sam drives.

MARY BETH

But Daddy to the rescue.

SAM

Yeah, I guess.

7	1	OTS	OTS shot from backseat cross angle showing close-in on ring.

8. LOCATION: TOLL BOOTH ENTRY TO THE BAY BRIDGE—DAY

A shot shows the toll booth ahead.

8-9-10-11	1	OTS	Cross shot OTS from backseat of Sam at toll booth.

9. LOCATION: EXT. INTERIOR OF CAR—DAY

ACTORS: Sam

Sam looks up.

10. LOCATION: EXT. INTERIOR OF CAR—DAY

ACTORS: Sam and Mary Beth

Sam looks ahead, annoyed.

> SAM
> (Half aloud)
> Oh, shit.

11. LOCATION: EXT. INTERIOR OF CAR—DAY
Mary Beth looks up.

> MARY BETH
> What's wrong?

> SAM
> Ummm . . . I'm on the wrong road. I don't want to go to
> San Francisco. Damn. And I can't back up.

12. LOCATION: EXT. INTERIOR OF CAR—DAY
ACTORS: Sam
Close-in of Sam, grudging, grabs his wallet to pay.

11	1	OTS	Close-in on Sam's wallet.

13. LOCATION: EXT. TOLL BOOTH ENTRY TO THE BAY
BRIDGE—DAY
A close-in of the car shot suggests Sam is at the toll booth.
ACTORS: Mary Beth and Sam—Doing Voice-Overs

> MARY BETH (V.O.)
> (Annoyed)
> Geez. How could you end up here?

> SAM (V.O.)
> Don't worry. I'll just turn around.

13	1	OTS	Cross shot OTS from backseat of Sam at toll booth.

14. LOCATION: EXT. ROAD IN OAKLAND

Cutaway shows a sign that says: "Rough Road Ahead."

14	1	1	Shot of "Rough Road Ahead" sign.

15. LOCATION: EXT. CITY STREET—DAY

ACTORS: Mary Beth and Sam—Doing Voice-Overs

Sam is driving on a city street.

> MARY BETH (V.O.)
> Now we'll be late. If only you hadn't missed the turnoff.

> SAM (V.O.)
> Well, I was talking to you. I got distracted.

> MARY BETH (V.O.)
> Oh, so it's my fault! Anyway, you know how I hate being late.

15	1		Shot of city streets.

16. LOCATION: EXT. CITY STREET—DAY

Cutaway shows massive traffic jam or car crash on the road Sam didn't take.

16	1		Shot of traffic jam.

17. LOCATION: EXT. INTERIOR OF CAR—A FEW MINUTES LATER

ACTORS: Sam and Mary Beth
SPECIAL PROPS: Almost-Empty gas gauge
As Sam drives, he notices the gauge is almost empty.

> SAM
> Oh, gotta get gas. Tank's almost empty.

17	1	OTS	Shot from backseat over Sam's shoulder showing that the gas tank is almost empty.

18. LOCATION: EXT. INTERIOR OF CAR—A FEW MINUTES LATER

> MARY BETH
> Oh, what now? You should have remembered to fill the tank. We'll be so late.

Sam reaches over and squeezes her hand.

> SAM
> Don't worry. It'll be just a few minutes.

18 (5)	1	1	Shot of city streets or pick up from 5.

19. LOCATION: EXT. GAS STATION—A FEW MINUTES LATER

Passing traffic suggests this is a busy downtown gas station.

19	2	Wide	Shot of car pulling into gas station.

20. LOCATION: EXT. GAS STATION—A FEW MINUTES LATER

ACTORS: Sam, Station Attendant, Mary Beth
SPECIAL PROPS: Air Gauge, Low Tire
Sam is next to a pump, starting to pump gas.

20a	2	Medium	Sam getting out of car and starting to pump gas.

The STATION ATTENDANT comes over to him.

STATION ATTENDANT
Hey, did you know your tire looks really low?

20b	2	Medium	Reverse angle of station attendant coming up to Sam.

Mary Beth peeks her head out of the car.

MARY BETH
Oh no. We're in a rush.

20c	2	One	Mary Beth poking her head out of car.

STATION ATTENDANT
Oh, it'll just take a minute. Good thing you stopped, or
you could have had a blowout.

20d	2	Close-up	Station attendant

As the station attendant pumps air into the tire, Mary Beth glares at Sam.

20e	2	Close-up	Mary Beth

SAM

Hey, what can I do? I gotta put air in it.

20f	2	Close-up	Sam

21. LOCATION: EXT. SUBURBAN STREETS—A LITTLE LATER
ACTORS: Sam and Mary Beth—Doing Voice-Overs
Sam drives up and down the street.

SAM (V.O.)

I'm sorry, but I lost the address. It's been months since we've been here.

MARY BETH (V.O.)

Geez. I can't believe it. Can't you do anything right?

SAM (V.O.)

Well, maybe you'll recognize it from the street view. At least we're close.

21	3	Pick up	Car driving in suburbs.

22. LOCATION: EXT. SUBURBAN STREETS—A LITTLE LATER
ACTORS: Mary Beth
SPECIAL PROPS: Purse, PDA

MARY BETH
Yeah, sure.

Mary Beth pulls out her PDA and checks a map of the area.

22	3	OTS	Cross shot from backseat of Mary Beth getting out PDA.

23. LOCATION: EXT. SUBURBAN STREETS—A LITTLE LATER
SPECIAL PROPS: PDA

Close-in on PDA.

23	3	Ext. car	From driver's side Mary Beth using PDA.

24. LOCATION: EXT. HOUSE IN SUBURBS—STILL LATER
ACTORS: Sam and Mary Beth

Sam and Mary Beth pull up across the street from the house.

24	3	Wide shot	Car pulling into street near driveway.

25. LOCATION: EXT. SUBURBAN STREETS—MOMENTS LATER
ACTORS: Sam and Mary Beth

Sam and Mary Beth walk toward the house.

SAM
Well, we're finally here.

MARY BETH
Yeah, thanks to my PDA and my e-mail.

25	3	Two	Sam and Mary Beth get out of car.

26. LOCATION: EXT. HOUSE IN SUBURBS—STILL LATER
ACTORS: Sam and Mary Beth
Sam and Mary Beth walk toward the house, when Mary Beth stops.

MARY BETH
You know, we're so late and I'm so bummed out now, I don't even feel like going in.

SAM
But our friends, our announcement.

BETH
Look, I'm sorry. But I'm not in a party mood anymore. Okay?

26	3	Two	Sam and Mary Beth walking toward house.

Sam turns to head back to the car.

SAM
Sure. If that's what you want.
Sam and Mary Beth walk to the car.

27	3	Two	Sam and Mary Beth walking back toward car.

28. LOCATION: EXT: CITY STREET—LATER

28	4	Pick up	Car driving away, city streets.

29. LOCATION: EXT: CITY STREET—LATER
ACTORS: Sam—Doing Voice-Over
Sam passes a freeway entrance sign at 27th or 52nd Street, which have a jumble of signs. He realizes he missed the entrance.

> SAM (V.O.)
> Oh, sorry. I missed the turnoff again. But I'll turn around at the next street.

29	4	Pick up	Car driving away, city streets, signs on 27th or 52nd.

30. LOCATION: EXT: CITY STREET—LATER
ACTORS: Mary Beth and Sam
Mary Beth turns and glares at Sam.

> MARY BETH
> Yeah, you do that.

30 (5)	4	Close-up	Mary Beth glares at Sam.

31. LOCATION: EXT: CITY STREET—LATER
ACTORS: Mary Beth and Sam—Doing Voice-Overs
As Sam drives, Mary Beth is becoming more agitated.

> MARY BETH (V.O.)
> You know. I'm feeling so pissed right now. I thought things would change. But you can't seem to do anything right. How can you work for Daddy? He needs someone he can count on.

SAM (V.O.)

Hey, come on. I'm sorry. Please relax. We could stop for

ice cream. Like old times.

31.	4	Pick up	Car driving in city streets.

32. LOCATION: EXT. CONVENIENCE STORE—MINUTES LATER

ACTORS: Sam and Mary Beth

SPECIAL PROPS: "Closed" sign.

Sam pulls into the store lot, but a sign says, "Closed."

32	4	Wide shot	Car pulling into convenience store.

33. LOCATION: EXT. INTERIOR OF CAR—MOMENTS LATER

ACTORS: Mary Beth and Sam

SPECIAL PROP: Engagement Ring

Mary Beth reaches down to her ring.

MARY BETH

Look. I'm sorry. Just leave me here, and I'll call a taxi to

pick me up.

33a	4	Close-up	Mary Beth reaching for ring.

Mary Beth takes off her ring.

MARY BETH

I can't take this anymore. Ever since we started out, so
many wrong turns. And now this. You don't seem to
know what you're doing.

Mary Beth hands Sam her ring.

MARY BETH

So take this back. If you can't do anything right, I don't
want to end up doing the wrong thing either.

33b	4	Med. two	Mary Beth hands Sam the ring.

34. LOCATION: EXT. CONVENIENCE STORE—MOMENTS LATER

ACTORS: Mary Beth and Sam

SPECIAL PROPS: Cell Phone, Engagement Ring

Mary Beth gets out, leaving the door open, and pulls out her cell
phone. Sam looks stunned.

SAM

Yeah, okay.

Sam looks at the ring, dazed, as Mary Beth walks around the corner
with her phone.

34a	4	One	Mary Beth getting out of the car and pulling out her cell phone.
34b	4	Close-up	Hands pulling cell phone out of purse.

35. LOCATION: EXT. CONVENIENCE STORE—MOMENTS LATER

ACTORS: Sam, Young Woman

SPECIAL PROPS: Wild Flowers, Cell Phone

Sam sits in the car looking stunned. Suddenly, a knock on the car door

35a	4	Car Ext.	Shot of Sam sitting in driver's seat. Out-of-focus knock on the passenger side window. Rack focus to young woman.

Sam looks up to see an attractive YOUNG WOMAN, late 20s, with long, flowing hair, in a loose-fitting dress. She holds some flowers.

> YOUNG WOMAN
> Hi! I'm sorry to bother you. But I took the wrong turn and my car ran out of gas. And this store is closed and my cell phone died.

Sam looks at her, obviously attracted and intrigued.

> YOUNG WOMAN
> So can you give me a lift?

35b	4	Close-up	Young woman asking for a ride.

Sam perks up and smiles broadly.

> SAM
> Sure. Anywhere you want.

35c	4	Medium shot	Sam from young woman's POV.

The young woman gets in.

35d	4	Medium	Shot of young woman getting into the car.

36. LOCATION: EXT. CITY STREET—A LITTLE LATER
ACTORS: Sam

Sam is driving away.

36	4	Wide	Car driving away.

37. LOCATION: EXT. FREEWAY—A LITTLE LATER

Sam passes a sign with an uplifting message, such as "Happy Valley."

37	4	Close-up	Shot of "Happy Valley" Road sign.

Rearranging the Shots in a Sequential Scene Breakdown to Create a Shooting Order Scene Breakdown

After you integrate the shot list with the scene breakdown, the final step is to rearrange the chronological order of shots to correspond to the expected shooting order. For example, a good approach—if it makes sense to do so, as we did in this case—is to film the scenes with the minor or supporting characters first. This way they don't have to hang around while you do the scenes with the main characters. Then we consolidated all of the scenes of driving around in a suburban area in order to take them from different angles outside and in the car.

Later the director/DP planned to do the remaining pick-up or B-roll shots of exteriors where the actors weren't needed.

19. LOCATION: EXT. GAS STATION—A FEW MINUTES LATER

Passing traffic suggests this is a busy downtown gas station.

19	2	Wide	Shot of car pulling into gas station.

20. LOCATION: EXT. GAS STATION—A FEW MINUTES LATER

ACTORS: Sam, Station Attendant, Mary Beth
SPECIAL PROPS: Air Gauge, Low Tire
Sam is next to a pump, starting to pump gas.

20a	2	Medium	Sam getting out of car and starting to pump gas.

The STATION ATTENDANT comes over to him.

> STATION ATTENDANT
> Hey, did you know your tire looks really low?

20b	2	Medium	Reverse angle of station attendant coming up to Sam.

Mary Beth peeks her head out of the car.

> MARY BETH
> Oh no. We're in a rush.

| 20c | 2 | One | Mary Beth poking her head out of car. |

STATION ATTENDANT

Oh, it'll just take a minute. Good thing you stopped, or you could have had a blowout.

| 20d | 2 | Close-up | Station attendant |

As the station attendant pumps air into the tire, Mary Beth glares at Sam.

| 20e | 2 | Close-up | Mary Beth |

SAM

Hey, what can I do? I gotta put air in it.

| 20f | 2 | Close-up | Sam |

32. LOCATION: EXT. CONVENIENCE STORE—MINUTES LATER

ACTORS: Sam and Mary Beth

SPECIAL PROPS: "Closed" Sign

Sam pulls into the store lot, but a sign says, "Closed."

| 32 | 4 | Wide shot | Car pulling into convenience store. |

33. LOCATION: EXT. INTERIOR OF CAR—MOMENTS LATER

ACTORS: Mary Beth and Sam

SPECIAL PROP: Engagement Ring

Mary Beth reaches down to her ring.

> MARY BETH
> Look. I'm sorry. Just leave me here, and I'll call a taxi to
> pick me up.

33a	4	Close-up	Mary Beth reaching for ring.

Mary Beth takes off her ring.

> MARY BETH
> I can't take this anymore. Ever since we started out, so
> many wrong turns. And now this. You don't seem to
> know what you're doing.

Mary Beth hands Sam her ring.

> MARY BETH
> So take this back. If you can't do anything right, I don't
> want to end up doing the wrong thing either.

33b	4	Med. two	Mary Beth hands Sam the ring.

34. LOCATION: EXT. CONVENIENCE STORE—MOMENTS
LATER
ACTORS: Mary Beth and Sam
SPECIAL PROPS: Cell Phone, Engagement Ring
Mary Beth gets out, leaving the door open, and pulls out her cell
phone. Sam looks stunned.

SAM
Yeah, okay.

Sam looks at the ring, dazed, as Mary Beth walks around the corner with her phone.

| 34a | 4 | One | Mary Beth getting out of the car and pulling out her cell phone. |
| 34b | 4 | Close-up | Hands pulling cell phone out of purse. |

35. LOCATION: EXT. CONVENIENCE STORE—MOMENTS LATER
ACTORS: Sam and Young Woman
SPECIAL PROPS: Wild Flowers, Cell Phone
Sam sits in the car looking stunned. Suddenly, a knock on the car door.

| 35a | 4 | Car Ext. | Shot of Sam sitting in driver's seat. Out-of-focus knock on the passenger side window. Rack focus to young woman. |

Sam looks up to see an attractive YOUNG WOMAN, late 20s, with long, flowing hair in a loose-fitting dress. She holds some flowers.

YOUNG WOMAN
Hi! I'm sorry to bother you. But I took the wrong turn and my car ran out of gas. And this store is closed and my cell phone died.

Sam looks at her, obviously attracted and intrigued.

> YOUNG WOMAN
> So can you give me a lift?

35b	4	Close-up	Young woman asking for a ride.

Sam perks up and smiles broadly.

> SAM
> Sure. Anywhere you want.

35c	4	Medium shot	Sam from young woman's POV.

The young woman gets in.

35d	4	Medium	Shot of young woman getting into the car.

24. LOCATION: EXT. HOUSE IN SUBURBS—STILL LATER

ACTORS: Sam and Mary Beth
Sam and Mary Beth pull up in across the street from the house.

24	3	Wide shot	Car pulling into street near driveway.

25. LOCATION: EXT. SUBURBAN STREETS—MOMENTS LATER
ACTORS: Sam and Mary Beth
Sam and Mary Beth walk toward the house.

SAM

Well, we're finally here.

MARY BETH

Yeah, thanks to my PDA and my e-mail.

25	3	Two	Sam and Mary Beth get out of car.

26. LOCATION: EXT. HOUSE IN SUBURBS—STILL LATER

ACTORS: Sam and Mary Beth

Sam and Mary Beth walk toward the house, when Mary Beth stops.

MARY BETH

You know, we're so late and I'm so bummed out now, I
don't even feel like going in.

SAM

But our friends, our announcement.

BETH

Look, I'm sorry. But I'm not in a party mood anymore.
Okay?

26	3	Two	Sam and Mary Beth walking toward house.

Sam turns to head back to the car.

SAM

Sure. If that's what you want.

Sam and Mary Beth walk to the car.

27	3	Two	Sam and Mary Beth walking back toward car.

Time: 11:30 on—Shots at my house and around neighborhood first; lunch break about 12:30-1:00.

1. LOCATION: EXT. FREEWAY OAKLAND LEADING TO BAY BRIDGE—DAY

ACTORS: None

SPECIAL PROPS: None

A pan shows cars driving toward the toll booth.

1	1	Car Ext.	Shot of traffic approaching the toll booths.

2. LOCATION: EXT. CITY STREET NEAR FREEWAY RAMP IN EAST BAY—DAY

ACTORS: Sam and Mary Beth

SPECIAL PROPS: Ordinary Sedan

DRESS: Casual weekend wear for professionals.

SAM, 30s, is driving with MARY BETH, 30s, toward San Francisco. They are both dressed casually, as business professionals might on a day off.

Sam stops at a light.

2	1	2 shots in car	Two shot from driver's side window.
3	1	2 shots	OTS from backseat showing actors silhouette with stop light framed in center of windshield.

3. LOCATION: EXT. INTERIOR OF CAR—DAY

ACTORS: Mary Beth

SPECIAL PROPS: Engagement Ring

Mary Beth holds up her hand to admire her ring.

MARY BETH

It's so nice. I can't wait to show it off at the party.

4	1	OTS	OTS shot from backseat cross angle showing side profile with rack focus from face to ring.

4. LOCATION: EXT. INTERIOR OF CAR—DAY

ACTORS: Mary Beth and Sam

Mary Beth leans over and plants a kiss on Sam's cheek.

MARY BETH

And finally after two years.

Sam looks up at the light, trying to concentrate on the road and listen to Mary Beth.

SAM

Yeah, it'll be nice to finally announce it.

5. LOCATION: ENTRANCE TO FREEWAY RAMP—DAY

The light changes and Sam heads onto the freeway ramp.

5	1	1	All dialogue shot from four angles: (1) Ext. car from driver's side focused on passenger. (2) External car from passenger side focused on driver. (3) Backseat cross shot OTS shooting driver. (4) Backseat OTS shooting passenger.

6. LOCATION: EXT. FREEWAY IN OAKLAND HEADING TO THE BAY BRIDGE—DAY

A long shot shows cars on the freeway.

ACTORS: Mary Beth and Sam—Doing Voice-Overs

> MARY BETH (V.O.)
> (A little shrewish)
> Yes. Mom and Daddy will be so pleased. And I'm sure you'll enjoy working for Dad. So much better than the crappy jobs you've had for the past year.

> SAM (V.O.)
> I know. But it's been so hard being a writer.

6	1	Car Ext.	Close shot of toll booths ahead.

7. LOCATION: EXT: INTERIOR OF CAR—DAY

ACTORS: Mary Beth and Sam

SPECIAL PROPS: Engagement Ring

Mary Beth waves her hand around, looking at her ring, as Sam drives.

> MARY BETH
> But Daddy to the rescue.

> SAM
> Yeah, I guess.

7	1	OTS	OTS shot from backseat cross angle showing close-in on ring.

8. LOCATION: TOLL BOOTH ENTRY TO THE BAY BRIDGE—DAY

A shot shows the toll booth ahead.

8-9-10	1	OTS	Cross shot OTS from backseat of Sam at toll booth.

9. LOCATION: EXT. INTERIOR OF CAR—DAY
ACTORS: Sam
Sam looks up.

10. LOCATION: EXT. INTERIOR OF CAR—DAY
ACTORS: Sam and Mary Beth
Sam looks ahead annoyed.

> SAM
> (Half aloud)
> Oh, shit.

11. LOCATION: EXT. INTERIOR OF CAR—DAY
Mary Beth looks up.

> MARY BETH
> What's wrong?

> SAM
> Ummm . . . I'm on the wrong road. I don't want to go to
> San Francisco. Damn. And I can't back up.

12. LOCATION: EXT. INTERIOR OF CAR—DAY
ACTORS: Sam
Close-in of Sam, grudging, grabs his wallet to pay.

12	1	OTS	Close-in on Sam's wallet.

13. LOCATION: EXT. TOLL BOOTH ENTRY TO THE BAY BRIDGE—DAY

A close-in of the car shot suggests Sam is at the toll booth.

ACTORS: Mary Beth and Sam—Doing Voice-Overs

> MARY BETH (V.O.)
> (Annoyed)
> Geez. How could you end up here?

> SAM (V.O.)
> Don't worry. I'll just turn around.

13	1	OTS	Cross shot OTS from backseat of Sam at toll booth.

14. LOCATION: EXT. ROAD IN OAKLAND

Cut away shows a sign that says: "Rough Road Ahead"

14	1	1	Shot of "Rough Road Ahead" sign.

15. LOCATION: EXT. CITY STREET—DAY

ACTORS: Mary Beth and Sam—Doing Voice-Overs

Sam is driving on a city street.

> MARY BETH (V.O.)
> Now we'll be late. If only you hadn't missed the turnoff.

> SAM (V.O.)
> Well, I was talking to you. I got distracted.

MARY BETH (V.O.)

Oh, so it's my fault! Anyway, you know how I hate being late.

15	1	1	Shot of city streets.

16. LOCATION: EXT. CITY STREET—DAY

Cutaway shows massive traffic jam or car crash on the road Sam didn't take.

16	1	1	Shot of traffic jam.

17. LOCATION: EXT. INTERIOR OF CAR—A FEW MINUTES LATER

ACTORS: Sam and Mary Beth

SPECIAL PROPS: Almost Empty Gas Gauge

As Sam drives, he notices the gauge is almost empty.

SAM

Oh, gotta get gas. Tank's almost empty.

17	1	OTS	Shot from backseat over Sam's shoulder showing that the gas tank is almost empty.

18. LOCATION: EXT. INTERIOR OF CAR—A FEW MINUTES LATER

MARY BETH

Oh, what now? You should have remembered to fill the tank. We'll be so late.

Sam reaches over and squeezes her hand.

SAM

Don't worry. It'll be just a few minutes.

18 (5)	1	1	Shot of city streets or pick up from 5.

21. LOCATION: EXT. SUBURBAN STREETS—A LITTLE LATER
ACTORS: Sam and Mary Beth—Doing Voice-Overs
Sam drives up and down the street.

SAM (V.O.)
I'm sorry, but I lost the address. It's been months since we've been here.

MARY BETH (V.O.)
Geez. I can't believe it. Can't you do anything right?

SAM (V.O.)
Well, maybe you'll recognize it from the street view. At least we're close.

21	3	Pick up	Car driving in suburbs.

22. LOCATION: EXT. SUBURBAN STREETS—A LITTLE LATER
ACTORS: Mary Beth
SPECIAL PROPS: Purse, PDA

MARY BETH
Yeah, sure.

Mary Beth pulls out her PDA and checks a map of the area.

22	3	OTS	Cross shot from backseat of Mary Beth getting out PDA.

23. LOCATION: EXT. SUBURBAN STREETS—A LITTLE LATER
SPECIAL PROPS: PDA
Close in on PDA

23	3	Ext. car	From driver's side Mary Beth using PDA.

28. LOCATION: EXT: CITY STREET—LATER

28	4	Pick up	Car driving away, city streets.

29. LOCATION: EXT: CITY STREET—LATER
ACTORS: Sam—Doing Voice-Over
Sam passes a freeway entrance sign at 27th or 52nd Street, which have a jumble of signs. He realizes he missed the entrance.

> SAM (V.O.)
> Oh, sorry. I missed the turnoff again. But I'll turn
> around at the next street.

29	4	Pick up	Car driving away, city streets, signs on 27th or 52nd.

30. LOCATION: EXT: CITY STREET—LATER
ACTORS: Mary Beth and Sam
Mary Beth turns and glares at Sam.

MARY BETH
Yeah, you do that.

30 (5)	4	Close-up	Mary Beth glares at Sam.

31. LOCATION: EXT: CITY STREET—LATER
ACTORS: Mary Beth and Sam—Doing Voice-Overs
As Sam drives, Mary Beth is becoming more agitated.

MARY BETH (V.O.)
You know. I'm feeling so pissed right now. I thought
things would change. But you can't seem to do anything
right. How can you work for Daddy? He needs someone
he can count on.

SAM (V.O.)
Hey, come on. I'm sorry. Please relax. We could stop for
ice cream. Like old times.

31.	4	Pick up	Car driving in city streets.

36. LOCATION: EXT. CITY STREET—A LITTLE LATER
ACTORS: Sam
Sam is driving away.

36	4	Wide	Car driving away.

37. LOCATION: EXT. FREEWAY—A LITTLE LATER
Sam passes a sign with an uplifting message, such as "Happy Valley."

37	4	Close-up	Shot of "Happy Valley" road sign.

About the Author

Gini Graham Scott is a screenplay writer, indie producer, TV game/reality show developer, and the author of over fifty published books. She writes scripts and books for others as well. She has written and produced several TV game, reality, and talk show pilots as well as trailers for over a dozen documentaries, scripts, and feature films. Scott has also written, produced, cast, and sometimes directed over four dozen short films, including music videos and book chapters.

Her scripts include action/adventure scripts, suspense thrillers, psychological character films, and contemporary dramas. Several projects are being packaged with attachments for funding. She has written eight scripts for clients, adapted from their novels, memoirs, or script ideas. Client testimonials are on her company website for Changemakers Productions at www.changemakersproductions.com /clients.htm.

Scott organizes monthly film industry networking events through a number of film groups she founded, which have more than 3,000 members, and she helps others connect to the film industry through the Film and TV Connection (www.filmandtvconnection.com).

She has hosted and produced the *Changemakers Radio* show featuring changes in society, the film industry, business, science, and technology. More details are at www.changemakersradio.com.

Scott is a speaker, workshop leader, and business consultant. Some of Scott's recent books focus on social trends, work, creativity, and change. Her latest books include *Want It, See It, Get It!* and *Enjoy!: 101 Little Ways to Add Fun to Your Work Every Day*.

Scott has been a featured guest on hundreds of TV and radio programs and networks, including *Good Morning America, The Oprah Winfrey Show, The Montel Williams Show*, and CNN. She has a PhD in sociology from the University of California at Berkeley, a JD from the University of San Francisco Law School, and MAs in anthropology, in pop culture and lifestyles, and in mass communications and organizational/consumer/audience behavior from Cal State University, East Bay. She expects to get an MS in recreation and tourism in 2013.

Biographical and promotional details are at www.ginigrahamscott.com; information on film production and scripts at www.changemakersproductions.com. Her website on writing, publishing, and promoting books and scripts for clients is www.changemakerspublishingandwriting.com. Her IMDB profile and resume are at www.imdb.com/name/nm2592609.